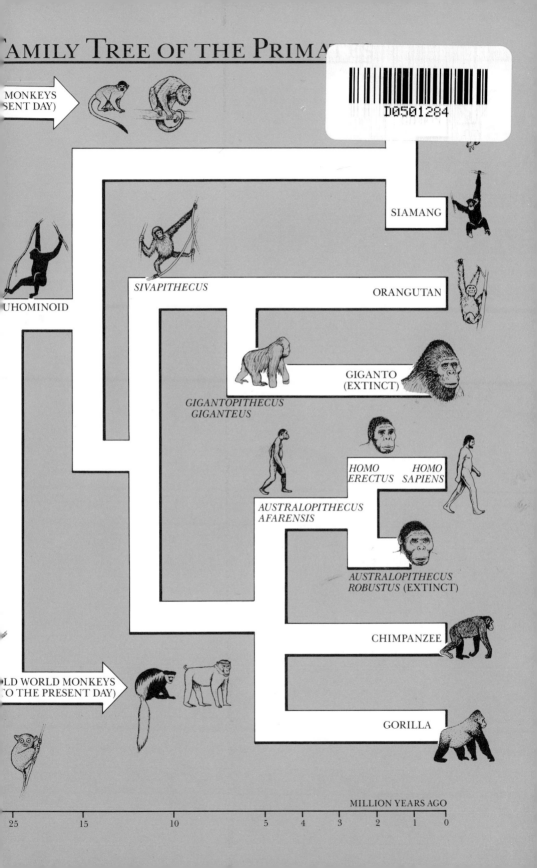

ᴀMILY TREE OF THE PRIMATᴇ

MONKEYS
(SENT DAY)

SIAMANG

SIVAPITHECUS

ORANGUTAN

UHOMINOID

GIGANTO
(EXTINCT)

GIGANTOPITHECUS
GIGANTEUS

HOMO   HOMO
ERECTUS   SAPIENS

AUSTRALOPITHECUS
AFARENSIS

AUSTRALOPITHECUS
ROBUSTUS (EXTINCT)

CHIMPANZEE

LD WORLD MONKEYS
(O THE PRESENT DAY)

GORILLA

MILLION YEARS AGO

25   15   10   5   4   3   2   1   0

D0501284

OTHER ORIGINS

OTHER ORIGINS

THE SEARCH FOR THE
GIANT APE IN HUMAN PREHISTORY

Russell Ciochon, John Olsen,
and Jamie James

BANTAM BOOKS
NEW YORK · TORONTO · LONDON · SYDNEY · AUCKLAND

OTHER ORIGINS
A Bantam Book / November 1990

BOOK DESIGN BY MARIA CARELLA.

MAPS DESIGNED BY GDS / JEFFREY L. WARD

Drawings of living primates and reconstructions of extinct
primates by Stephen D. Nash.

Library of Congress Cataloging-in-Publication Data

Ciochon, Russell L.
    Other origins : the search for the giant ape in human prehistory /
Russell Ciochon, John Olsen, and Jamie James.
    p.   cm.
Includes bibliographical references and index.
ISBN 0-553-07081-9
    1. Gigantopithecus.   I. Olsen, John W.   II. James, Jamie.
III. Title.
GN282.6.C56   1990
569'.8—dc20   90-38913
                                                                           CIP

Published simultaneously in the United States and Canada

PRINTED IN THE UNITED STATES OF AMERICA

RRH   0 9 8 7 6 5 4 3 2 1

Contents

Acknowledgments

We wish to extend our sincerest appreciation first to our colleagues in the Socialist Republic of Vietnam for their continuing cooperation and openness. Ha Van Tan, Director of the Institute of Archaeology in Hanoi, and his staff deserve our thanks for their scientific professionalism and unflagging attention to our well-being and comfort in the field.

Our research in Vietnam was made possible through the able assistance of Nguyen Van Ku, Vice-Director of International Cooperation for the Vietnam Committee on Social Sciences; Nguyen Hoang An and Vu Dang Dzung of the Foreign Ministry, posted at the Vietnamese Embassy in Bangkok; Dr. Vo Quy, Dean of the Faculty of Biology at Hanoi University; Ha Nam Ninh, District Leader of the Ba Thuoc region, western Thanh Hoa province; and colleagues from the Thanh Hoa Provincial Museum in Thanh Hoa City.

Ambassador Emrys T. Davies of the British Embassy in Hanoi and his wife, Angela, provided invaluable assistance to our party in the absence of local American diplomatic representation. We thank them for allowing us to invade their official residence on various missions having to do with typewriters, telex machines, and spaghetti dinners.

Jodi Darragh of Americans for International Aide and her colleague, Lynn Oros, deserve recognition for their careful and efficient handling of our complex travel arrangements, including transshipment of large quantities of field equipment.

In China, our work was greatly facilitated by the kind assistance of Zhang Xingyong and Li Kunsheng of the Yunnan Provincial Museum; Jiang Tinyu and Xie Guangmao of the

Museum of the Guangxi Zhuang Autonomous Region; Yi Guangyuan of the Bailiandong Cave Science Museum, Liuzhou, Guangxi; and Wu Rukang, Huang Wanpo, Gu Yumin, and Zhang Yinyun of the Institute of Vertebrate Paleontology and Paleoanthropology in Beijing.

The L.S.B. Leakey Foundation in Oakland, California, the National Geographic Society, and the Old Gold Summer Fellowship Program of the University of Iowa have provided the financial assistance for our Vietnamese investigations and their support is gratefully acknowledged.

We are very grateful to Henry Schwarcz of McMaster University for dating the Lang Trang cave samples by electron spin resonance, and to the National Science Foundations for supporting this research.

For access to facilities and for other support of research undertaken on the University of Iowa campus we acknowledge the Center for Electron Microscopy Research, the Dows Dental Research Institute, the Graduate College, the Museum of Natural History, and the Departments of Anthropology, Biology, Botany, Geology, and Pediatric Dentistry.

Many people contributed in many ways to the implementation of our research and to the production of this book. Among the most important are our agents, John Brockman and Katinka Matson; Leslie Meredith, our editor; Richard Greenwell of the Tucson-based International Society for Cryptozoology; artists Bill Munns, Stephen Nash, and Will Thomson; and colleagues Eric Delson, Dennis Etler, John Fleagle, Clark Howell, Mark Morgan, Judith Moses, Richard Nisbett, Bob Thompson, and Tim White.

We reserve final acknowledgment for Dr. Judy Ladinsky of the U.S. Committee for Scientific Cooperation with Vietnam. Dr. Ladinsky's expertise, enthusiasm, and personal charm, more than any other factors, are responsible for the successful implementation of our research in Vietnam. We are very much in her debt.

RUSSELL CIOCHON
JOHN OLSEN
JAMIE JAMES

Foreword

Everything interesting that happened in human prehistory happened in Africa—everyone knows that. Charles Darwin theorized that the earliest humans evolved in Africa because, he argued, man's closest relatives, the chimpanzee and the gorilla, live there. By all accounts, he was absolutely right, and the date currently given to our earliest origin is about seven million years ago. Moreover, our ancestors first acquired an enlarged brain in Africa: that happened with the evolution of the genus *Homo,* probably about two and a half million years ago. And, if what certain molecular biologists infer about an arcane aspect of human genetics is correct, then Africa was also the place where modern humans—you and I—first evolved, maybe one hundred fifty thousand years ago.

So what were Russell Ciochon, John Olsen, and Jamie James up to when they took themselves off to Asia—and to Vietnam of all places? If they were interested in the *really* important pieces of the story of human evolution, their destination should have been Kenya or Tanzania or Ethiopia, surely?

Well, Russ Ciochon has never been one to be constrained by what others thought he should be doing, a quality that has raised eyebrows among some of his colleagues. But it is just that quality of doing the unexpected that sometimes produces great and, of course, unexpected rewards. That is precisely what happened in this case.

Teaming up with archaeologist John Olsen and writer Jamie James, Ciochon put together a bold expedition that would explore an aspect of human prehistory that no one else had addressed. More important, it's an aspect of human prehistory that no one else had even *thought* of addressing. The result is a novel insight into a critical juncture of human origins, some three quarters of a million years ago: the time during which our ancestors, *Homo erectus*, were first moving through Asia, the time when they would have had their first encounter with *Gigantopithecus*, a giant of an animal, the largest primate that ever lived.

Why is this interesting? Because it puts our ancestors in a very real environmental context that nevertheless has the stuff of fantasy about it. It makes us think hard about how very different the Asian world was for our ancestors, a world where bamboo might have been even more important than stone in their technological sphere. It makes us wonder at the possible role that our ancestors played in the final extinction of *Gigantopithecus*. And it tempts us to imagine what role the giant ape might have played in the origin of the almost universal myth of the Giant Ape—the yeti, Bigfoot, and others.

The story of the expedition combines elements of adventure, hardship, frustration, and, of course, the excitement of discovery. It was a team effort, we are told, and we get a frank and often humorous glimpse of how this most unusual of sciences—paleoanthropology—is really done out there in the field. Not quite the death-defying antics of Indiana Jones, but close. Jamie James, whose fractured French helped to stave off a diplomatic incident at one crucial point in the expedition, has done a wonderful job in putting it all together for a lay audience.

In these days of increasing political sensitivities, it can be difficult at best and virtually impossible at worst for anthropologists and archaeologists to obtain the required research permits from host governments, even in the best regulated of countries. Quite correctly, host countries whose resources for education and research may be limited are beginning to require visiting scientists to contribute some of their time and funding to helping students of those countries. In a very real sense, it is an opportunity for visiting scholars from rich nations to give something back to the host countries, from whose archaeological and paleontological resources they are benefiting. But it all makes for bureaucracy, and bureaucracy, as we all know, is a consumer of time and patience par excellence.

To attempt in the 1980's a scientific venture in Thanh Hoa, a western province of northern Vietnam, therefore invited bureaucratically inspired frustration, if not complete disaster, of the most exquisite nature. Even if the United States had not blasted the host country with the most devastating weapons of war, short of nuclear annihilation, a decade earlier, the task would have been challenging enough. As it was, the fact that the authors achieved anything at all is a tribute to their persistence and to the forgiving nature of the Vietnamese. It also helped that Olsen speaks fluent Mandarin.

The "proper" place for paleoanthropology has been Africa, of course, at least for the past half-century. The late Raymond Dart discovered the first early human fossil in South Africa in 1924; and he and his associate, Robert Broom, continued for twenty years to uncover more and more evidence of human prehistory in various sites in the region. For those twenty years the apelike fossils that Dart and Broom were recovering from various cave sites were dismissed by most authorities as having nothing important to do with the human story. Not until the late 1940's did the rest of the paleoanthropological world begin to take Dart and Broom—and Africa—seriously. The proper place for paleoanthropology at that time, you see, was Asia. The eminents in the science in both the United States and Britain had their eyes on the Asian continent as the birthplace of mankind. So it took a lot of powerful evidence to swing their gaze to the Dark Continent, but swing it did.

And when the Leakeys—first Louis and Mary and then their son, Richard—began to make their mark, from the early 1960's onward, East Africa became the focus of attention. For good reason, because the record of human history, written in fossil bones and stone tools, that came from the famous Olduvai Gorge in Tanzania (Leakeys senior) and along the shores of Lake Turkana in northern Kenya (Leakey junior) is truly stunning. Add to this Don Johanson and his French colleague's remarkable discoveries from farther north, in Ethiopia, which included the famous skeleton, Lucy, and you really are witnessing a revolution in a science.

As the authors of this book point out, the business of paleoanthropology has too often been about finding the oldest "this" or the most complete "that." What it really should be about is putting together the story of human origins from the most fragmentary of information: assembling a mosaic when most of the pieces are missing, as the authors put it. Nevertheless, that mosaic is steadily filling out, with tantalizing images beginning to emerge. How much more is left in order to complete the picture, no one knows, for how can you know what you don't know?

As a cautionary tale, it is salutary to read the writings of prominent paleoanthropologists of the early decades of this century, because one frequently comes across statements such as, "The outline of human prehistory is now clear, merely the details are missing." There was a tremendous confidence that The Truth had been wrested from the depths of prehistory. Now, of course, we know that nothing was clear, and it wasn't just the details that were missing.

What are we to say now, after the recent Africa-inspired revolution that I mentioned? That the outline is now clear, with merely the details missing? Almost certainly not. The outline looks good, it's true, especially as other sciences have recently begun to contribute significantly to paleoanthropology. Among these is behavioral ecology, which seeks to put human origins within a biological context, and genetics, which adds an extra dimension to seeking relationships in the family tree. A clearer picture therefore *is* emerging, one in which we see our forebears as animals among other animals, members of a biological environment in which naturalistic rules govern success and failure, in which some species survive while others do not.

But what of that element of specialness that used so much to pervade the thinking of paleoanthropologists, the notion that humans and their forebears somehow stood out from the rest of the naturalistic world, right from the beginning? Perhaps inevitably, there has been an overreaction to that position, so that many scholars now regard anything less than fully modern *Homo sapiens* as somehow crude and primitive, lacking entirely those elements that make us feel human. Compassion, consciousness of self and death, moral judgments, ritual and mythology—is every glimmer of these qualities restricted to the last few seconds of the evolutionary clock that measured our arrival? Surely not.

By making Asia the venue of their expedition, Ciochon and Olsen are "bringing paleoanthropology back home again," as they say. And by focusing on the encounter between *Homo erectus* and *Gigantopithecus*, they bring us right back into the territory of our humanness, they force us to contemplate it in the most unusual of circumstances.

Imagine it: An ape standing 10 feet tall and weighing in at 1,200 pounds. That's the way the authors describe *Gigantopithecus*, or Giganto for short. No one has seen such a creature, of course, but with the aid of a great deal of skill and $150,000 bestowed on a realistic reconstruction, a moving model has been made of one. Hold a Giganto jaw in your hand—in fact, fossil jaws and teeth are all that is known about the creature—and the mind truly boggles.

I saw my first Giganto jaw in Beijing, right next to a jaw of *Homo erectus*, as it happens. The comparison is so great that it was almost shocking, with the human relic dwarfed alongside the immense ape's. But it was a comparison simply of size: See how much bigger Giganto was than *Homo erectus*, that sort of thing. What the authors of this book have done is make the comparison real, for Giganto and *Homo erectus* are not just fossils, objects of paleontological interest and fascination: They were part of each other's worlds. And, just possibly, Giganto is still part of the modern world, our world, probably not as relict populations in remote places, but as part of our collective mythology: as the inspirer of the ubiquitous and compelling Bigfoot myth.

Which, of course, will send many professional scientists screaming for their *Handbook of Proper Scientific Procedures*, which, unfortunately, doesn't have an entry under "myth." Except, perhaps, to say that it has no place in science. Myth is not necessarily a synonym for fiction, as many seem to imagine. In the context of human culture, it is an essential part of the human condition, an embodiment of important things, a method of transmitting collective truths. Myths have a grasp on the human imagination that goes beyond the allure of fantasy.

Even in science itself—and especially in paleoanthropology— myth sometimes plays a part. The notion, mentioned earlier, that humans were somehow special from their evolutionary inception derives from the mythology of our special place in the world. And the current reaction to that, which makes humans special only in recent evolutionary time, is part of the making of modern myths that nevertheless has to do with coping with our place in the world. As long as we contemplate ourselves, whether as philosophers or as paleoanthropologists, that same question will intrude. That is the nature of being human.

Whether collective memory of events from deep in our past also contributes to modern mythology is open to question, open to the reader to contemplate. Did the encounter between *Gigantopithecus* and *Homo erectus* that we now know did, in fact, occur imprint itself so deeply in the human psyche that it was transmitted through thousands of generations, to be expressed still in modern folklore? Whatever answers one comes up with, *Other Origins* and the courageous venture that inspired it should at least make one reflect a little attentively on the nature of human history. For me, human history will never be quite the same again.

ROGER LEWIN
Washington, D.C.

The Illustrations

Page 8: (top) Nguyen Van Binh climbing in a cave in Ba Thuoc.
(bottom) Binh displaying a fossilized pig jaw excavated from Lang Trang II.

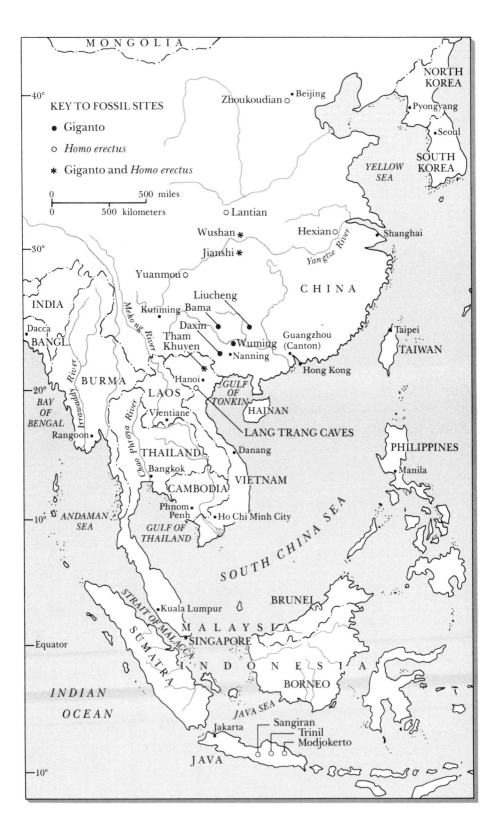

KEY TO FOSSIL SITES

● Giganto

○ *Homo erectus*

✳ Giganto and *Homo erectus*

| 0 | | 500 miles |
| 0 | 500 kilometers | |

MONGOLIA

NORTH KOREA

Zhoukoudian ○ • Beijing

• Pyongyang

• Seoul

YELLOW SEA

SOUTH KOREA

○ Lantian

Wushan ✳

Jianshi ✳

Hexian ○

Shanghai

Yangtze River

Yuanmou ○

CHINA

Liucheng

Kunming Bama

Daxin ●

Tham Khuyen

Wuming ●

Nanning

Guangzhou (Canton)

Taipei

TAIWAN

Hong Kong

INDIA

Dacca

BANGL.

Mekong River

Irrawaddy River

BURMA

Hanoi •

GULF OF TONKIN

LAOS

HAINAN

LANG TRANG CAVES

BAY OF BENGAL

Rangoon •

Vientiane •

Chao Phraya River

THAILAND

Bangkok •

CAMBODIA

VIETNAM

Danang •

PHILIPPINES

Manila •

ANDAMAN SEA

Phnom Penh •

• Ho Chi Minh City

SOUTH CHINA SEA

GULF OF THAILAND

Equator

STRAIT OF MALACCA

SUMATRA

• Kuala Lumpur

BRUNEI

MALAYSIA

SINGAPORE

INDONESIA

BORNEO

INDIAN OCEAN

JAVA SEA

Jakarta

Sangiran

Trinil

Modjokerto

JAVA

40°

30°

20°

10°

10°

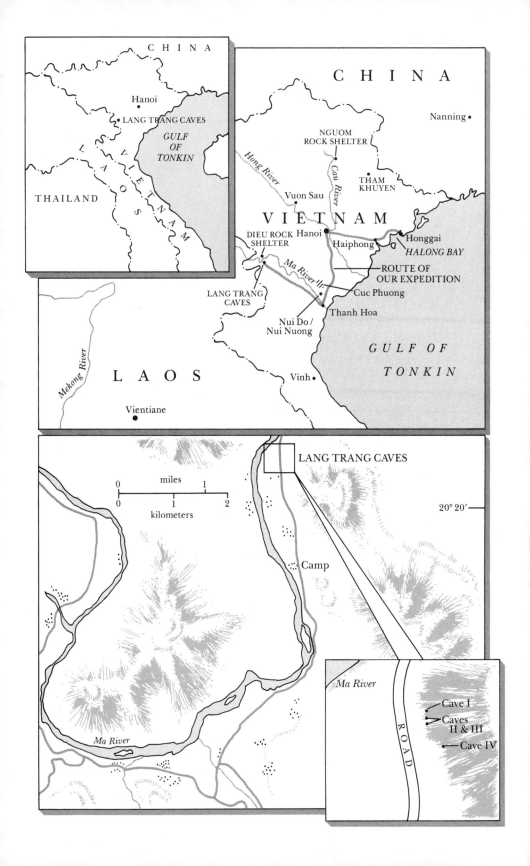

CHINA

Hanoi
• LANG TRANG CAVES

GULF OF TONKIN

LAOS

VIETNAM

THAILAND

CHINA

Nanning •

NGUOM ROCK SHELTER

Hong River

Cau River

Vuon Sau •

THAM KHUYEN

VIETNAM

DIEU ROCK SHELTER

Hanoi

Haiphong •

Honggai •
HALONG BAY

Ma River

ROUTE OF OUR EXPEDITION

LANG TRANG CAVES

Cuc Phuong

Nui Do / Nui Nuong

Thanh Hoa

GULF OF TONKIN

Mekong River

LAOS

Vinh •

Vientiane •

LANG TRANG CAVES

0   miles   1
0   1   2
kilometers

20° 20'—

Camp

Ma River

Ma River

Ma River

ROAD

Cave I

Caves II & III

Cave IV

First Contact

A Tale of Two Species

A few hundred thousand years ago, sometime during the Ice Age, as the early morning mists cleared over the semitropical jungle of what is now called Southeast Asia, perhaps somewhere in modern South China or northern Vietnam, our direct ancestor *Homo erectus* had a momentous first encounter with another primate—a huge extinct ape called *Gigantopithecus*, the largest member of our own taxonomic order, the Primates, that ever existed on earth.

A brave, hardy band of *Homo erectus* has broken off from a larger group of their kind and left them far behind. They are a migrating people, always on the move, searching for food— and also, perhaps, driven by curiosity to see what is on the other side of the horizon. By the modern standard our ancestors would seem to us brutish, but they are unmistakably human: standing fully erect, as their name implies, clear-sighted, and bold. They are encamped under a rock overhang, which affords protection from the elements. On this early morning, the older women of the group are hunkering in the mouth of the overhang, rocking on their heels in just the same fashion as their modern Asian descendants. They are milling wild rice between two stones, preparing a breakfast gruel. An adolescent girl tends the fire, periodically feeding it old, weathered bamboo culms, which crackle and spark when they make contact with the flames. Sitting near the fire is an old woman, who is plaiting a sleeping mat from dried bamboo leaves.

The little children, whose job is to gather bamboo shoots and other edible greens from the edge of the jungle for the day's meal, have wandered out of their grandmothers' sight. Two little boys have flushed a sleeping bamboo rat from its burrow and are gleefully chasing it. Suddenly an orangutan, hidden in a nearby stand of bamboo, utters a strange, loud call. The ape's cry frightens one of the very young children, who begins wailing to attract his mother's attention.

The young women of the group are gathered in a wild patch of rice they had recently discovered near the overhang. They are grunting and shaking their heads in disgust: a herd of elephants, or perhaps of *Stegodon,* an even more enormous kin of the elephant, passed through during the night and trampled the tender shoots. They resignedly begin picking through the damage done by the huge mammals, to see if any of the young plants are still edible.

Meanwhile, their mates, the young men, are preparing to go out for the hunt. The thick-muscled youths pull down the sturdiest culms of bamboo and, using sharpened stones from the nearby riverbed, fashion them into weapons. It is a painful, laborious process, and their fingers are bleeding by the time they have finished, but they need a good supply of projectiles and skinning tools for the day's hunt. One of the young men indicates—perhaps with a specialized guttural sound, or merely a gesture—where they will go today in search of game. One of the elders might perform a bit of shamanic magic to invoke the protection of a hunt god.

They have not had a kill for a long time: twenty days before, they killed a mother panda and her cub, which provided the group with meat and fat for several days. But after a week of nothing to eat but wild rice, bamboo shoots, and bitter greens, they are hungry for meat. This morning, the youths head toward the river, where one of the group recently saw some pandas. They fan out and sweep quietly through the jungle, searching the dim undergrowth for a vibration in the cover, a swish of fur. As they approach the river, they hear a loud racket of bamboo being trampled. Debouching from the thick cover of the bamboo forest into the riverside clearing, they take in an amazing sight—something utterly unlike anything ever before seen by their species.

In a clump of bamboo at the edge of the clearing, a troop of giant apes is foraging, snapping huge stalks of bamboo as easily as so many bits of straw. They hear the approach of the men, and turn. The two species are eyeball to eyeball for the first time. The apes loom to a height of ten feet—more than twice the height of the men!—and weigh well over a thousand pounds. They are covered with golden hair that is a bit grayer on their backs and shoulders, and of a reddish, auburn cast on the arms. They are fist-walkers; one of them lopes forward a few gigantic steps to get a closer look at the group of men. Its head is enormous, with a thickset jaw. The crown of its head looks almost diminutive atop the huge mandible. Small yellow eyes burn in its skull as it takes in the sight of its furless distant cousins. A half-eaten bamboo stem hangs from its gaping maw.

The men sense that they are not in danger from the apes. They have had experience with other great apes, such as the orangutan, and they intuit that these *Gigantopithecus*, immense and fearsome as they appear, are not interested in killing them. Yet they are amazed, awestruck. As the vanguard in the human dispersion through Asia, they are brave and clear-minded, but they are making first contact with something utterly new. After a moment, they collect their wits and begin shouting and gesticulating, brandishing their weapons. They have no intention of engaging in hostilities with the apes; it is only an instinctive defensive reaction. The huge apes amble slowly into the forest, away from the band of our ancestors, who race home to communicate what they have seen to the women and the old men as best they can.

That is no tale told by Edgar Rice Burroughs or H. G. Wells. Exactly how fanciful our version is, or in how many details it diverges from the "truth"—what really happened— we shall never know. Nor can we say with certainty exactly where the meeting took place or what happened afterward, as the two species learned to live side by side.

Yet we do know that something like this happened: *Giganto-pithecus* is native to South Asia, while *Homo* originated in Africa and migrated eastward, finally arriving in what is now called

Southeast Asia no later than 800,000 years ago. Incontrovertible evidence that some such contact took place was supplied in 1965 by Vietnamese excavators: in a cave in northern Vietnam, at a site called Tham Khuyen, some fossil teeth of *Gigantopithecus* were found alongside human remains. In addition, two recent finds in China, in Hubei and Sichuan provinces, have bolstered the plausibility of the human-Giganto nexus. At both sites, fossils of the giant ape were found in depositions that also contained human remains.

The details of our scenario of this first encounter between our ancestors and Giganto, to use the nickname that has gained currency among those of us who are on speaking terms with the great beast, range from dead certainties to educated guesses. We know, for example, that pandas and orangutans were present, because we ourselves have excavated their fossil remains, but the premise that they were hunted by *Homo erectus* with bamboo weapons is a logical conclusion, based upon a web of analogy and inference. As to whether *Gigantopithecus*, like the orangutan and other Asian primates, actually had golden hair, a grayish back, and auburn arms—that is just a guess. But at this point we feel that we are entitled to make a few educated guesses: we have spent the better part of the past three years traveling throughout Asia trying to bring to life this scenario of the existence of our ancestors, to fill in the blank of this particular canvas of prehistory.

Paleoanthropology and archaeology can rarely be done in comfortable, modern places where you can use your credit cards. For some reason, this kind of work is usually accomplished in places where beds come draped with mosquito nets, where bush jackets and pith helmets do not look ridiculous. Yet even by the standards of modern field excavation, our search for remains of *Homo erectus*, a direct human ancestor, and of *Gigantopithecus*, the largest ape that ever existed, took us about as far off the beaten track as it was possible to go: to the remote and beautiful uplands of western Thanh Hoa province, in northern Vietnam.

In 1989, just fourteen years after our two countries had been at war, we were digging side by side with specialists from the Institute of Archaeology in Hanoi, on the first joint field expedition ever mounted by scientists from the United States and Vietnam. The excavation we have undertaken with the Vietnamese, at a cave system called Lang Trang (the name comes from a tiny hamlet nearby), has yielded a fossil discovery of major importance: in January 1989 we discovered the first firmly dated specimen of *Homo erectus* in Southeast Asia (actually, there are five of them!). *Homo erectus* was long known to have existed in mid-China and in Indonesia, under the familiar names of Peking Man and Java Man, but between the two there yawned a gap. Now that gap has been closed, and what might be called Lang Trang Man can take his place next to his more famous contemporaries.

We have recovered more than a thousand fossil specimens to date from the Lang Trang caves, and we have literally only scratched the surface. The fossils from Lang Trang are creating, piece by piece, the best picture yet available to science of Southeast Asia in the Ice Age.

Assembling the Human Mosaic

The disembodied "we" leading you on this tour through the life and times of our prehistoric ancestors in Asia are three: Russell Ciochon, a professor of paleoanthropology at the University of Iowa, whose profession it is to put flesh on the fossilized bones of the fauna that lived in the prehistoric environment; John Olsen, an archaeologist from the University of Arizona, to glean as much information as possible about the life of early man from the artifacts he left behind; and Jamie James, a writer to put it all together for the ordinary reader.

Of the three of us, Russell Ciochon is the dogged, relentless doer, the determined soul of the expedition. He is our equivalent of what football color commentators call the Motivator. Although Ciochon has traveled in Asia on more than thirty field trips, he has managed not to absorb the first thing of how they do business in that part of the world. He simply does not take no for an answer, and Communist Asia is a place where "no" is a way of life. Whenever things begin to look bleak, when the bureaucratic dissembling and delays seem to be simply insurmountable, Ciochon hangs tough and says, "Look,

I'm not leaving here until you . . . ," and then he explains in precise terms what he needs. Sometimes that stubbornness is embarrassing, and on a few, rare occasions it has created problems for us. Yet more often it is a way out of problems: Asians are not accustomed to powerful personalities like Ciochon's, and his deep, abiding belief that he is going to get his way usually inspires the same belief in the people we are dealing with. His mind is a quick instrument, and those not accustomed to his rapid, wide-ranging speech are sometimes bewildered by him. But listen to him, and you will learn a lot—especially if it has to do with paleoanthropology. The man knows his bones.

John Olsen is utterly different from Ciochon, and the two complement each other perfectly as professional colleagues. John is a cool, phlegmatic intellectual, thorough in his preparation and cautious in reaching conclusions. Yet when he does make up his mind, everyone stops talking to hear what he has to say. Olsen has become particularly adept at smoothing over the ruffled feathers that Ciochon sometimes leaves behind him. A second-generation archaeologist who received his Ph.D. at twenty-four, his dedication to the field of prehistoric archaeology is absolute. He has a devilish sense of humor—particularly if Ciochon is the butt of the joke. Whenever the Big Guy, as Ciochon is affectionately known, gets to be a little too big for his britches, no one else can deflate him with a deft, well-aimed barb as can Olsen.

Jamie James is perhaps the most incongruous member of the group: an inveterate city slicker from New York, a subscriber to the Metropolitan Opera who collects first editions, he does not resemble anyone's idea of an outdoorsman. But he found camp life quite congenial, and soon carved out a niche for himself as the expedition's chef. James joined Ciochon and Olsen as a journalist coming along to cover their story; a former *Discover* staffer, he had developed a diverse portfolio. In addition to scientific subjects, he has written on themes as diverse as South American literature, polo, and German opera. A quick study, James immersed himself in the Giganto assignment, taking a serious, scholarly approach to his role. The coauthor of a book about archaeology in Cyprus who had also traveled extensively to sites in Mexico and Peru, James was well suited to the assignment. Yet he soon found that the quest for Giganto was becoming more than just an assignment, and he became deeply involved in the expedition as a participant, not just an observer.

In many fields scientists must learn to make the most of very sparse information. However, perhaps only cosmologists must go quite as far down the treacherous path of inference as do we who spin stories about human prehistory. The data are scarce and unreliable, and so are prized all the more. Scientists in the last generation have made extraordinary advances in wringing the last drop of information from the rare scraps of evidence that are available. Yet despite the quickened pace of scientific discovery, our ignorance remains vast.

For several million years before the emergence of modern man, hominid ancestors were making tools. The earliest cultural artifacts that have been found so far are some African stone tools dated to 2.5 million years B.P. ("before the present," the standard abbreviation now used by scientists when dates extend too far back into the past for a biblical time standard to be useful). Between that time and the first tentative scratchings of written history, which were made at the earliest around 5,000 B.P., lies 99 percent (99.8 percent, not to put too fine a point on it) of the story of the human race. The job of prehistoric archaeologists is to reconstruct that story, to reconstitute intellectually and imaginatively the world inhabited by our ancestors from the available evidence.

The archaeological record, all known cultural remains taken as a whole, is a reflection of human life in the past, but it is a warped, skewed reflection. Think of a cracked mirror, with the silver peeling off the back and dirt covering the front surface. Such a mirror would provide a recognizable, reasonably accurate reflection of the person gazing into it, but it would be far from precise. The archaeological record reflects the prehistoric world in much the same way.

Owing to a wide variety of factors, the archaeological record preserves some aspects of culture better than others. These factors are known collectively as formation processes, because they delineate the parameters within which archaeological artifacts may outlast the many forces that conspire to destroy them, and, just as important, determine in what form they survive to us. In plain language, archaeologists must confine their interpretations to those artifacts that have survived the passage of the years. A culture that we know only from its bones and stones and perhaps its ceramics might very well have made a whole variety of things from organic raw materials. If their writing system had employed an organic ink on dried leaves, for instance, we would have absolutely no record of it. An archaeologist who was not thinking carefully might say, based upon the record, that it was a nonliterate culture; a good archaeologist simply notes that there is no evidence that the culture had a writing system.

The study of the remains of the living world falls under the purview of paleontology, of which paleoanthropology, the study of the fossil remains of man and the other primates, is a subspecialty. In the prehistoric world, *Homo* was just another member of the animal kingdom, competing for survival with the others; and his lot was made easier or more difficult by the abundance or scarcity of plant and animal life in the environment. Such is still the position *Homo* occupies in the living world, though that basic circumstance of our generic existence has become considerably more complicated: as a species we have learned ways of transforming raw materials into entirely new substances, suitable for the manufacture of the necessities of life—a revolution that is wreaking havoc on our global environment. For most of the time that people have existed, they have not lived in houses or had plentiful supplies of durable clothing, nor has their supply of food been at all certain. Man lived very much as a part of the natural world. That is not to say that prehistory was ever a golden age: on the contrary, it was a wild and woolly place. The fossil record, the paleontological counterpart of the archaeological record, provides a window onto the world of our ancestors, showing first exactly who they were, and second which animals and plants shared their environment.

The picture of prehistoric life told by the fossil record must be pieced together within the same restrictions as those that operate in the archaeological record, described above. The fossil record covers virtually the entire planet, in most cases buried under the surface of the earth, though occasionally it is exposed by erosion. The number of scientists trained to look

for fossils is very small, and paleontology as a systematic enquiry is a relatively young enterprise, scarcely a hundred years
old. Thus the discoveries that enlarge the fossil record are, to an
enormous extent, a matter of dumb luck.

The limitations real life places on a scientist—urgent logistical
matters such as finding a place to plant a spade, getting permission to do so from the local politicians and landowners, and
then finding the money to pay for it all—take up an inordinate
amount of time. When the day finally arrives that digging can
actually begin, all the surveys and geological reports in the
world cannot guarantee that anything more than dirt will be
found. Nonetheless, it is a sort of axiom in paleontology that
you make your own luck; or, in the words of Branch Rickey,
the former owner of the Dodgers, "Luck is the residue of
design." It almost always turns out that good paleontologists
have good luck, and, conversely, those who never seem to find
anything of interest are not the good paleontologists.

Yet the discovery of interesting new fossils is not even the
most important aspect of our science. Since, to a really overwhelming extent, the vast majority of fossils will never be
excavated, the art of interpretation is much more important
than the mechanics of excavation. Practically speaking, the
discovery of any new fossil, regardless of how "major" it is,
enlarges our understanding of the overall picture by only a
small degree.

Paleontology is an attempt to piece together a mosaic. We
are missing almost all of the tiles, though we do not know
exactly how many; we do not even know which side is up on
the tiles that we do have; and we have no clues as to what the
design of the mosaic will ultimately turn out to be (rather like
trying to solve a jigsaw puzzle without the box lid). Thus the
fossils we do discover are precious, and we must exercise
caution—and, to the extent that we can, wisdom—in interpreting them. The archaeological and fossil records, combined
with what information may be gleaned about climate from
geological studies, tell us all that we will ever know about the
world inhabited by the human race before the historical era. It
is a never-ending process; as each new discovery adds another
fragment to the design, most of our preexisting notions must
be revised to accommodate the new bit of evidence.

Myths of the "Man-Ape"

Paleoanthropology, despite its sesquipedalian name, is one of the most popular of the sciences, and the reason is not hard to find: it is about ourselves and our relatives in the mammalian family tree. Those of us who poke around in the earliest days of the human race grow accustomed to people taking a keen interest in our work. When Ciochon's group in Burma in 1978 found the fossil remains of *Amphipithecus*, the earliest known anthropoid predecessor, their discovery was on the front page of the *New York Times*, and *Time* did a story about it. Even *People* magazine called him up.

Yet even on the paleoanthropological scale of things, the amount of interest our research into Giganto has stirred has been extraordinary, not only among our professional peers, which is gratifying, of course, but also among the public. And that, in a way, is a part of our subject. There is something in us that simply cannot resist the tale of our direct ancestors barging into the presence of a ten-foot-tall ape, and that itself is a proper subject for anthropology. Anthropology per se is the study of humanity, from our first appearance on the evolutionary stage to the complexity of our present social condition: a big subject, to say the least. So it is commonly divided into a myriad subordinate "—ologies," which fall into two main areas, cultural anthropology and physical anthropology (with archaeology as a sister discipline floating somewhere between the two, perhaps nearer to cultural than physical). At times the two anthropologies seem to have about as much in common as do botany and astrophysics. Cultural anthropology is the study of human societies, a discipline pioneered by Franz Boas, Margaret Mead, and others. Physical anthropology is concerned with the biological aspects of the human organism, the study of human variation and human adaptation. It encompasses paleoanthropology, which may be defined as the study of the evolutionary history of our ancestors as visualized through the examination of their fossilized remains and through comparative anatomy of the human body with specimens of the other primates, both fossil and living.

Our study of *Gigantopithecus* brings the two fields together in a unique and compelling juncture, for myths of great hairy manlike creatures are a part of the folklore of most primitive cultures. In recent years many studies on the recurrent motif of the man-ape in our history have been published, ranging from the seriously scientific to the quasi- and semiscientific and the downright silly. Two of the more reputable tenants of the Bigfoot bookshelf are *Manlike Monsters on Trial,* published by the University of British Columbia Press, consisting of papers presented at the university at a symposium on the subject; the other is *Still Living? Yeti, Sasquatch, and the Neanderthal Enigma,* by Myra Shackley, a lecturer at the University of Leicester. Shackley's book traces the phenomenon back to the tablets of Gilgamesh, the Babylonian epic that is one of the earliest works of literature extant.

One of the epic's principal episodes, worth setting forth in detail here, concerns the meeting between Gilgamesh, the hero, and a hulking wildman called Enkidu. In Joseph Campbell's version of the epic, in *The Masks of God: Occidental Mythology,* Enkidu is described like this: "The whole of his body was hairy and his locks were like a woman's, or like the hair of the goddess of grain. Moreover, he knew nothing of settled flocks or of human beings, and was clothed like a deity of flocks." Enkidu, who was brought into the world by the mother goddess (or a potter, depending on how one reads the tablets), was cavorting with the gazelles at their waterholes and terrifying the local folk. Gilgamesh, the king, advised his people to tempt the man-beast with the sexual charms of the priestess of Ishtar. The strategy succeeded, and Enkidu was eventually tamed and lived peaceably with the Babylonian shepherds. Gilgamesh, however, being a hero, had to do battle with Enkidu; he won, naturally, but he spared the wildman, and the two became inseparable companions.

As Shackley points out, the interesting thing about the tale is its homely ring of truth, particularly the detail about the man-beast at the waterholes terrifying the local gentry: there is something unmistakably *observed* about the incident. It is axiomatic in the modern study of myth that certain elements are imaginary, and certain other elements are based on real experiences, even if at a great temporal and experiential remove. In Homer, for example, while the faithfulness of Penelope and the disorderly clamor of her suitors are clearly based on life, the giant one-eyed Cyclops is just as obviously the invention of the poetic imagination (although the poet's imagination could certainly have been sparked by a real-life freak of nature). The impact of Heinrich Schliemann's discovery in the late nineteenth century of the historical Troy upon the interpretation of myth is difficult to overestimate. Until then the city of Troy was almost universally assumed to be as much an invention of Homer as the Cyclops. We are not suggesting that the Trojan question, as it is known to classicists, is settled, but certainly a consensus exists among scholars that Troy was a real city, which is now known to archaeology as the site near the modern town of Hissarlik, in western Turkey.

Shackley also enumerates the vast catalog of classical and medieval references to satyrs and wildmen, which are more easily dismissed as purely literary figments. Nevertheless, among preliterate cultures belief in the existence of a threatening anthropomorphic beast, typically covered with hair, is virtually universal. In addition to the familiar sasquatch of North American Indians and the yeti of the Himalayas, there are remarkably similar legends around the world: the *almas* of central China, various hairy giants of Central America, the *didis* of Guiana, the *sedapas* of Sumatra, and many more, in every quarter of the globe, all fit the same description. In a later chapter, we shall explore the myths of the giant ape that persist even today.

We are not proposing here a defense of the existence of the Abominable Snowman; he has enough advocates already. Yet the preponderance of worldwide legendary material, essentially so similar, makes it natural to look for a common source of some kind. There are the two main schools of thought on the subject of how legends arise. The Swiss psychoanalyst Carl Jung articulated the view that myths issue from within the psyche, from what he called the collective unconscious of the human race. From that point of view, it might be postulated that it is inevitable that similarities exist among the legends and fairy tales of widely distributed cultures, because they are the creations of deep-seated human needs. In this case, many would suggest that the frightful bogeyman image of the hairy man-beast is an objectification of man's profound and inchoate libidinal (if we may change psychological-theoretical horses in midstream) instincts.

The alternative view is most cogently expressed by Claude Lévi-Strauss, who propounded the theory that myths are handed down from person to person, and culture to culture, and that while this process continually transforms the legendary material, the underlying structures remain the same. Like Homer's Troy, foundations for universal myths can be found in the *real* experiences of our ancestors.

One of Russell Ciochon's graduate students at Iowa, Brenda Sutherland, has compiled an encyclopedic survey of anthropomorphic legends throughout the world, which powerfully supports the supposition that they must have some common origin— whether of a psychic or an experiential nature is more difficult to say. Sutherland also addresses in her research the question of how long a legend can survive. The aborigines of Australia have a cultural tradition that extends back more than 38,000 years. Their legends, passed down in a continuous storytelling chain, tell about bizarre creatures that the aborigines believe lived in a golden age they call the *kadimakara,* the dreamtime. Some paleontologists such as Patricia Rich, of Australia's Monash University, believe that these legends are based on the tribal memory of animals now extinct but which have turned up in the fossil record. For example, some aboriginal stories concern a man-eating monster called the *bunyip,* which bears a strong resemblance to *Palorchestes,* a bull-sized marsupial with massive claws and a short trunk that became extinct at the end of the last Ice Age.

That figure of 38,000 years may seem excessive, but several corroborating instances exist of the persistence of folk tales beyond the 10,000-year mark. In his reminiscences about life with the Indians of Panama, Leon DeSmidt relates that the Cuna tribe have a legend about a giant demon with a long snout trailing down to the ground—very similar to an elephant that had been extinct in the New World for at least 10,000 years. On the other side of the Pacific Ocean, the Chukchee people of the eastern Soviet Union, according to a study published at the turn of this century, told tales about lost tribes who emigrated beyond the sea but sometimes swim back. These legends indicate a cultural continuity with the prehistoric era before human ancestors crossed the Bering land bridge, which was cut off only 8,000 to 10,000 years ago.

An even more cogent case that may be interpreted as demonstrating the persistence of tribal memory can be found in the lore of the Tehuelche Indians, in Patagonia. Several travelers have reported that the Tehuelche tell tales of a giant nocturnal beast, "as big as an ox" but with short legs and a coat of short coarse hair. No living animal in the New World resembles this nameless legendary creature. However, scientists since the eighteenth century have known about the fossil remains of a huge sloth that became extinct less than 30,000 years ago, which would have matched the Tehuelche's creature rather closely. The famous natural historian Georges Cuvier (1779–1832) examined one such fossil and named the animal *Megatherium,* which means simply "large mammal." *Megatherium* certainly deserved its prefix: the animal was at least fifteen feet tall when it stood on its hind legs, which it probably did in order to eat leaves, and it had terrible curved claws the size of a reaper's sickle.

Scientists in the nineteenth century were reluctant to concede that man could ever have known *Megatherium* at first hand, for they supposed the animal's antiquity to be much greater than it actually was. Likewise, it was long believed that the mammoths, the enormous Ice Age elephantids, could never have been known by man—until Paleolithic cave paintings of the animals in Europe proved that they were. A third example may be found in the case of *Glyptodon,* the giant armadillo-like animal that flourished in the Americas during the last Ice Age. Armored carapaces of *Glyptodon* have been excavated that reach lengths of up to twelve feet. It was always assumed that this monstrous creature became extinct long before the crossing of the Bering land bridge—until 1881, when a natural historian named Santiago Roth found human remains underneath, or next to, a *Glyptodon*'s carapace at an excavation site near Buenos Aires. Other scientists have turned up carapaces with hearths underneath them: the evidence suggests that Ice Age Patagonians used *Glyptodon* carapaces as houses, or perhaps as tombs.

We make no claims for what is unprovable and even unassertable, but it is certainly within the bounds of legitimate conjecture to postulate that the encounter between *Gigantopithecus* and early man, which we know took place, might have had an impact on the primary matrix of tribal memory. It is a fascinating thought to keep in the back of the mind, as we venture forward on our exploration of the life of early man, that the source for the worldwide legend of the anthropomorphic bogeyman might well have been a real creature that left behind real fossil remains. The study of human prehistory is one, we have asserted, that needs no popularizing or "livening up": we are all enthralled by the enigma of the dawn of our kind. The direction of our studies into *Gigantopithecus* and *Homo erectus* in Asia, by placing us toe to toe as a species with what might well be the source of one of the most fundamental of archetypal myths, proceeds to the very heart of human science. Our work could potentially bring us to a direct confrontation with ourselves.

CHAPTER 2

Asian Geneses

An African Obsession

Probably the most compelling question that can ever be put to paleoanthropology, the issue that underlies our field, is, Where did we come from? As is the case with all big questions, it is much more easily posed than answered. That is not to say that we cannot answer it; the problem, rather, is that there are so many answers, depending on how you define and modify the terms. Still, most paleoanthropologists can agree on the very broad outlines of the answer: our genus, *Homo,* emerged in Africa sometime around two million years ago, descending from the same ancestral primate stock that produced the African great apes—the chimpanzee and the gorilla. If you attempt to clarify the picture much beyond that very sketchy point, you will hear as many explanations, and see as many family-tree diagrams, as you have paleoanthropologists.

To begin with, there is great uncertainty as to what we mean by "we" when we ask, Where did we come from? or, to put it another way, What does being human really mean? It is a deeply subjective issue, and the answer you get depends on whom you ask: an archaeologist will define humanness in terms of toolmaking or the use of fire, perhaps, while a paleoanthropologist will express it in terms of the morphology of fossil bones and teeth. While controversy has raged in prehistoric studies, with repercussions reaching far beyond our immediate field, in recent years some firmly held convictions on the subject of human origins have gained general acceptance—yet even these, like most firmly held convictions, are well worth reexamining with a skeptical eye.

Paleoanthropologists, as much as the public, have for years held a prejudice that breaks down into two overly simplistic formulas: first, that older is always better, and second, that Africa is the place for all interesting investigations into the emergence of man. The two assumptions go together: since Africa is earliest, in terms of human remains, it follows that it must be best.

The idea that older is better has taken a surprisingly firm grip on the field of paleoanthropology, but under even the mildest light of logical scrutiny, it becomes almost nonsensical. The principal way of coming up with the oldest possible hominid fossil is to bend the definition of what we call human. This has been carried far beyond any sensible limit. If you saw Donald Johanson's prehuman "Lucy," *Australopithecus afarensis,* her appearance, aside from her upright posture, would be in no sense human (nor, it ought to be pointed out, has Johanson ever claimed that she was). Johanson's discovery of Lucy was certainly a major find, not least because such a large portion of the specimen (40 percent) was unearthed, yet it has been the focus of sometimes misguided popular attention, simply because it pushed back the hominid "envelope" to a point even further than the three-million-year mark it had previously reached.

The "older is better" fetish is just that, a fetish, but age is utterly irrelevant if what interests us is to come up with some idea of what life was like for our ancestors in the mysterious span of prehistory. In fact, some of the most exciting work going on right now is in the area of determining where and when completely modern *Homo sapiens* first arose, the last major event of paleoanthropology.

As for the second assumption, that Africa is inherently more interesting than the rest of the world, it ought to be freely conceded that from one point of view that is a valid generalization. For the past twenty or thirty years, some of the most spectacular finds in the history of paleoanthropology— the discoveries made by the Leakeys in Tanzania and Kenya, and Donald Johanson's work in Ethiopia—have been coming out of that continent. Furthermore, as we have stated, every responsible thinker in the field believes that *Homo* arose in Africa. Setting all "fetishism" aside, nothing is more fascinating to contemplate than that first day when a creature who was recognizably and identifiably one of us existed on the planet. Yet that is only the beginning.

Paleoanthropology's obsession with Africa, and scorn for the study of the spread of *Homo* out of Africa, would be analogous to a modern historian turning up his nose at the saga of the discovery and settlement of the New World. Yet in many quarters, among both academics and the lay public, African studies has an ineluctable snob appeal and a disdain for Asian studies in human prehistory flourishes.

It was not always so, however. Throughout most of the history of paleoanthropology and archaeology as sciences, scarcely a hundred years, it was widely assumed that Asia would be the focus of the study of early man. Many of the most important names in paleoanthropology—Eugene Dubois, Roy Chapman Andrews, Davidson Black, Pierre Teilhard de Chardin, and Ralph von Koenigswald, to mention a few—did their work in the great triangle roughly described by Calcutta, Beijing, and Java. They made some of the most significant discoveries of our science there, as we shall see in the next chapter.

The Eve Hypothesis vs. Regional Continuity

During the past two years, Africa has once again been thrust into the paleoanthropological limelight, this time in connection with new thinking about the most recent common ancestor of all modern peoples. The press has nicknamed this new interpretation the Eve hypothesis, because the ancestor scientists have experimentally identified is a woman, "the mother of us all." To arrive at this startling conclusion, scientists compared the structure of mitochondrial deoxyribonucleic acid (mtDNA) in living human cells of various populations living throughout the world. Why did they use DNA from the mitochondria, the powerhouse of the cell, which is located in the cytoplasm? In the 1970's biochemists discovered that the DNA of the cell's mitochondria does not result from a mixing of both parents' genes, as is the case with other DNA, but rather is passed down directly from the mother to the offspring. Thus it preserves a family record that can be traced back many generations through the female line.

Over the course of many generations, random changes occur in the structure of mtDNA, as they do in other parts of the cell, as the result of genetic mutation. Biochemists Rebecca Cann, Mark Stoneking, and Alan Wilson hypothesized that by examining the structure of mtDNA from women from all over the world, it would be possible to reconstruct the last common ancestor of all those individuals, by determining the degree to which they differed in their DNA structure. When this analysis was performed, using samples from 147 women, the common ancestor of them all was postulated to be an African woman who lived some 200,000 years ago—"Eve." As the first representative of our own species, this hypothetical Eve presumably would have looked and behaved, in all essential respects, like a modern African woman. The theory's proponents derived this date from estimates of the average mutation rate for mtDNA over the course of time. *Homo erectus* was already flourishing throughout Eurasia by that time, but according to the Eve hypothesis, modern *Homo sapiens* arose in Africa, then migrated quickly throughout the Old World, and completely supplanted the preexisting hominid species. Some proponents of the theory will admit privately, however, that the data and mathematical probabilities only slightly favor Africa over Asia as the source continent, the home of Eve—though none of them has conceded that somewhat compromising aspect of their analysis in print. Is it possible that the African mystique is at work again?

Since this provocative thesis was first advanced, amid all the hoopla that generally accompanies a bold new theory about human origins, dissenters have cast grave doubts on the conclusions of the mtDNA analysis. Foremost among them is paleoanthropologist Milford Wolpoff. Wolpoff advocates an alternative view of the rise of modern *Homo sapiens,* which is usually known by the catchphrase "regional continuity." This view of the emergence of modern man, based on direct observation of the fossil record, is that *Homo,* in the form of *Homo erectus,* originally migrated out of Africa about one million years ago and spread throughout the Old World. Modern man, *Homo sapiens,* then evolved simultaneously in different regions. The theory has two advantages over the Eve hypothesis: first, it accounts for the regional variations that may be observed in human fossils everywhere in the Old World, throughout the whole time span covered by the human lineage; and second, it postulates a more gradual process of evolution than the Eve hypothesis, which rests upon the notion that *Homo sapiens* was a brand-new species that emerged 200,000 years ago and completely supplanted *Homo erectus,* which became an evolutionary dead end.

In the first place, the fossil record shows that other populations of *Homo sapiens* were living in Europe and Asia prior to the 200,000 B.P. date for "Eve." What happened to these populations? Were they totally wiped out by the African populations of *Homo sapiens,* without leaving a trace? Moreover, as Milford Wolpoff points out, there are no firmly dated African specimens of *Homo sapiens* from the critical time period of around 200,000 years B.P. In fact, he asserts, there are not even any equivocally dated African specimens that support the Eve hypothesis. The most convincing support for regional continuity comes from a careful analysis of the earliest fossils of *Homo sapiens* recovered from different regions of Eurasia: in every case, according to Wolpoff, they bear stronger morphological affinities with their local predecessors, the various firmly dated specimens of *Homo erectus,* than they do with anything African.

The central problem with the Eve hypothesis, according to the proponents of regional continuity, is that it rests on some very sweeping, and questionable, assumptions. In a long, comprehensive paper published in 1989, Wolpoff summarized the widespread criticism of the underpinnings of Cann, Stoneking, and Wilson's theory in this way:

> The genetic basis for the Garden of Eden [Eve] hypothesis is most widely attributed to the interpretation of mtDNA variation. This interpretation rests on the reading of a genetic clock from the mitochondrial variation, which requires the assumptions that (1) the main source of mtDNA variation is mutations (selection and drift can be discounted);

(2) the rate of mutations is constant everywhere, and mutation accumulation is linear with time; (3) the colonization events used in rate-determinations are accurately dated, singular, and unidirectional. It is unlikely that *any* of these assumptions are correct.

Those are strong words. However persuasive the Eve hypothesists may be, there is always something a bit more compelling about a chain of reasoning based on the tangible fossil evidence than on algebraic interpretations of statistics. Perhaps Wolpoff's most convincing single argument against the Eve hypothesis is his postulation that the complete replacement of one human population by another has never been possible, because there is always a process of admixture at work. The classic case of admixture is the colonization of the New World, where, even conceding the catastrophic effects on native populations of the war and disease brought to the New World by Europeans, as well as the latter's technological superiority, admixture clearly was the result. In North America the ultimate result has been the virtual extinction of American Indian populations, but the vast majority of the modern inhabitants of the New World constitute an admixture of Indian and Old World gene pools.

In order for the Eve hypothesis to make any sense, we would have to accept the premise that there was never any sexual contact between the preexisting archaic *Homo sapiens* and the emergent breed of modern *Homo sapiens,* a rather improbable notion. After all, the theoretical "Eve" must have had her "Adam," and he could only have come from some preexisting stock. The process of admixture must therefore have been at work from the very beginning. In the place of admixture, the Eve hypothesists would have us believe that the new African *Homo sapiens* carried out a relentless campaign of extermination of archaic *Homo sapiens* throughout the world, without ever establishing a single point of genetic contact. As Wolpoff says, "Admixture between invading and indigenous populations would invalidate the interpretation of [the Eve hypothesis], because it would result in the introduction of more ancient mitochondrial lineages into the ancestry of modern populations." While the Eve hypothesis works brilliantly as a model, it may not thrive as well in the real world as it does in the computer programs that spawned it.

A Dental View

Yet another theory of the emergence of *Homo sapiens,* based, like the Eve hypothesis, on an interpretation of statistical data, is advanced by a dental anthropologist named Christy Turner. Turner has undertaken a huge, worldwide study of human teeth samples, which has led him to conclude that the first anatomically modern people arose not in Africa but in Southeast Asia. Turner's finding is based on twenty years of research into human dental features, including measurements of what he terms secondary traits—the bumps and ridges on teeth, and the number of roots they possess.

Profiling dental ridges is not quite as "sexy" for the media as finding an African mother of us all, and so Christy Turner is not likely to appear on the cover of *Newsweek*; yet the evidence he has compiled is in its own way as persuasive as the Eve hypothesis. His sample is mighty impressive. He has studied more than 12,000 individuals from around the world (as opposed to 147 in the genetic study of Cann, Stoneking, and Wilson). Most of his sample is archaeological, but a few specimens are from modern people. Like the Eve hypothesists' mtDNA studies, Turner's conclusions are based entirely on probabilities derived from statistical analysis. Of the eighty-three population groups identified in his study, the Southeast Asian sample contained the fewest specialized features. Turner is working on the assumption that the random genetic mutations responsible for such specialized adaptations are themselves the results of ecological stress associated with the emergent species' migration. Thus, the more specialized features a population has— that is, the more it diverges from the earliest exponent of the new species—the farther it is from the point of the species' emergence. Since the Southeast Asian sample has the fewest such divergences, and is in fact less "evolved," it is hypothetically the point from which the new species' migrations originated.

Inevitably, the question arises, How can we reconcile Christy Turner's statistical analysis with the Eve hypothesis? The underlying principles of both approaches appear to be sound, and both analyses also appear to have been well carried out. Appearances can be deceiving however, and if experience is our guide, we can be sure that, with time, flaws in one or the other, or both, of these studies will be brought to light by independent researchers. In the meantime, we are tempted to pull a bit of logical legerdemain and postulate that the two cancel each other out, and that we should go with regional continuity, at least for the moment. The beauty of regional continuity is that it offers scope for modern *Homo sapiens* to have emerged both in Africa and in Southeast Asia, which would harmonize the two conflicting theories.

A Family Tree

A sense of wonderment must have struck our ancestors the first time they confronted *Gigantopithecus,* the largest primate that ever lived. They had seen other, much larger animals—the elephants and stegodons, for instance, and the rhinoceros are several times more massive than Giganto. Yet when *Homo erectus* met the great ape, the confrontation must have resonated on a deeper level than merely that of marveling at the creature's great size. We may assume that our ancestors experienced the same instinctive sense of kinship that man has always felt toward the other members of his taxonomic order. (See the family tree on the endpapers of this book.)

From the accounts of medieval travelers who came back with tales of strange men of the jungle to the fascination of modern television viewers with the films about Dian Fossey and Jane Goodall and their work with the great apes, we respond to the primates with a strong sense that they are not entirely "other." If we cannot quite say that the light of reason shines in their eyes, we may at least say that, in the words of the eighteenth-century French naturalist the Comte de Buffon, writing about the orangutan, "It is a brute of a kind so singular, that man cannot behold it without contemplating himself."

Before we embark on our voyage of Asian discovery, we should clarify the relationships among the members of the primate family tree. Although, as we have stated, there are as many versions of this tree as there are paleoanthropologists, which is close enough to being true, we can nonetheless sketch in a picture accepted by most modern scholars.

The great split in the primate family tree is between the lower primates or prosimians (lemurs, lorises, and tarsiers) and the higher primates or anthropoids (monkeys, apes, and man). The anthropoids are divided into two main groups: the New World monkeys of South and Central America, and the Old World monkeys and apes of Africa and Asia. The apes can be divided into two large groups, the lesser apes and the great apes. The human line descends from the latter group, and can actually be thought of as a subgroup of the great apes.

The lesser apes include the acrobatic, arboreal gibbon and the siamang, which live in the tropical forests of Southeast Asia. The surviving great apes are three in number: the knuckle-walking chimpanzee and the gorilla, both of which inhabit the tropical forests and savanna-woodlands of Africa, and the rather reclusive orangutan, a tree-dwelling ape that once ranged throughout Southeast Asia but is now found only in Indonesia, in shrinking areas of the islands of Sumatra and Borneo. In order to understand this family tree better, we must make room for a fourth great ape: *Gigantopithecus*.

On the basis of anatomical and biochemical analyses, our closest relatives of all the apes are the chimpanzees. Ninety-eight percent of the genetic material in human DNA is identical with that of chimps. Another way of looking at it is to say that all the visible and developmental differences between people and chimpanzees are attributable to our unique 2 percent. Genetically, the gorilla is only slightly more removed from us. These similarities are so striking that some paleoanthropological theorists have proposed that the chimpanzee, gorilla, and man be grouped together in a separate taxonomic family. The more distantly related orangutan would be a member of a different family, which would include *Gigantopithecus*.

In order to understand fully the family tree of the primate order, we must project it into the fourth dimension. No consideration of interspecific relationships is valid without taking into account the descent of the various species through time. Scientists measure time with the geological clock: terms such as Pliocene and Pleistocene are as basic to paleoanthropology as Thursday and noon are to daily life.

To oversimplify a highly complicated matter, scientific timekeeping, insofar as biology is concerned, begins around 3.5 billion years ago, when it is believed that life first arose on this planet; for nearly 90 percent of the time since the bioclock started ticking, the earth was populated by mere specks of living matter. Without going into all the intervening eras, periods, and epochs, the conventional temporal subdivisions, we may simply say that the primates, the order to which we belong, have existed on earth for perhaps 65 million years (that is, since the time of the Cretaceous extinction, which wiped out all the dinosaurs except for the birds). After the end of the Cretaceous period, we enter the Cenozoic era, which is subdivided into epochs called the Paleocene, the Eocene, the Oligocene, the Miocene, and the Pliocene (these five are known collectively as the Tertiary period, which ended about two million years ago).

Then comes the Quaternary period, divided into the Pleistocene epoch, which is the time of the last Ice Age, and then our own epoch, the Holocene, which begins just 12,000 years ago, when the last glacier retreated and wholly modern climates and biota (animal and plant life taken together as an ecological unity) emerged. The Pleistocene is conventionally divided into three periods: the early Pleistocene, from 1.8 million years to 700,000 B.P.; the middle Pleistocene (when the confrontation between *Homo erectus* and *Gigantopithecus* took place), from 700,000 to 125,000 B.P.; and the late Pleistocene, which finishes off the epoch until the advent of the Holocene. (See the time line on the endpapers of this book.)

Now, forget about missing links. The business of drawing a primate family tree ought to be thought of as reaching back into time for common ancestors; the farther back in time we go, the more far afield we may discern cousinage. For example, the first branching in the primate line, the bifurcation into the prosimian and the anthropoid lines, may have taken place in the Eocene or perhaps even the Paleocene—in any case, more than 50 million years ago. The first evidence of the anthropoid line is the fossil primate *Amphipithecus,* which evolved in Asia around 45 million years ago. (Ciochon discovered a jawbone of *Amphipithecus* in Burma in 1978, which landed him on the front page of the *New York Times*.)

The Hominidae, our own family, emerged about five million years ago, at the beginning of the Pliocene epoch. What happened further down the hominid family tree is the subject of endless controversy and revision, so we shall set that aside for the moment. The branch leading to the gorilla and chimpanzee (descended from fossil apes called the African dryopiths) originated around the same time. In Asia, another group of fossil apes, the sivapiths, gave rise to the orangutan and *Gigantopithecus*. The orangutan and Giganto share as a common ancestor an extinct primate called *Sivapithecus*, which is best known from an eight-million-year-old skull discovered in Pakistan in 1979 by an American paleoanthropologist named David Pilbeam.

Gigantopithecus is the only ape known to have become extinct in the Pleistocene epoch. All of the other great apes and, of course, the human lineage, survived the most recent Ice Age, yet *Gigantopithecus* became extinct. Why? What is unique about Giganto? How similar was it to the other Asian great ape, the orangutan—or how different? What differences were there about *Gigantopithecus* that might have led to its evolutionary downfall? Why is it important for us to know about Giganto?

To answer these questions, we were drawn inexorably to Asia. For if you review this skeletal family tree, an interesting fact emerges. Setting aside the gorilla-chimpanzee-human cluster—which, as we have said, may even constitute a separate family—all of the other principal primate lineages are Asian in origin. While major paleoanthropological discoveries in Africa over the past forty years were making international news headlines, Chinese scientists were quietly working at localities throughout the central Asiatic plateau and southward all the way to the provinces bordering Burma, Laos, and Vietnam. Publishing their discoveries in hard-to-find Chinese journals, these pioneering Chinese scholars were documenting an extensive and hitherto unknown fossil record that substantiated the view of Davidson Black and others that Asia played a central role in the history of the primate order. This record of the Asian genesis of the primates has remained largely unknown in the West; only now is it beginning to be translated and discussed by paleoanthropologists in the world community.

One recent fossil find in China indicates that Asia may have been the place where the entire primate order arose. Traditionally, scientists have thought that the very first primate ancestor, a hypothetical animal called the "euprimate," emerged in North America. The euprimate was the evolutionary stem from which evolved all the living primate species, the common ancestor of prosimians, monkeys, apes, and man. The fossil discovery that has changed that view, a primate called *Docoredon anhuiensis,* was recovered in a deposit dating to the middle Paleocene (approximately 60 million years ago), north of the Yangtze River in Anhui province, China. *Docoredon,* identified on the basis of several upper and lower jaws, has been shown by American paleoanthropologist Fred Szalay and Chinese paleontologist Li Chuankuei to be the earliest euprimate. The placement of euprimate origins in Asia has some interesting implications. Identification of *Docoredon* as the earliest euprimate yet recovered indicates that the Asian continent was likely the early primate dispersal center for North America via the Bering land bridge, and for Europe via a southern land corridor across the Paleocene epicontinental sea, which covered parts of what is now Central Asia.

In much the same fashion, the finds of the first anthropoids such as *Amphipithecus* indicate that the higher primates arose in Southeast Asia some 45 million years ago, whence they dispersed throughout the tropical regions of the Old World. They most likely entered Africa in the latter Eocene across the narrow, swamplike Tethys Sea, which then separated northern Africa from southwest Asia. Other populations crossed the then narrow equatorial Atlantic Ocean by island-hopping along a series of volcanic islands that were strung across the ocean. Thus, early anthropoids from Southeast Asia were able to colonize South America (by way of Africa), where they evolved into the New World primate species.

Only at this point does the scene switch to Africa. Moreover, some recent fossil discoveries by Chinese excavators even suggest that while the dryopith hominoid line (stem ancestor of the African ape–human group) was emerging in Africa, an even earlier, nearly identical dryopith hominoid line, unrelated to the

Asian sivapith apes, was evolving in southern Asia. If that hypothesis is substantiated by further fossil discoveries and supporting analysis, it could revolutionize paleoanthropological thought, for the dryopith hominoid line, which ultimately led to the emergence of man, could have had an Asian origin. None of this ought to be construed, however, to mean that there is any doubt that *Homo* arose in Africa; that is almost sure to remain as one of the few certainties in a field fraught with uncertainty. Nonetheless, taking the primates as a whole, positing Africa as the focal point of their origins relies upon the exception rather than the rule: By returning to Asia to seek some answers, we were, in a sense, bringing paleoanthropology back home again.

The Great Leap East

While the thrust of our work has been to flesh out, with scientific evidence, the first contact between *Gigantopithecus* and our human ancestors, carrying out that objective has entailed a first contact of an altogether different sort: our work has brought us face to face with the former enemy of our country, in the first scientific field expedition ever carried out between the United States and the Socialist Republic of Vietnam.

Vietnam in the mid-1980's was among the most wretched and remote places in the world. It was, for an American, a particularly exotic place. Still quite devastated physically by the war, its meager resources were at that time still being drained by its military occupation of Cambodia. Diplomatically and economically isolated from most of the world, Vietnam was a geopolitical disaster area. Scientific research, understandably, was just about the nation's lowest priority. Vietnam was, and is, an exceptionally difficult place to accomplish anything, particularly anything as devoid of demonstrable practical benefit as digging up old bones and stones. So, why go there?

There were quite valid scientific reasons for us to go to Vietnam, which we shall explain presently, but we may as well admit that part of the attraction for us was precisely the fact that Vietnam was so remote and challenging a destination. Before our Vietnamese adventure, Olsen had done much of

his fieldwork in the Taklamakan Desert, a virtually uninhabited wasteland in northwest China and in Tibet, where he
continues to work. Olsen was one of only a handful of foreign
archaeologists with a regular field niche in China. He and
Ciochon met in China in the seventies, when the Middle Kingdom first opened its doors to foreign scholars. Ciochon had
done extensive paleoanthropological fieldwork in Africa, India,
and Southeast Asia—notably in Burma (where he discovered
the remains of *Amphipithecus*), which has been virtually closed to
outside researchers for over twenty years. Yet the Taklamakan,
Tibet, and Burma seemed almost commonplace alongside post-
war Vietnam.

We are the first ones to smile at the romanticized image of
the khaki-clad archaeologist, trudging through the jungle, ma-
chete in hand, in search of lost civilizations. Yet there will
always be an allure in forbidden places. The thirst to experience the unknown that attracts explorers to the ends of the
earth remains unquenched. Even if geographers long ago
charted the last square inch of the globe, there will always be
places that are unknown in other senses, destinations for the
incurably curious. Paradoxically, for Americans, that place in the
mid-1980's was Vietnam. Because so many of our countrymen
had been fighting a war there in the very recent past, Vietnam
was surely the last place on earth we might have been expected
to go to pursue our work. So, once the idea presented itself, it
immediately became the most irresistibly seductive of goals.

Fortunately, there did exist a compelling scientific reason
for us to go to Vietnam. Indeed, once we had set as our goal
the search for data to flesh out that scenario of first encounter
between *Homo erectus* and *Gigantopithecus*, and thus to arrive at
a better understanding of both creatures, Vietnam became, by
a process of elimination, the only place, or certainly the best
place, we could go.

Gigantopithecus is known to science from about a thousand
fossil teeth and four jawbones. The great majority of these
materials came from China—most, indeed, from one locality,
Liucheng cave (also known as *Gigantopithecus* Cave) in the
Guangxi Zhuang Autonomous Region, which borders Vietnam
on the northeast. One of the jawbones, it is true, is from
northern India, but it is an isolated specimen, taxonomically

distinct and somewhat smaller than all the other known remains of *Gigantopithecus*. In fact, the Indian variety has been
assigned a different name altogether, *Gigantopithecus giganteus,*
as opposed to *Gigantopithecus blacki,* the Southeast Asian species.

Setting aside for the moment the isolated Indian find, all of
the fossil discoveries of Giganto are from China and Vietnam.
Now, one might suppose that the logical place for us to start
would be China, considering not only how well connected and
well known Ciochon and Olsen are there, but also the fact that
in the mid-1980's Sino-American relations were at an all-time
high. Yet although China had made great strides toward re-
joining the rest of the world, a nearly insuperable xenophobia
was still flourishing there. The principal reason that Olsen had
been able to establish himself in the Taklamakan was that
Xinjiang, as an autonomous region, has an archaeological in-
frastructure different from that of China's other provinces. If
he or any other Westerner had in the mid-eighties sought
permission to excavate in a province with stronger scholarly
ties to the central authorities in Beijing, and that includes most
of China, he would almost certainly have been turned down.
Besides, all but the hardiest Chinese excavators were daunted
by the arduous field conditions of the Taklamakan.

We finally chose Vietnam because of a peculiarity of Chinese folk culture. For thousands of years, Chinese pharmacists
have used fossils, which they call dragon teeth and dragon
bones, as one of many ingredients to concoct various medicinal
potions, which are intended to cure ailments ranging from
backache to sexual impotence. The fossil-rich caves of South
China have been sedulously mined by peasants for these medicinal treasures, which they sell to apothecaries in the cities.
Even though the government in Beijing frowns on the practice, it still flourishes today. Anyone may purchase the precious fossil remains of extinct species in a well-stocked pharmacy
in any large Chinese city. However, if you try it, be sure to tell
the clerk not to grind up the fossils into a powder for you! In just
such a pharmacy, in Hong Kong in 1935, the German paleoanthropologist Ralph von Koenigswald found the first evidence
of *Gigantopithecus*; he came across a fossil tooth that did not
belong to any known primate species. As he dug deeper, not in
the earth but in the drawers of Chinese apothecaries throughout
Asia, he was able to establish the ape's existence conclusively.

Thus there were grounds for serious doubts as to the likelihood of finding more remains of the animal in a region that had been so thoroughly mined. All the promising sites had been reserved by Chinese paleoanthropologists affiliated with the strong regional museum system in China. There was no particular reason to think that we would get anywhere with the scientific community in Vietnam, but at least we had no reason to be sure that we would fail. Additionally, in contrast to China, Vietnam has no history of exploiting fossiliferous caves for dragon bones. That fact alone accounts for the importance of Vietnam in our work.

Paleontologists refer to the process by which animal bones are transformed into fossils and become a part of the geological record as taphonomy, from the Greek root meaning "tomb." Taphonomy is concerned with all the processes that bring about the preservation of bones, from the time the animal dies until its remains are recovered by the paleontologist from the earth in the form of fossils—including events such as the systematic mining of caves in South China for dragon bones. Vietnam is thus a rich source of Pleistocene fossils because the circumstances of cave taphonomy in that area are so different from those of its neighbor.

Our discovery of Vietnam began in 1983. Ciochon's studies into the great ape *Gigantopithecus* had led him to conclude that Vietnam was the best place to look for it, and he invited John Olsen to join him in the search. Olsen was remotely aware of Vietnamese archaeology through his work in China; a number of his close colleagues at the Chinese Academy of Sciences in Beijing had conducted research in Vietnam before the Sino-Vietnamese schism in the late seventies, under the auspices of the Institute of Archaeology in Hanoi. By the eighties the split had become so profound that we found ourselves, once we had established our initial relationship with the Vietnamese, in the bizarre position of supplying copies of recent Chinese publications in archaeology and paleoanthropology to our colleagues in Hanoi, who in some cases had known the authors quite well before their countries fell out. What changes the last decade and a half have seen in East Asian politics: American scholars acting as the go-between for Chinese and Vietnamese scientists, who can no longer communicate directly with one another!

Beyond the simple fact that the Institute of Archaeology in Hanoi existed, scarcely anyone in the West knew what sort of work was going on there. Yet if Ciochon and Olsen were going to make a scientific visit to Vietnam, they would have to be guests of a local scientific institution, and the Institute was the logical choice. However, they could not pick up the telephone in the United States and ring up the Institute of Archaeology in Hanoi; the American government forbids it. Nor could they write a letter and drop it in the mailbox on the corner. Since the war, Vietnam has been an outcast from the international postal convention, which regulates mail throughout most of the world.

The first direct contact we had with the Vietnamese occurred in July 1983, when Ciochon was in Bangkok, on his way home from an expedition in China. At the suggestion of an American foreign service officer (formerly a C.I.A. operative) posted there, Ciochon decided to approach the Vietnamese about collaborative research. At the Vietnamese embassy, right next door to the American embassy on Wireless Road, he met with the science attaché, Nguyen Hoang An. The two men spoke for several hours about life in Vietnam—and life in America— and about what kind of research Ciochon wanted to undertake in Vietnam.

Eventually, they got onto the topic of the war. Mr. An asked Ciochon what he had done during the war. Ciochon told him that he had been a student at the University of California at Berkeley, and had participated in many antiwar demonstrations. He admitted that he had been able to escape the war through his student deferment.

An replied, "No one in my country escaped the war."

At the end of the conversation, An promised Ciochon that he would do all he could to help him establish communications with the Institute of Archaeology in Hanoi, and referred him to the U.S. Committee for Scientific Cooperation with Vietnam. The only direct line of communication between American and Vietnamese scientists, the committee was founded in 1977 by Edward Cooperman, a physics professor from California State University at Fullerton who had been a vigorous, outspoken opponent of the American involvement in the war. The initial purpose of the committee was to facilitate the introduction of scientific humanitarian services, particularly medical aid. Before Ciochon approached them, the committee had not been involved in supporting field expeditions—mainly because no one had suggested such a course.

A doctor and public health expert named Judith Ladinsky, who is now in charge of the committee, undertook to arrange our visit. Ladinsky has played the part of go-between for other American physical and social scientists besides our team; however, no other Western scientists have yet established an ongoing field research relationship comparable to the one we have with the Institute of Archaeology.

In 1985 Ladinsky approached the Vietnamese, who said that they would certainly consider inviting American archaeologists for a visit, with an eye toward developing a program of cooperative field research. It took nearly two years to translate that generalized sentiment into reality, but in December 1986, Ciochon and Olsen were at the Vietnamese embassy in Bangkok to pick up their entry visas to the Socialist Republic of Vietnam.

Thus began the long and tortuous road that would ultimately end in Lang Trang, a remote village in northern Vietnam, where we would discover a cave system that has proved to be one of the most productive fossil sites in all Asia. There, in the misty jungles of an idyllic valley that had been bombed repeatedly by American A-4 jet fighter bombers just fifteen years before, we have recovered one of the most complete fossil assemblages of the middle Pleistocene in Southeast Asia. Some of the animals represented by the fossil remains we have found are now extinct in Vietnam, such as the orangutan and the panda, and that bears significantly on our understanding of how the great ape *Gigantopithecus* became extinct.

Whatever else the future may hold for our scientific partnership with Vietnamese scientists as we continue our joint quest for evidence relating to the life of early man and Asia's giant fossil ape, our dig has already carved out its own niche in paleoanthropological history: at Lang Trang we discovered the only firmly dated fossil remains of *Homo erectus* in Southeast Asia—which makes them perhaps the oldest specimens of man yet identified from that part of the world.

CHAPTER 3

A Search for Origins

The Way East

When we decided to go to Asia to search for evidence of the world of early man, we were returning to the locus of most of the interesting investigations in our discipline since its emergence just over a hundred years ago. Indeed, for most of the time that scientists have been looking for evidence and insights into the biological past, they have been coming to the mother of continents, Asia.

One of the most fundamental concepts of evolutionary biology is that the evolution of a group of animals usually begins in a single center of origin, geographically isolated from other regions; and then the species disperses outward from that center. The concept was articulated by Darwin in *The Origin of Species,* in 1859: "Hence, it seems to me, as it has to many other naturalists, that the view of each species having been produced in one area alone, and having subsequently migrated from that area as far as its powers of migration and subsistence under past and present conditions permitted, is the most probable." Once the center-of-origin concept took hold, and as more and more new species were demonstrated to have arisen in Asia, the continent came to be nearly universally accepted as the place of human genesis.

The first proponent of the Asian genesis of man was the outspoken German embryologist and evolutionist Ernst Haeckel.

Writing in the latter nineteenth century, Haeckel considered man to be more closely related to the Asian anthropoid apes, the gibbon and the orangutan, than to the African apes, and on that basis he hypothesized an Asian center of origin for man—located, prophetically, in Southeast Asia. He was so confident of this that he coined the name *Pithecanthropus alalus* ("speechless ape-man") for the proposed ancestor. Haeckel's notions about the close relationship between man and the Asian apes have since been disproved, yet his postulation of man's Asian origin was to be the most widely accepted theory in the field for the next half century.

One of Haeckel's disciples, a fiery redheaded Dutchman named Eugene Dubois, believed so implicitly in the existence of this ape-man that he shipped out as an army surgeon in order to get to the Dutch East Indies, where he could look for its remains. And he promptly found them—in 1891, four years after he set out, which is quite prompt by paleoanthropological standards—in middle Pleistocene deposits near a Javanese village called Trinil, on the Solo River. When young Dubois presented the skullcap, thighbone, and teeth he had found, to which he had given the name *Pithecanthropus erectus,* to the International Zoological Congress of 1895, he was ridiculed by the assembled establishment. How could they have known they were looking at the first discovery of *Homo erectus,* at that time the oldest human remains ever recovered?

Yet not everyone was skeptical: Henry Fairfield Osborn, the head of the American Museum of Natural History in New York, was a believer; influenced by Haeckel and Dubois, he created a famous map of the world indicating the global regions where all the major groups of mammals had originated. In 1900 he wrote an article for the journal *Science* which predicted that Asia would ultimately prove to be the source of fourteen orders and countless species of mammals. Osborn particularly favored the central plateau of Asia, because of its central location in relation to the other continental land masses and its detailed geological record of climatic changes.

He argued that the uplift of the Himalaya Mountains to the south would have caused periods of desiccation in Central Asia. Such environmental change, Osborn reasoned, would have forced the higher primates to adapt to unaccustomed habitats, and the biological stress imposed by these changes would have channeled evolution toward the development of fitter and better adapted species, ending in the origin of man. Such a theory seems simplistic in light of our current understanding of evolutionary biology, but Osborn was a good scientist, and at the time his theories were extremely influential.

In 1915 paleontologist William Diller Matthew published an influential book entitled *Climate and Evolution,* which propounded the thesis that primitive human species and many other mammalian groups were constantly being thrust out from a center of dispersal, which, like Osborn, he located in the central plateau of Asia. This remote region was beginning to take on a legendary mystique as the hypothetical locus of the evolutionary Garden of Eden. The consensus was growing that Asia, in addition to being the mother of continents was also the cradle of man.

In search of the "Garden of Eden": the American Museum's Fourth Central Asiatic Expedition, led by Roy Chapman Andrews, heads into the Gobi Desert, in 1928. *(Photo: Shackleford. Courtesy Department of Library Services, American Museum of Natural History)*

The Great Fossil Hunt

From 1916 to 1930, the naturalist and world explorer Roy Chapman Andrews organized and led a series of expeditions under the aegis of the American Museum of Natural History into Tibet, Mongolia, China, and Southeast Asia, in search of fossil evidence that would support the Asian hypothesis of Haeckel, Osborn, Matthew, et al. Andrews's First Asiatic Expedition of 1916–17 began its overland trek in Hanoi, traveling from there by train across northern Vietnam (then known as Tonkin) to Kunming, in South China, and finally on to Tibet. The Second Asiatic Expedition, in 1919, concentrated on the exploration of the fossiliferous regions of Mongolia. In 1921, the Third Asiatic Expedition journeyed to eastern Sichuan province to explore the Pleistocene karst caves and fissures above the gorges of the Yangtze River. On this trek Andrews, accompanied by paleontologists Walter Granger and William Diller Matthew, discovered a rich Pleistocene mammalian fauna in a limestone cave fissure in Wushan county. This fauna was the first excavated evidence of what we now call the *Stegodon-Ailuropoda* fauna. Though the Granger-Matthew team recovered more than twenty species of mammals, there were no ape or human remains among them. From 1987 to 1989, paleontologist and Chinese wildman enthusiast Huang Wanpo and his wife, paleoanthropologist Gu Yumin, returned to these same limestone fissures in Wushan and discovered a specimen of *Gigantopithecus* contemporary with *Homo erectus* in what we now regard as the type locality for the *Stegodon-Ailuropoda* fauna.

In 1922, the first of five American Museum expeditions ventured into the Gobi Desert of Mongolia; the others took place in 1923, 1925, 1928, and 1930. Called the Central Asiatic Expeditions by Andrews, these intrepid multidisciplinary projects recovered fossils of numerous Cretaceous dinosaurs, the first dinosaur eggs, complete skeletons of the unique Miocene shovel-tusked mastodon elephants, and nearly complete remains of the colossal Miocene rhinoceros named *Baluchitherium*, which stood seventeen feet high at the shoulders and was thirty-four feet in length—without doubt the largest mammal

that ever walked the earth. Thanks to the collecting abilities of
Pierre Teilhard de Chardin, the Central Asiatic Expeditions
also identified several late-Pleistocene archaeological sites, where
they found many stone tools. These expeditions substantiated
that Asia had indeed been a major theater of mammalian
evolution—but they found no fossil human remains.

As a matter of fact, it turns out that the excavation of early
human fossils had been going on for many years—though the
excavators had no idea what it was they were digging up—to
supply the extensive pharmaceutical trade in "dragon bones"
in China. The magnitude of the dragon-bone trade at that time
is revealed by a customs inspector's report dated around 1900,
which states that in excess of twenty tons of fossil bones and
teeth were being loaded at Chinese ports annually; and this
figure reflected only those fossils being shipped to Chinese
apothecaries abroad—to the Philippines, Singapore, and so
forth—which amounted to only a small fraction of the quantity bought and sold inside China.

The first Western scientist to make use of this fossil source
was Max Schlosser, of Munich, who in 1903 published a detailed description of a large number of mammalian fossils, over
sixty species in all, that had been purchased in pharmacies by a
German colleague during a tour of China. Among the specimens was a "peculiar apelike, manlike" upper molar tooth.
Unfortunately, the way it was procured made it impossible
to determine the exact locality (the technical term for an
archaeological site) from which it had been extracted, and thus
its geologic age. Nonetheless, the specimen was certainly Chinese, confirming that China was the place to search for
Pleistocene man. As we saw earlier, the existence of the great
ape came to light in just the same way, when the German
paleoanthropologist Ralph von Koenigswald serendipitously discovered the first Giganto specimen while patiently combing
through dusty drawers full of dragon bones.

Nearly fifteen years after Max Schlosser's first publication
describing the existence of "apelike, manlike" fossil teeth in
Chinese apothecary shops, a Swedish geologist named J. Gunnar
Andersson, who was working in Beijing as a mining advisor,
searched the pharmacies there for clues that might lead him to
the source of the dragon bones. Obviously influenced by

Schlosser's work, Andersson recognized the essential importance of establishing where the dragon bones had been
unearthed. His investigation led him to a limestone quarry
near the town of Zhoukoudian (formerly spelled Choukoutien),
thirty miles from Beijing, where he found a system of fossil-
filled crevices and caverns; it would ultimately yield one of the
largest collections of early human fossils in the history of the
science.

In 1926, Andersson announced to the world the first unequivocal evidence of truly ancient man in China, in the form
of two isolated hominid teeth. The need for a full-scale excavation cried out, and a Canadian anatomist named Davidson
Black heard the call. Black, whose interest in paleoanthropology
had been kindled by the fraudulent but as yet unexposed
Piltdown Man, had come to China in 1919 because he shared
Osborn and Matthew's conviction that early man had originated in Central Asia. Black organized the first full-scale excavation of Zhoukoudian, which began in April 1927. Two years
later, with the support of the Rockefeller Foundation, he established the Cenozoic Research Laboratory, where scientists from
eight different nations worked together in a spirit of international cooperation until it closed its doors in 1941.

Davidson Black was the first director of the Cenozoic Research Laboratory. Under his leadership, excavations at Zhoukoudian yielded many human fossils, including several nearly
complete skulls. Black originally assigned them a new name,
Sinanthropus pekinensis ("Chinese man of Peking," or Peking
Man), but after certain taxonomical similarities with Eugene
Dubois's finds in Java were noticed, it was gradually accepted
that Peking Man and Java Man were both examples of the
same species, *Homo erectus.* Black adduced all this as evidence
that the Hominidae, the zoological family to which man belongs, had arisen in central Asia.

In 1934, at the age of fifty, Davidson Black was found dead
in his laboratory, slumped over a skull of *Homo erectus* he had
been working on. Franz Weidenreich, a German anatomist
lecturing at the University of Chicago, took over as director of
the Cenozoic Research Laboratory. He continued Black's work
of collecting and studying fossils of Peking Man until the
Japanese invasion at the outbreak of World War II forced the

laboratory to disband. Weidenreich then returned to the United States, bringing with him his beautifully executed casts of all the fossils of *Homo erectus* excavated from Zhoukoudian, 175 specimens representing at least forty individuals. It was a good thing he did: all of the original remains of Peking Man were lost soon after Weidenreich's departure. The fossils had been carefully packed into crates and loaded onto an evacuation train headed for the docks at Tianjin—and were never seen again. There have been any number of investigations, not to mention trashy novels and hoax "discoveries," but no trace of the specimens has yet been uncovered, and the mystery seems no closer to a solution now than the day the specimens disappeared.

While the Chinese discoveries of *Homo erectus* were taking place, a new wave of research had begun in Java. In 1931, Ralph von Koenigswald took a post with the geological survey of the colonial administration in the Dutch East Indies, in fulfillment of his boyhood ambition to go to the tropics to search for remains of early man. It had been nearly forty years since Dubois had made his big finds, and a great deal of work remained to be done there. In 1936 Koenigswald discovered the skull of a hominid infant in early Pleistocene deposits, making the site even older than Dubois's in Trinil, which had been of middle Pleistocene vintage. In 1937, in the Sangiran region of Java, he made another major discovery: an adult skull, identical to Dubois's specimen, and a very well-preserved mandible. Koenigswald continued working in Java until 1941, when the war in the Pacific forced him to quit, as it had Weidenreich in China. But Koenigswald did not time his escape as well as his colleague, and he was captured by the Japanese and incarcerated in a prison camp. He had hidden his fossils in several safe places on Java, however, and after the war he went back for them and brought to the United States the fossil remains of some twenty-five *Homo erectus* specimens.

In the 1930's and 1940's, *Homo erectus* was generally viewed as an ape-man, occupying an intermediate position between anatomically modern man and the apes. The original name proposed for Java Man was *Pithecanthropus,* which literally means "ape man." Koenigswald used this terminology until the 1950's. At the time of their discovery in the twenties and thirties, the finds of *Homo erectus* in Java and China were considered to be the oldest fossil evidence of the human family. The major finds of *Australopithecus* had not yet been made, and the few that were known were not considered to be a part of the hominid family until 1947, when British anatomist Wilfred Le Gros Clark presented his analysis of the South African finds at the First Pan African Congress, in Nairobi. In addition, the archaeological record of stone tools today associated with *Homo erectus* was not well known, and thus the cultural and mental abilities we now ascribe to the species were not generally accepted: indeed, many reconstructions of *Homo erectus* from this period depicted him as virtually an upright ape.

The Rise and Fall
of *Ramapithecus*

Meanwhile, in the Siwalik Hills of northern India, on the doorstep of Indochina, important paleoanthropological investigations had been taking place. As early as 1879 primate fossils, some remains of extinct dryopithecine apes, had been found here, but no hominids. Then in 1910 the English paleontologist Guy Pilgrim discovered two parts of a lower jaw. Pilgrim, an official with the Geological Survey of India, did not realize the significance of the find at the time, but that fragmentary mandible would later become the type specimen of *Ramapithecus*, the Miocene primate once believed by many paleoanthropologists to be the first hominid, the last link between man and the apes. The first scientist to recognize the importance of Pilgrim's find was a paleontologist named G. Edward Lewis; while on a dig with the Yale North India Expedition in 1932 he discovered an upper jaw of *Ramapithecus*, which he was the first to describe as the common ancestor of the Hominidae.

The subsequent history of *Ramapithecus* is long and checkered. After Lewis's initial argument for its transitional ape-to-human status, in the 1930's, *Ramapithecus* sank into paleontological oblivion in the forties and fifties. Then, in the early 1960's, Elwyn Simons of Yale University revived interest in *Ramapithecus* by claiming that it was the earliest hominid, the true "missing link." Throughout the sixties and the early seventies, *Ramapithecus* held center stage in virtually every anthropology textbook as the earliest human ancestor.

In the mid-1970's, the support for *Ramapithecus* again began to wane, when Donald Johanson's discovery of *Australopithecus afarensis* showed that the hominid family most likely arose in Africa, not in Asia. Further erosion of the hominid status of the ramapithecines came with Sarich and Wilson's biomolecular studies of the blood proteins of living primates, which demonstrated that man, the chimpanzee, and the gorilla form a tightly knit group with a common ancestor, from which they diverged perhaps as recently as 5 million years ago. Since *Ramapithecus* was a Miocene species that lived some 10 million to 14 million years ago, it could not be the earliest hominid and sole human ancestor, as Elwyn Simons had argued so strongly in the 1960's. The final nail in the coffin of *Ramapithecus* came in 1979, when David Pilbeam, of Yale University—who was also working in the Siwalik Hills where Pilgrim had found the original remains of *Ramapithecus*—discovered a complete skull of a closely related ape species. This skull had decidedly orangutanlike features. Soon it became clear that most if not all of the hominid characteristics of *Ramapithecus* were actually the result of reconstructive wishful thinking rather than hard fossil evidence.

In 1922, the American Museum sent its ace fossil hunter, Barnum Brown, to the Siwalik Hills, which had certainly proved their worth as a source of fossils. Working with Guy Pilgrim, Brown unearthed cartloads of fossils in the Siwaliks, and later along the Irrawaddy River in Burma, but there were no

---

FACING PAGE: Half a century ago, American archaeologist Hallam Movius advanced the theory that the paleolithic cultures of the Old World can be divided between those that made elaborate stone hand-axes, in the West, and the "pebble tool cultures" in the East, which manufactured less sophisticated stone choppers and chopping tools. The so-called Movius Line, shown here, purports to mark that cultural divide. The sites indicated on the map were influential to Movius's thinking. Also shown is the distribution of bamboo in Asia, with the Movius Line superimposed, which argues strongly in favor of the thesis that paleolithic Asians might have used bamboo tools—which would not have survived in the archaeological record—to fill the needs for which Western cultures created hand-axes and other finished stone tools.

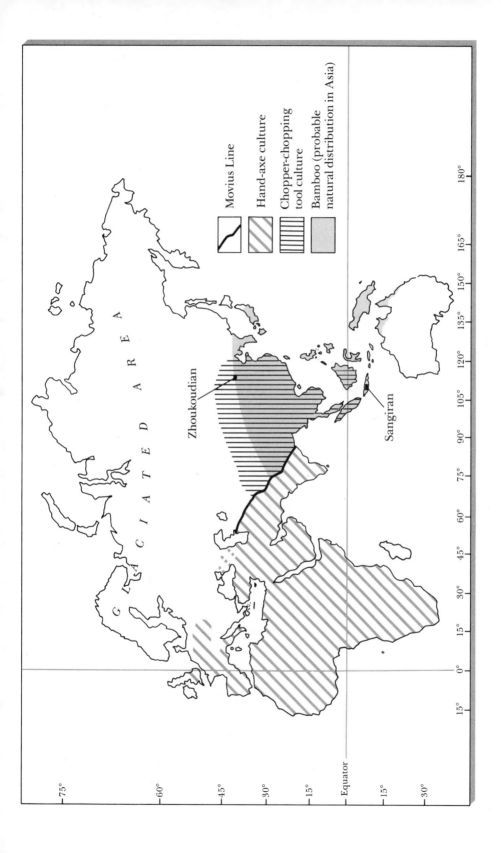

Movius Line

Hand-axe culture

Chopper-chopping
tool culture

Bamboo (probable
natural distribution in Asia)

Zhoukoudian

Sangiran

GLACIATED AREA

Equator

early human remains among them. In 1937, another American team, the Joint American Southeast Asiatic Expedition for Early Man, undertook an extensive excavation in Burma; they did not find any hominid fossils either, but the expedition is noteworthy because it brought together some of the most original minds in the history of paleoanthropology. The team was led by Helmut de Terra, a geologist from the Philadelphia Academy of Sciences. His staff included Pierre Teilhard de Chardin, the French Jesuit paleontologist and mystic, and Hallam L. Movius, Jr., then a young archaeologist from Harvard.

Even though some of his basic concepts proved to be wrong, Movius is nonetheless one of the most influential theorists in modern paleoanthropology. He advanced the theory that the early European cultures, like that of Neanderthal man, used relatively well developed stone tools such as hand axes, while the early Asian cultures tended to use technologically less developed "pebble tools," consisting primarily of choppers and other chopping tools. He went so far as to draw a line down the middle of the Eurasian supercontinent, which came to be known as the Movius Line, to divide the hand-axe users from the pebble-chopper peoples. While this distinction is not without its grain of validity, there are so many exceptions as to render its original implications virtually null.

Movius's ideas have greatly irritated Asian scholars, who contend that they carry the implicit racist message that carefully finished hand axes are bigger and somehow better than simple pebble tools—implying that European people were bigger and better, too. Pham Huy Thong, the Vietnamese archaeologist who, as we shall see, proved to be one of the principal personalities in our own drama, wrote witheringly about some stone-tool discoveries in Thanh Hoa province, where we would carry out our own excavation: "Hard by Ham Rong Bridge, which the U.S. tried in vain to destroy, losing 99 supersonic aircraft there in the attempt, a rich Paleolithic site was revealed ... These discoveries have dealt a telling blow at the racist thesis advanced by some American archaeologists, H. L. Movius, Jr., in particular, who insist on making a distinction between a white civilization, which used worked stones, and the 'pebble culture' of other races."

Teilhard de Chardin
and the Piltdown Hoax

Pierre Teilhard de Chardin is one of the most colorful figures in twentieth-century science. In the tradition of the Society of Jesus, Teilhard (who was a direct descendant of Voltaire) brought to his priestly calling a deep curiosity about this world, and a strong interest in making his mark in it. Shortly after taking his solemn vows, he wrote: "Gradually (though we cannot yet say in what terms, but without the sacrifice of a single one of the facts, whether revealed or definitely proved), agreement will be reached, quite naturally, between science and dogma in the burning field of human origins. In the meantime, let us take care not to reject the least ray of light from any side. Faith has need of all the truth." Given the continuing debate about evolution and "creationism" in our public schools, Teilhard's prediction, unfortunately, has not come true; the argument between science and dogma still continues to burn quite as hotly now as it did seventy years ago, when he was writing.

Teilhard first achieved fame by his role, the exact nature of which will perhaps never be known, in the century's most notorious scientific hoax, the Piltdown affair. Paleoanthropology, still virtually an infant science, was thrown into an uproar by the discoveries, made over a period of years beginning in 1908, of what were believed to be very early human remains in Piltdown, Sussex. Fragments of what was identified as a fossil human skull were found in association with a jawbone that closely resembled that of a modern chimpanzee. Teilhard's contribution was the discovery of a canine tooth that also resembled that of an ape but clearly belonged with the jawbone. Scientists tore out their hair for years, trying to make sense of the anomalous finds. Not until 1953 were the fossils revealed to be fraudulent. The skull fragments actually were human fossils, but the mystifying jawbone turned out to be that of a modern orangutan, skillfully treated with potash and iron to resemble a human fossil. And Teilhard's tooth, which had been one of the most compelling elements of the forgery, turned out to be an orangutan tooth, carefully filed down and stained to resemble an early human tooth.

The authorship of the hoax has never been determined and probably never will be; the evidence is simply too scanty. Teilhard, because of the importance of his contribution, has often been accused, but he is not a particularly good candidate. He was certainly an unswerving advocate of Darwinian evolution, and a thoroughly unprankish man. Even so, many persist in trying to pin it on him, perhaps because of his religious vocation, and the Church's official hostility to Darwin. Yet his subsequent career would tend to vindicate him: he spent most of the rest of his life on paleoanthropological digs—with de Terra in India, Burma, and Java; with Davidson Black at Zhoukoudian; with Roy Chapman Andrews in the Gobi Desert; and on many other projects in Ethiopia, South Africa, and throughout Europe.

In 1951 Teilhard went to South Africa to see the world-famous discoveries made in the limestone caves of the Transvaal by Raymond Dart. Dart, who called his specimens *Australopithecus* ("southern ape"), believed that he had found remains of a "man-ape" that was intermediate between the living apes and modern people—in other words, the long-sought missing link. Yet Europeans who had studied Dart's finds believed that they were in fact the earliest hominids yet discovered. Wilfred Le Gros Clark, in particular, concluded after his trip to the Transvaal that there were several key resemblances between the australopithecines and modern humans, and that the ape-like qualities were just what one would expect in the early Hominidae.

Teilhard, as the first scientist familiar with the *Homo erectus* specimens from Java and Zhoukoudian to see Dart's discoveries, served as a sort of paleoanthropological referee; he was able to confirm that *Australopithecus* was indeed a hominid. Teilhard saw Dart's specimens as morphologically bridging the gap between the apes and China/Java early man. This judgment and evidence from elsewhere on the African continent led Teilhard to conclude that on paleontological and cultural grounds, Africa, not Asia, was the probable birthplace of *Homo*—the *true* Garden of Eden, as Darwin himself had predicted in 1871. As significant discoveries of fossil hominids continued to be made in the Great Rift Valley of eastern Africa, Asia slipped more and more into the shadows, paleoanthropologically speaking.

A Portrait of *Homo erectus*

Who was *Homo erectus?* What was our predecessor link in the chain of evolution really like? If we look first at his skull, we encounter a creature with a receding forehead, projecting brow ridges, a prominent nose, and almost no chin. Yet despite its somewhat brutish profile, this creature had a posture and mode of locomotion that was altogether human. Our best overall anatomical view of *Homo erectus* comes from one of the earliest members of the lineage, the nearly complete skeleton of a twelve-year-old male youth recovered in 1984 from a site called Narikotome, near the western shore of Lake Turkana, in Kenya. This skeleton, which is firmly dated to 1.6 million years B.P., was discovered by the famous Kenyan fossil collector Kamoya Kimeu, who has been responsible for many of the important fossil finds made by Richard Leakey's team. Since the species appears to have changed only slightly over the course of its 1.3-million-year history, this specimen, which is nearly complete, gives us a unique view of what the Asian descendants of *Homo erectus* who first encountered Giganto might really have been like.

The sex of the skeleton was determined by the masculine shape of its pelvic bones and the facial robusticity (thickness and heaviness) of the skull; the boy's age was estimated by comparisons with modern *Homo sapiens* tooth-wear stages and dental eruption patterns. The specimen, nicknamed "the strapping youth," measures five feet four inches in height, which means that *Homo erectus* was big, as early hominids go. Since considerable growth occurs after the age of twelve, it is safe to say that his adult stature would have been about six feet, exceeding the mean for standing height in modern human males.

In terms of brain size, the strapping youth has a cranial

capacity of 900 cubic centimeters, slightly above the mean for
Asian and African *Homo erectus* populations, whose cranial capacity ranges from 750cc to 1,225cc. At the upper end of its
range, the brain size of *Homo erectus* was comparable with that
of modern people (in which the range is from about 1,150cc to
1,900+cc). It has proved very difficult to correlate brain size
with intelligence, but clearly an ancestor species whose brain
size extends into the range for modern man must have been
capable of many of the same behaviors.

One significant dissimilarity between *Homo erectus* and modern people is in the number and extent of physical differences
between the sexes, a phenomenon biologists call sexual dimorphism. The most obvious manifestation of sexual dimorphism
in our genus is in relative size, which in modern populations
averages .93: that is, modern *Homo sapiens* females are, on
average, 93 percent the size of modern males. In *Homo erectus*,
the size difference between male and female was much more
pronounced, about .75. In addition, the male of the species
had bones that were much more robust, especially in the skull,
than those of the female. The much greater extent of physical
differences between men and women in *Homo erectus* were not
known until 1969, when an Indonesian paleontologist named
Sartono discovered a very large skull of a male *Homo erectus* at a
site called Sangiran, in Java. That discovery helped to resolve
some long-standing confusion: forty years before, Ralph von
Koenigswald had concluded that a large and robust male *Homo
erectus* jaw he had discovered should be allocated to a distinct
genus, which he called *Meganthropus paleojavanicus* ("the large
man of ancient Java"). In fact, the jaw only seemed extremely
large because he was comparing it with female specimens. More
recently, it was found that sexual dimorphism in hominids pre-
dating *Homo erectus*, such as *Australopithecus afarensis*, is even more
pronounced than the .75 value observed in our direct ancestor.

Though *Homo erectus* would likely have been as tall as we
are and would have walked in a bipedal fashion nearly identical to ours, our ancestors would have looked quite different in
the upper torso region. Analysis of the strapping youth shows
he had a conical thorax, with narrow shoulders and a rib cage
tapering outward, like that seen in *Australopithecus* and modern
African apes, rather than the barrel-shaped chest of modern
man. The Narikotome *Homo erectus* also provides an important

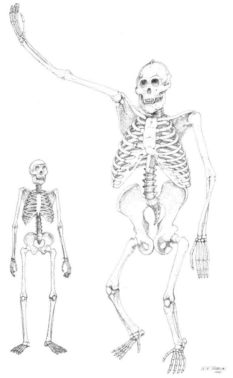

Reconstructed skeletons of *Homo erectus*, at left, and *Gigantopithecus*, which is shown erect for comparison. *(Drawing by William Thomson)*

clue concerning the pelvic region that enables us to make some deductions about the size of the birth canal. In early *Homo erectus,* the pelvic outlet was significantly smaller than that seen in modern people. Even given the smaller mean brain size, *Homo erectus* could not have delivered a baby the size of a modern infant. Thus it seems likely that fetal development continued after birth, with brain growth occurring throughout infancy as seen in *Homo sapiens.* As in our species, pronounced infant dependency and a host of related behavioral adaptations must have been present in *Homo erectus.* On the basis of the fossil record alone, we can be reasonably certain that despite the striking differences in appearance between *Homo erectus* and ourselves, and as much as we would have found their lives to be rough and brutal, our ancestor species was profoundly human.

CHAPTER 4

Break On Through
to the Other Side

Touching Down

As our Russian-built Illyushin jet began to descend from
the muggy Vietnamese sky to the landing strip at the airport in Hanoi in January 1987, we were finally struck by
the enormous significance of what we were doing. We fancy
ourselves pretty cool customers, but for the first time in our
professional lives, we were setting off on a scientific adventure
for which we were completely unprepared. True, we had
been to China when it was still a vast terra incognita, the
far side of the moon, but on that occasion we had been
surrounded by other American scientists, and had followed
an iron-clad itinerary that we had helped to establish. This
visit to Hanoi was something entirely different. For one
thing, not so many years before our government would have
considered the simple act of deplaning at Hanoi's Noibai International Airport an act of treason. Our arrival in Hanoi
was in every sense an excursion through the looking glass—
as both Lewis Carroll and John Le Carré might use the
phrase. When the plane landed on the tarmac, Olsen whis-
pered to Ciochon, "Toto, I don't think we're in Kansas
anymore!"

Actually, we felt more like Darwin sailing into the South
Pacific aboard the *Beagle*: come what may, this was going
to be an exceptionally instructive journey of discovery. We
were the first American scientists invited to Vietnam to

50

carry out a joint program of fieldwork. In fact, our visit must have been approved from high up in the bureaucratic chain of command. Our work would be quite visible, and while we had great confidence in our ability to keep our wits about us, occasionally we feared that we would be watched over too carefully and prevented from doing what we wanted to do—whatever that might turn out to be! Although we had made no specific preparation for the visit— we had not been able to communicate with our prospective hosts to set out a detailed agenda—in a sense our whole careers up to that time were our preparation for what was to come.

Southeast Asia has always been of pivotal importance to prehistorians, as the potential bridge across the great gap between the known *Homo erectus* localities. In recent years, it has also become increasingly essential to our understanding of the worldwide dispersion of human culture—witness Christy Turner's radical new theory that Indochina is where modern man arose. Yet we have far less archaeological information about this area of the world than almost any other. Because of the isolation imposed on this part of Asia by political events, modern fieldwork methods and theory were almost unknown here until we began our partnership with the Institute of Archaeology in Hanoi. Likewise, Western archaeologists were for the most part entirely ignorant of the work that had been going on here, except for occasional reports that filtered into scholarly publications in Eastern Europe. Yet just as Asia had held an extraordinary importance in paleoanthropology throughout most of the history of our field, the same held true in the field of prehistoric archaeology. Vietnam, particularly, was vital in the study of early man, for many of the prototypes of the earliest Asian civilizations were identified there. Now we would have the chance to meet the scientists carrying out archaeological work in this part of the world, and to see what we might be able to accomplish here ourselves.

We were met at the airport by the two scientists who would come to be our closest professional colleagues and, ultimately, friends: Nguyen Van Hao and Nguyen Van Binh. They represent two eras of Vietnamese archaeology in terms of their professional training. Hao,* who is now in his late fifties, received his specialized instruction in archaeology at Peking University (as it is still called, despite the fact that the city is now more commonly designated Beijing), during the epoch when Vietnam was still a client state of the People's Republic of China.

Hao has the simple, down-to-earth style that is typical of the Vietnamese, yet there is something dignified and even courtly about him. Like the majority of his countrymen he is scarcely five feet tall, but unlike most of them he is a bit portly, with plump arms and hands like those of a little boy. His prematurely graying hair falls over his face in a great shock. Hao, a senior member of the staff who soon after we met him became the vice-director of the institute, was unfailing in his polite attention to our needs, but he was also punctiliously conventional. Like everyone in a position of responsibility in Vietnam, he was a rigid rule-follower. These two competing priorities sometimes resulted in conflicts for him: he very much wanted to be a good host and grant us our every request, but when we asked for things that would have required him to bend the rules a tiny bit—something we, especially Ciochon, never hesitated to do—Hao was thrown onto the horns of a dilemma. We eventually learned to respect his position, and to ask for favors only when they were of real importance to us.

Nguyen Van Binh, in his thirties when we met him, is probably exactly midway in age between Ciochon and Olsen. He had received his training at the University of Sofia, in Bulgaria, and in Moscow in the recent period of Vietnam's gravitation toward the Soviet sphere of influence. Because of his proficiency in Bulgarian, Russian, and English, Binh managed to remain au courant in many developments in archaeological theory and method at a time when his country was

---

* A word about Vietnamese proper names: unlike many other Asian languages, in Vietnamese a person's last name really is his last name. However, as in Chinese, first names are used only by the most intimate family members, parents and spouses. Thus we would call Nguyen Van Hao "Professor Hao" and Nguyen Van Binh "Mr. Binh." When we grew friendly with people, we would drop the honorifics and call them by their family names, schoolboy style. Thus, while Professor Hao would retain his honorific, because of his age and position, Nguyen Van Binh, who is our age and a more informal person, became simply Binh.

profoundly isolated from most of the world, and he is quite conversant in a wide range of topics in Old World prehistoric studies.

Binh is a very boyish-looking man, with a Tom Sawyer-like cowlick always sticking up on the back of his head. He is a hot-blooded person with a tremendous drive and dedication to his profession; perhaps more than Hao, he sees doing archaeology as his first priority, and he suffers through agonies whenever the system prevents us, as scientists, from accomplishing exactly what we would like. Because of his studies in Bulgaria and Russia, he is more sophisticated than most Vietnamese people, and he chafes at the extreme deprivations and limitations placed on his life because of his country's isolation and poverty. When, at the conclusion of our excavation in 1989, Jamie James gave him a Beatles cassette tape, Binh wept with grateful joy.

When we arrived in Hanoi, we met the man who was the director of the Institute of Archaeology at that time, Professor Pham Huy Thong. Without doubt the best-known archaeologist in Vietnam, he had also had a successful career as a poet. As a student in Paris in the thirties, he had been a close friend of Ho Chi Minh's, and for many years he had been a member of the party. When we met Thong, he was a wizened old man in his seventies, with a detached smile constantly playing across his lips. It was he who had sent the cable inviting us to Hanoi.

An Archaeological Tour

Our first week in Hanoi, we spent eight to ten hours a day at the Institute of Archaeology, which occupies a charming building in the style of a villa on the French Riviera, a rambling three-story structure with porches and terraces and a red tile roof. The institute is the central coordinating point for all archaeological and paleoanthropological research throughout Vietnam, north and south. Our time at the institute was spent exchanging information and viewpoints through a series of lectures and group discussions.

Communications proved to be somewhat laborious, because nearly all of our conversations had to be translated from English to Vietnamese and back again by our official translator, Tran Kim Nga, a delightful twenty-six-year-old woman with a shy, fetching smile. Madame Nga's conversational English was good enough, but she was completely unfamiliar with most of the subjects we were discussing. Phrases like "Lower Paleolithic biface industry" and "radiocarbon dating" were not a part of her vocabulary. However, Hao, who had studied in Beijing, speaks Chinese; and this enabled him to communicate directly with John Olsen, who also speaks fluent Mandarin, and helped us to overcome the linguistic difficulties posed by the occasional inadequacies of our translator. It also proved to be of great importance later on, when we were carrying on delicate negotiations about our continuing relationship with the Institute of Archaeology.

After this initial period of getting acquainted and exchanging notes, we set out on an archaeological tour of northern Vietnam. On our first day in Hanoi, a highly detailed itinerary for this trip appeared as if by magic; it was evident from the start that a great deal of behind-the-scenes planning had gone on before our arrival. At the end of this first trip, we would remark that we accomplished more in the way of science in these weeks in Vietnam than we had often done in several months on other expeditions.

As we pursued our circuitous journey through northern Vietnam, we found ourselves tracing the course of prehistoric archaeology in peninsular Southeast Asia. Traveling in a Russian-built minivan, we were accompanied by Professor Hao, Binh, Madam Nga, and Nguyen Van Ku, a representative of the Social Sciences Committee, the government agency that oversees the Institute of Archaeology and our official host. Mr. Ku, although impeccably polite, was clearly there to keep an eye on us. A tall, silver-haired man with a canny expression on his face, he was very quiet and self-effacing, but whenever any important decisions had to be made, or when money needed to be doled out, he asserted his control over the expedition.

Our first destination was Cuc Phuong National Park, a high, densely forested valley surrounded on all sides by limestone towers (also known as karst topography). In a tropical climate a paleontologist must carry out his search for fossils in karst landscape, for these limestone towers typically are

The douc langur is now one of the rarest monkeys in Southeast Asia, in large measure because of the devastating effects of napalm and Agent Orange attacks during the war. *(Photograph by Lois K. Lippold)*

filled with caves and fissures where fossils have a chance first to form, and then to be protected from the elements that would conspire against their survival. Located at the conjunction of Ha Son Binh, Ha Nam Ninh, and Thanh Hoa* provinces, Cuc Phuong receives some hundred inches of rain annually. It is a thick rain forest of broad-leaved trees, with a canopy reaching up to nearly two hundred feet in places. It has a rich primate fauna that includes several species of macaque monkeys, the black gibbon (*Hylobates concolor*), and several colobine

---

*Throughout this book, all diacritical marks have been omitted from words and proper names in Vietnamese, which is standard practice in journalistic and scholarly publishing. These names, for example, properly cited, would appear thus: Hà Sòn Bình, Hà Nam Ninh, Thanh Hóa. Even "Vietnam" ought properly to be rendered "Việt Nam." To a Vietnamese person, these words are meaningless without their dense overlay of accents, slashes, and underlining dots. However, some of the diacritical marks in Vietnamese do not even exist in orthodox Roman typography; and in any case the chances of a nonnative speaker ever getting all those names right, practically speaking, approach nil.

monkeys, including the very rare douc langur, *Pygathrix nemaeus*. Many southern populations of the douc langur, which is now an endangered species, were wiped out during the war by American air attacks using napalm and Agent Orange. The rich present-day distribution of primate species throughout this stretch of Vietnam was an important factor in our decision to come to Thanh Hoa province in search of primate fossils.

Our reason for visiting Cuc Phuong was to study an important rock shelter of the Hoabinhian culture. The existence of the Hoabinhian was first established in 1926 by Madeleine Colani, one of the great names in Indochinese archaeology, who excavated the Stone Age site in Hoa Binh province that gives the culture its name. A brief excursion into the history of archaeological studies in Vietnam at this point will perhaps be useful in sorting out the different stages of early human culture there. P. I. Boriskovskii, himself one of the brighter lights in the field in recent years, in 1966 published a detailed book in Russian about that history, which was later translated into English and published in the journal *Soviet Anthropology and Archaeology*. It is a lucid work, unusually free of doctrinaire axe-grinding and point-making.

Archaeology in Vietnam

The first semblance of modern archaeology in Vietnam begins with the arrival of the French, who in 1899 established in Hanoi the Ecole Française d'Extrême-Orient, which was not a school at all but a research institute and the focus of scholarship for all of French Indochina. Boriskovskii points out that the early investigation of many important archaeological sites was entrusted to rank amateurs, dilettantes who were more interested in collecting knick-knacks than in science (of course, exactly the same comment might be made about the early history of European archaeology). As an example, he cites the excavation of Dong Son, one of the most important Bronze Age sites in East Asia, which was carried out by a man named Pageot, whom Boriskovskii describes as "a man with no education whatever, a circus performer, later a seaman, and, finally, for a number of years a French customs official in Thanh Hoa province."

Things got onto a more solid foundation with Henri Mansuy (1857–1937), who first pushed back the Vietnamese archaeological record to the early Neolithic period with his discoveries of polished stone tools in the Bac Son mountain range, on the northern edge of the Red River delta. The Bacsonian culture, as it is called, is distinguished by edge-ground tools and the first appearance of pottery in the region. The major cultural adaptations of hill rice agriculture and the domestication of dog and buffalo are also attributed to the Bacsonian culture, or late Hoabinhian, dated between 8,000 and 6,000 B.P.

Archaeologists working in Vietnam, as everywhere, have tended to progress steadily from later cultures to ever earlier ones as the science becomes more and more sophisticated (and also for the simple reason that older artifacts often are deeper down in the ground). After Mansuy's, the next major contribution was made by Madame Colani, as she is usually called, one of the earliest professional female archaeologists anywhere. Her discovery of the Hoabinhian culture was the first to establish the Paleolithic in Vietnam. According to Boriskovskii, who approvingly notes that Madame Colani worked with Vietnamese assistants, then quite a rare practice, "She made many exploratory trips, primarily in the inaccessible mountain regions of the country, and discovered about one hundred caves and other habitations of primitive man." It ought to be pointed out that the names Dongsonian and Hoabinhian as cultural identifiers are now in use throughout Southeast Asia.

Discoveries of early Paleolithic man were made in the era of the Socialist Republic of Vietnam, after the establishment of the Institute of Archaeology. That was accomplished by decree number 65, which was signed by Ho Chi Minh in 1945, just a few months after the founding of the republic (and nine years before Dienbienphu, when the Communists finally kicked the French out of northern Vietnam). Ho Chi Minh was a great booster of archaeology, for what he perceived as its propaganda potential and its ability to establish the ethnic identity of the Vietnamese people.

He believed that archaeology was an efficient means of providing the Vietnamese people with hard evidence of their unique cultural heritage. Vietnamese archaeologists mean something particular when they call themselves "unique"—that their culture is not merely a watered-down by-product of that of their dynamic neighbor to the north. China has had a profound influence on the economic, political, and social development of Vietnam for the past two thousand years. This fact, coupled with the recent history of antagonistic relations between the countries, has placed a premium on archaeological data, because of their ability to trace the separate cultural heritages of the Vietnamese and the Chinese peoples. As a broadly based social thinker, Ho Chi Minh saw the importance of instilling in the Vietnamese people a recognition of their heritage, a powerful and continuous entity despite the fact that Vietnam has been a vassal state of both Asian and European powers for the greatest part of its two-thousand-year history.

Mao Zedong also recognized early on the potential of archaeology to promote Chinese nationalism, since a fundamental part of his theory of planned social change involved the notion that societies must "let the past serve the present." By this Mao meant that in socialist societies such as China and Vietnam, archaeology does not exist simply to provide a fuller understanding of the past per se, as an end in itself, as it does in Western societies. Rather, archaeology's sole function is seen as the means by which direct links may be forged between the past and the present.

In the eyes of Vietnamese archaeologists, these links demonstrate two important tenets of human culture. First, the inevitability of the Marxist view of history is acknowledged by showing how present social circumstances derive directly from the past. Second, the unique ethnic heritage of the Vietnamese people is indicated by contrast with the archaeological records of China, Thailand, Laos, Burma, Cambodia, and other neighboring societies.

Since archaeology in Vietnam is not a pursuit of knowledge for knowledge's sake, as it ideally is in non-Marxist societies, it is logical that the science should be thoroughly integrated with other aspects of social enquiry and reform, and carried out in

Here, at Tham Khuyen Cave, Vietnamese scientists in 1965 found fossils of the giant ape *Gigantopithecus* and remains of early man side by side— one of the most important fossil discoveries ever made in Asia. *(Photograph by Russell Ciochon)*

close collaboration with scholars from other socialist nations. Most of the pioneering excavations in search of remains of ancestor cultures have been undertaken in concert with archaeologists from the Soviet Union (most important, Boriskovskii himself), Bulgaria, and East Germany. To that list the United States may now be added.

For us, the single most important fossil discovery in Vietnam took place in 1965 at a site called Tham Khuyen, in the northern province of Lang Son, near the Chinese border. There, in an area originally surveyed by East German scientists, Vietnamese paleontologists excavated remains of Pleistocene fauna, including *Gigantopithecus,* and *Homo erectus,* in the same cave. In 1970, Chinese excavators in Hubei province also recovered remains of *Gigantopithecus* and *Homo erectus* side by side; more recently, paleoanthropologists in Sichuan province came up with yet another such association of Giganto and *Homo erectus*. Also recovered at Tham Khuyen was the skull of a gibbon with the complete face and much of the cranial vault, and a partial skull of the giant panda, which is now extinct in Vietnam.

The discoveries at Tham Khuyen were what had prompted us to come to Vietnam in the first place. They were major finds, yet were almost entirely overlooked by the world archaeological community. If such discoveries had been made in India or Indonesia, they would have been front-page news. Boriskovskii makes a tantalizing reference in his historical sketch to a strikingly similar paleontological discovery made more than fifty years ago by two members of the French Indochina Geological Service, Jacques Fromaget and Edmond Saurin. From 1934 to 1936, Fromaget and Saurin excavated caves in Upper Laos, just across the border from Thanh Hoa province, Vietnam—where we began excavating in 1989. According to Boriskovskii, the Frenchmen found "fossil Pleistocene fauna along with bones that may have belonged to a man of the *Sinanthropus* [i.e., Peking Man, *Homo erectus*] type . . . The question was opened as to whether Indochina had been populated by ape-like men at the beginning of Paleolithic."

A Debate over Stone Tools

Meanwhile, back at Cuc Phuong: the Hoabinhian rock shelter we had come to visit, dating from the late Pleistocene, is located on the side of a karst tower, in dense forest, about a hundred feet above the valley floor. Originally excavated in 1966–67 by a Vietnamese–East German team, the Cuc Phuong site yielded a tightly flexed (that is archaeologese for crouching, usually in the fetal position) human burial in a slab-lined pit and masses of mussel shells, a typical feature of Hoabinhian burial sites. The significance of the Hoabinhian culture in Southeast Asia is its role in the origins of agriculture and the genesis of the region's ethnic mosaic. As far as we know, the Hoabinhian culture in Malaysia and other parts of southern Asia were the first to engage in simple food production based on the cultivation of fruit and root crops in garden settings. The Hoabinhian development of this early form of agriculture, which may be described as horticultural, suggests to archaeologists that human populations may have been subject to substantial changes during this period in Southeast Asia, which would have influenced the development of alternative means of subsistence. Most Hoabinhian sites in Vietnam date from 9,000 to 15,000 years B.P., which means that such evidence of horticulture in Southeast Asia is most likely as old as the earliest known record of food production in the fertile crescent of the Middle East, the proverbial cradle of civilization.

Then we pushed on to Thanh Hoa, the first of several visits to this desperately impoverished province. There, we visited two localities that were originally investigated by Boriskovskii, Nui Do and Nui Nuong. Nui Nuong today is a barren, boulder-strewn hill covered with scrubby vegetation—a world apart from the lush verdure of Cuc Phuong. While we were poking around here, we found one of the large core tools described by Boriskovskii as a cleaver, similar to those associated with *Homo erectus* in Africa. Since most of the determinations of the age of Nui Nuong and Nui Do have been based on the shapes of the tools discovered there and their supposed similarity to known, dated middle-Pleistocene tools found elsewhere in the Old World, we were surprised to see that this particular artifact bore all the signs of a relatively late date of manufacture. In fact, upon returning to Hanoi, we saw identical specimens in the National Museum of History, where they were clearly labeled as having been found in Neolithic sites in the same province as Nui Nuong and Nui Do.

From Nui Nuong, we set out on our way to Nui Do, about twelve miles away on the banks of the Ma ("Horse") River. Our van broke down halfway there, so we had to hike the last eight miles through the countryside. The rice paddies were bustling with activity, for the planting season was at its height, yet as we walked by, like the Pied Piper we attracted a large following of children, and many adults as well, only too happy to abandon their work to wander along behind us. They accompanied us right to the foot of Nui Do (which translates as Mount Do, though it is no mountain), where we encountered the same boulder-strewn, lunar landscape we had seen at Nui

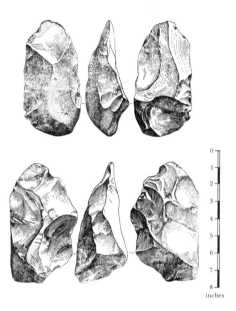

These stone tools were discovered at the Nui Do site by Vietnamese archaeologists, who believe that they may have been made by *Homo erectus*. *(Courtesy of Institute of Archaeology, Hanoi)*

Nuong. Looking out across the flooded rice paddies toward the distant karst towers, we could see villages that had been bombed during American air attacks on a nearby petroleum refinery and a bridge over the Ma River. One of the young archaeologists in the party pointed out his native village and recounted to us his childhood memories of fleeing American bombs and machine-gun fire.

Nui Nuong, Nui Do, and similar open-air sites in western Thanh Hoa province, especially the assemblages of stone objects they have yielded, have been the source of a great deal of controversy since their discovery in the 1960's. While Soviet and Vietnamese archaeologists maintain that the sites are remnants of Vietnam's earliest known inhabitants—going back at least 300,000 years, to the middle Pleistocene—many Western archaeologists who have viewed the sites and the artifacts collected there disagree. They believe that either these objects are not tools at all, that they are in fact nothing more than random assemblages of broken rocks, or that they date to a much younger period of time, to the late Neolithic or Bronze Age, several thousand years ago. Since one of our primary goals in Vietnam was to examine all available evidence of the presence of middle-Pleistocene human ancestors in this area of Indochina, the controversy surrounding these sites in western Thanh Hoa province captured our attention.

We were fortunate in being able to visit the Nui Nuong and Nui Do localities in the company of several of the archaeologists from Hanoi and Thanh Hoa who are responsible for the ongoing investigation there. Supplementing our close examination of stone tools from these sites housed in Hanoi, we now had a chance to see first hand the geological context in which they had been discovered. The geological context of stone tools is of paramount importance in the correct interpretation of their true age. Previously published Vietnamese reports on the subject were sketchy and ambiguous, so we relished the opportunity to see the artifacts, if that is what they are, and their original locations on the same trip.

After our study of the tools and the sites, we concluded that some of the claims offered by the Vietnamese and Soviet archaeologists for the early Paleolithic antiquity of these finds are valid. However, these judgments are based on difficult-to-define characteristics, such as the shape and degree of weathering of individual tools. No independent method of corroborating the age of these finds has yet been offered. At the same time, we feel that many of the chipped stones that are called Paleolithic tools are actually just chipped stones and nothing more. The geological conditions of the western Thanh Hoa localities make them prime candidates for the production of naturally fractured splinters of stone that can often mimic, in a superficial way, those made by human hands.

We also believe that among those objects from Nui Nuong, Nui Do, and related sites that can be confidently attributed to the deliberate stone-working activities of human ancestors, more than one period of time is represented. In fact, sites such as Nui Nuong and Nui Do most likely functioned as quarry workshops where people exploited the exposed and readily flakable basalt and quartzite outcrops over a very long period of time. Thus, these sites *may* contain evidence of some of Vietnam's earliest human inhabitants, but until such finds are

made in association with fossils of animals (including, if possible, human fossils) or other datable materials, sorting out
the time range represented by the sites will remain nearly
impossible.

"A City of Delightful Surprises"

After that first field trip to Nui Nuong and Nui Do, we returned to Hanoi for a brief layover, in order, among other
things, to have our van repaired. Hanoi is still a beautiful city,
despite everything that mildew and Soviet architects have done
to it. A British journalist would tell us a couple of years later
that in his opinion, Hanoi was the most beautiful capital in the
world. That is an exaggeration, but it is impossible not to see
what he means. The city certainly made a favorable impression
on Roy Chapman Andrews when he visited it in 1916 at the
beginning of the First Asiatic Expedition. He wrote, "Hanoi is
a city of delightful surprises. It has broad, clean streets, over-
hung with trees which often form a cool green canopy overhead, beautiful lawns and well-kept houses, and at the center
in the town is a lovely lake surrounded by a wide border of
palms."

Remarkably, Andrews's description still holds true seventy-
four years later, although the houses are now rather more
moldy than well kept. As must have been the case when Andrews was in Hanoi, there are almost no automobiles here;
everyone gets around by bicycle or motorbike. At night, Hanoi
takes on a rather eerie aspect, for the city is scarcely electrified.
The whirring of bicycle wheels fills the dark streets, and people
squat in doorways, backlit by kerosene lamps, quietly smoking
tobacco and playing cards.

We soon discovered that we were the only Westerners in
Hanoi who were not members of the diplomatic corps. The
other guests at our hotel were Libyans, Palestinians, Cubans,
and a boisterous group of East German tourists. We made
friends with a visiting Iraqi doctor, a friendly fellow named
Yassar, who was only too happy to practice his English and

show us the ropes—including how to get our hands on some dong, the currency of the Socialist Republic of Vietnam.

At that time, the discrepancy between the official and the black-market exchange rates was so enormous—the latter about ten times the former—that absolutely no one went to the official money changers. Indeed, no one seemed to know where dong could be got at the legal rate. There were, of course, government banks, but no one we met had ever been to one. When we asked Madame Nga about changing dollars to dong, she did not understand what we were talking about. Since she was a member of our official escort, naturally she could not acknowledge that there was such a thing as the black market, but on the other hand the idea of changing money at the government banks was just too outlandish to be grasped. At last she said, hesitatingly, "I don't think you can do it." We realized then that we would simply have to deal with Yassar's source, the chargé d'affaires at the Iraqi embassy. We were told later that many of the foreign embassies in Hanoi had arrangements with the Vietnamese government to exchange dollars for dong at the "official black-market rate." That amounted to an acknowledgment by the Vietnamese government of the actual value (i.e., the worthlessness) of the dong, and in addition it assured them access to the American dollar, the hard currency they needed badly.

Once our van was repaired, we set off again, to visit some sites of the Sonvian culture in Vinh Phu province. The first stop was a place called Vuon Sau, near Viet Thi, which is nothing more than a low hill overlooking the Red River, used for the cultivation of manioc. Here, in natural gullies, we found a number of artifacts including the Sonvian index fossil—an "index fossil" is an object typically found in localities associated with the culture, almost like its trademark—a split quartzite cobble that bears close affinities to later Hoabinhian tools.

The Sonvian, which takes it name from the culture's type site in the Red River valley, is slightly earlier than the Hoabinhian and may be its precursor, in the sense that both the Sonvian and Hoabinhian share a broadly similar approach to the manufacture of stone tools: namely the longitudinal splitting of river-worn cobbles to yield sharp stone flakes, and a more heavy-duty chopping edge on the cobble itself. The possible relationships between the Sonvian and Hoabinhian cultures are of interest not only in terms of their chronology, but also because the geographical location of their known habitations suggests that some fundamental differences exist. For the most part, Sonvian sites are in the open, along erosional terraces that flank river courses, and on the slopes of exposed hills. Hoabinhian remains, on the other hand, are known almost exclusively from cave deposits and shell middens (the archaeological term for garbage heaps) along the coastline of Southeast Asia. While there are exceptions to the rule, the pattern is so striking that archaeologists have speculated widely on what this geographical disparity means. Thus, we must rely not only on the typology of the stone artifacts discovered in Sonvian and Hoabinhian sites to judge the significance of this variability, but also on the contexts in which these cultural remains are found.

Herein lies one of the persistent dilemmas in the interpretation of the early archaeological record: because Paleolithic sites are most often characterized by large numbers of stone artifacts, which are very durable, and little else, the meaning of the variations among the stone tools found at different sites is extremely important in sorting out the relationships that might have existed among those sites when they were inhabited. In Western Europe, particularly in France, the birthplace of Paleolithic archaeology, it has long been recognized that this sort of variability could be explained in a number of ways, and that making a correct identification is complicated by the limited nature of the Paleolithic record itself—the fact that it consists almost entirely of stone tools. It is impossible to put an absolute date on a stone tool with any sort of chemical or physical lab test, since the age that would result from such a test, many millions of years, would be the age of the stone itself, not its date of manufacture.

In the 1960's archaeologists began trying to explain this variability in meaningful terms. François Bordes, the doyen of French Paleolithic archaeology, maintained that each of the distinctive sets of artifacts recovered in geographically or temporally distinct contexts represented a separate *cultural* entity. In other words, Bordes believes that typological variability among stone tools found together was actually a measurement of cultural variability.

The American archaeologist Lewis Binford disagreed. He pioneered the notion that the variability observable in Paleolithic sites in France might represent the remains of different activities carried out by the same group of people. Binford posited that a single culture, providing for its subsistence and doing other activities at different places at different times, might produce the same sort of archaeological record that Bordes had interpreted as the result of cultural variability. In fact, Binford stated that the organization of activities according to seasons, a common practice among preindustrial peoples, might yield clusters of sites with similar artifact groups that could mimic the variability of the sort described by Bordes.

This dilemma, sometimes called the Binford-Bordes debate, has yet to be resolved in many areas of the world, where the Paleolithic archaeological record is much sketchier than it is in southwest France, where the issues were first joined.

In Vietnam, the relationships between the Sonvian and Hoabinhian complexes are of exactly the type that engendered the Binford-Bordes debate. The more we know of these two industries, the less likely it seems that chronology alone can account for the similarities and differences discernible between them. Labeling the Sonvian as ancestral to the Hoabinhian simply because in some archaeological sites it lies in strata underneath remains of the latter, overlooks the fundamental difference in the distribution of most Sonvian and Hoabinhian sites. Even recognizing the disparities in the geographical location of the sites of the two does not resolve the issue. We are still unable to answer the fundamental question, Why are most Sonvian sites out in the open, while most Hoabinhian sites are found in caves? Whether these sites represent radically different cultural adaptations, or whether they preserve the remains of different activities of essentially the same group of people, has yet to be solved. One thing is clear: answers will not be forthcoming until we have a much larger sample of artifacts—including those we are recovering in our excavation in Vietnam.

Whatever its relationship with the Hoabinhian may be, the Sonvian culture is particularly important to us for an association found at Nguom Rock Shelter, in Bac Thai province. In a living floor there, Vietnamese scientists found Sonvian stone tools together with burned and broken bones of *Pongo pygmaeus,* the orangutan, along with other animal remains. The context of this discovery has been radiocarbon-dated to about 23,000 B.P., making it the last securely dated occurrence of the orangutan on the Indochinese peninsula.

Currently, the geographical range of *Pongo* is restricted to parts of the Indonesian islands of Sumatra and Borneo; yet we know from the fossil evidence that in the Pleistocene the orangutan ranged over modern South China, Burma, Thailand, Cambodia, Laos, Vietnam, Malaysia, and Java, as well as Sumatra and Borneo. The cause of the extinction of the orangutan in Southeast Asia has always been a perplexing mystery: Why do only insular populations of this great ape survive, when suitable tropical-forest habitats can be found throughout Indochina? It now seems likely, or at least plausible, that the people who made the characteristic split-quartzite cobble tools of the Sonvian culture were systematically hunting the orangutan. It is difficult to state with certainty that early human hunting caused the extinction of *Pongo* on the mainland of Asia, but it certainly contributed to its extinction. As we shall see in a subsequent chapter, this hypothesis about the extirpation of the orangutan on the Asian mainland serves as an interesting model for the extinction of *Gigantopithecus.*

The Riviera of Vietnam

Our final field trip was to Halong Bay, about sixty miles down the coast from the border with China, and eighty miles due east of Hanoi. The drive took us across Vietnam's lowland coastal plain to the Gulf of Tonkin, where the port of Haiphong is situated. As we crossed each of the dozen bridges along the way, Madame Nga would tell us how many American airplanes had been shot down in the war while trying to blow it up. She said that although the bridges were often damaged, they were easily rebuilt in a few days. When we reached the harbor of Haiphong, at dusk, we boarded a small ferry carrying people, trucks, and bicycles across the inlet.

Halong Bay is the Riviera of Vietnam. That may sound silly to those who have never seen it, but it is an apt comparison. We were astonished by the beauty of the place. Halong Bay has become a favorite playground of the Communist world; in the dead of European winter, Bulgarians, East Germans, and other Soviet-satellite snowbirds join the Russians in their retreat to this place, which can only be called a tropical paradise. You will not find luxury here—north Vietnam has not known luxury in any form since before the war with the French, which ended in 1954—but the beaches are lovely, the seafood superb, and the hotels comfortable enough (if you overlook the rats, which seem to thrive in all Vietnamese hotels). Yet the great attraction is the scenery. Limestone towers by the hundreds rise from the clear blue waters of the bay. Many of these rugged little islands are mantled with emerald green vegetation, some glitter nakedly in the sun, others have bizarre formations of natural architecture—bridges and arches, occasionally a hole right through the sheer side of a cliff.

We had come to Halong Bay to explore these tower karsts. When we returned to Vietnam for our excavation two years later, the expedition's geologist, a graduate student of Ciochon's named Katerina Semendeferi, conducted us on an intensive tour of the limestone topography of the bay, and in a later chapter we shall thoroughly explain the geological processes that formed this beautiful and unusual landscape.

Paleoanthropologists and archaeologists have a vital interest in karst, for it is typically filled with caves and fissures, which have been the source of almost all of the fossils and cultural remains that have been recovered in this part of the world. In karst towers exactly like the ones in Halong Bay, Chinese paleoanthropologists in the 1950's recovered the first jaws and teeth of the giant ape *Gigantopithecus* in situ, in the Guangxi Zhuang Autonomous Region, which adjoins Vietnam to the northeast.

The Social Sciences Committee had arranged for us to rent a large boat that could take us miles offshore among the more than three thousand karst islands that loom throughout Halong Bay. In the Pleistocene era, which began 1.8 million years ago, when much of the world's oceans were frozen in huge continental glaciers, many of the watery parts of Southeast Asia, as

far south and east as Java, in the modern Indonesian archipelago, were a part of the Asian mainland. The submerged plateau underlying these shallow waters is called the Sunda Shelf.
Ocean depth in this coastal area of Vietnam is less than 300
feet, and in the Pleistocene these islands were towers on the
coastal plain.

As we steamed among these towers, we could see a variety
of caves and fissures in their often perfectly vertical faces. We
saw over a hundred such caves and fissures in this brief survey;
in many of them, we saw breccia, the cementlike sediment in
shades of red, orange, and yellow that usually contains fossils.
We were unable to stop at any of them, for our ship was much
too big to land in such close quarters.

Yet we knew we would come back to Halong Bay. By this
time, all of our doubts and fears about coming to Vietnam had
completely vanished. We were on quite friendly terms with
Hao and Binh, and we sensed that they as much as we were
taking it for granted that this scientific partnership would
continue. When we returned to Hanoi, we negotiated the terms
of our return with Pham Huy Thong, the director of the
institute. Although Professor Thong made every effort to conceal the fact, it was clear that our coming to Vietnam was an
extraordinary event, which resonated far beyond the narrow
confines of the nation's scientific community. The Vietnamese
never wanted to let us know how difficult things were, apparently from a motive of politeness, but also no doubt from a
deep-seated secretiveness acquired during the war. At no time
did we feel like enemies—particularly with Hao or Binh, who
showed very little interest in political matters—yet it was also
apparent to us that many people higher up in the government
had to sign off on our visa applications.

Another aspect of our negotiations was the subtle, unstated
need for an acceptable form of baksheesh. The presumption of
equality between the two sides had to be maintained at all costs,
yet we were nonetheless perceived as the bearers of bounty;
on this first trip we brought with us a Kodak Carousel slide
projector, a Pentax 35 millimeter camera, and some professional books. As our conversations with Thong progressed, we
found ourselves promising the Vietnamese all sorts of things: a
photocopying machine (we were not sure that it would be legal

to give them that, as the United States government severely restricts the export of technological goods to Vietnam under the provisions of the Trade with the Enemy Act; later we learned that it was permissible), some expensive reference books, even a Vietnamese typewriter. The latter are manufactured in East Germany and, bizarrely, are more easily obtained in the West than in Vietnam.

Thong was very good at letting us know what might be a good thing to offer, without ever quite coming out and asking for it; and we were only too happy to oblige him. We knew that we wanted to come back, and if the price of admission was a few hundred dollars' worth of hardware, we would find the money.

CHAPTER 5

The Road to Ba Thuoc

Prehistoric Flora and Fauna

The topography of Southeast Asia a million years ago might not have had a tremendously different appearance from the way it looks today. A map of the region would have looked altogether different, of course—much of what is today underwater was then dry land—but the landscape would have been more or less the same. Northern Vietnam is basically one huge chunk of limestone that is constantly subjected to immense quantities of water: water in the atmosphere, water in the form of precipitation, water coursing through the region in rivers and underground streams. The result is some of the most beautiful and bizarre landscape in all Asia. In the Pleistocene, the topography would have been distributed differently. An observer comparing the landscape then with its modern appearance would see it at an earlier stage in the process of erosion. In other words, what were then shallow depressions are now fissures; what were then fissures are now caves; what were then mouths of caves are now natural arches, and so forth.

The vegetation on the ground was undoubtedly much thicker, since the populations of *Homo erectus* who lived here would not have made any clearings, having not yet mastered the art and science of food cultivation. Yet the plant species at that time, which included the giant taro, lemon grass, the red bean, and bitter cucumber, might not have differed much from what one sees today. One likely difference might have been that in the

Pleistocene the bamboo, which grows today in thick stands everywhere, would have been even more spectacularly abundant, because the land had not been cleared for agriculture.

The most startling difference would have been in the fauna. Since we have excavated over one thousand fossils, representing thirty-six mammalian species, we now have a rather clear picture of the animal life in this area at that time. Huge beasts of all kinds dominated the landscape. Carnivores such as the tiger and leopard were much more common then than now, and competed for food with species such as the Asiatic black bear (*Ursus thibetanus*) and other species that are no longer found in Vietnam. And they all competed with canines such as the wolf and the Asiatic wild dog in preying on the dozens of bovid and cervid species (cowlike and deerlike mammals, respectively). Yet of them all, the most dramatic megafauna ("megafauna" describes very large animals of the fairly recent past) would have been the Proboscidea: the elephant and its even more enormous cousin, the stegodon, now vanished from the landscape. Also present were the orangutan, tapir, and rhinoceros, all of which are now extinct in Vietnam.

Hanging in the bamboo forests, the giant panda would have been seen chomping away; nowadays it is found only in some remote highlands of central China, in terrain remarkably similar to that of northern Vietnam. The question of why the great white-and-black bear became extinct there and yet persisted in regions of China is a fascinating one, as yet unanswered by biologists, though as we shall see, it bears directly upon another unanswered question, that of *Gigantopithecus*'s disappearance.

To a modern observer, the most interesting sight would have been the multitude of primate species. In addition to the swarms of monkeys, such as the stump-tailed macaque, the rhesus macaque, and the langur, several varieties of gibbon were present, and the orangutan would have been swinging amongst the boughs of the trees. Presiding over them all, enormous and powerful, *Gigantopithecus* would have been a brooding presence in the jungle. Last of all, we would have seen our own ancestor, *Homo erectus*, huddled around his hearth fires and hunting in the valley. They were an ugly, hairy people, but with a genius for an entirely new way of adapting for survival.

As we drove through modern Thanh Hoa province for the first time, on our way to the site of our excavation, at first the landscape looked to us so primeval that we half expected to see *Homo erectus* camping out in the hollows in order to avoid roaming elephants and stegodon, or to catch a glimpse of the giant panda and *Gigantopithecus* munching bamboo peaceably, side by side in the bamboo forests. In fact, the face of the land has changed dramatically, owing to centuries of agriculture. As primitive as the occasional bamboo dwellings appeared to us, they were home to a society that has been tilling the soil and propagating domesticated animal species for millennia.

Communication Breakdown

After the success of our first visit to Vietnam, we thought that our invitation for a return visit would soon be forthcoming. Over the course of the year that followed, Ciochon wrote long letters to Pham Huy Thong, the director of the Institute of Archaeology, suggesting the itinerary and agenda for the next visit. As an earnest of our good intentions, the photocopying machine we had promised was purchased immediately and shipped to Haiphong via Hong Kong. We also arranged for Judy Ladinsky, head of the U.S. Committee for Scientific Co-operation with Vietnam, to bring the Vietnamese typewriter and the anthropological reference books Binh and Hao had requested. Yet we never received any sort of acknowledgment or reply for these things, nor did we receive an invitation to come back. A great silence emanated from Hanoi.

The assumption all along had been that we would return, at the latest, exactly one year after the first trip, in January 1988. We made all the preparations for the trip, while sending off terser and ever more urgent cables to Hanoi. Then, just a couple of weeks before we had planned to leave, we received a wire informing us that the January trip was off. In the absence of any explanation as to why our request had been turned down, we started from scratch. We wrote again, urging them to invite us to come in May for a period of three weeks, to visit Tham Khuyen or some other Pleistocene-epoch fossil locality,

Into this lush green valley in northern Vietnam we came to look for fossil remains of human ancestors and of *Gigantopithecus*, the largest primate that ever lived. The Ma River ("Horse River") flows serenely through the western district of Thanh Hoa province, about fifteen miles east of Laos. *(Photograph by Jamie James)*

Seen here through a fissure at the top of the towering limestone mountain in which we excavated, the Ma valley rolls out to the horizon. *(Photograph by Jamie James)*

Some 350 miles to the northeast, the Li River valley in South China has exactly the same sort of distinctive limestone topography as the area we excavated. Along the banks of the river, majestic stands of bamboo soar to heights exceeding forty feet. Bamboo played an essential role in early human adaptation in this semi-tropical environment. *(Photograph by Jamie James)*

This limestone tower contains at its base the cave system we excavated. Lang Trang I, the cave opening where we began working, is visible at ground level in the center of the photograph. At the right is the fissure we called Lang Trang III. *(Photograph by Russell Ciochon)*

Halfway through the season, we were the guests of honor at a feast held in the house of a family of Tai people, one of the principal ethnic minorities in Thanh Hoa province. These Tai girls are banging out a dance beat with bamboo rhythm blocks. *(Photograph by Jamie James)*

This limestone tower near Liucheng, in South China, yielded the greatest haul of *Gigantopithecus* fossils ever found—including the jaw and teeth pictured on page 7 of the black-and-white photo section. *(Photograph by Russell Ciochon)*

At left, former Hollywood make-up artist Bill Munns stands next to the life-sized model of Giganto he built to our specifications. Below, the head of Giganto peers through a mock jungle.

Below, Munn's model of *Homo erectus*, next to its "skull," which was based upon that of Peking Man, one of the original discoveries of the species.

(All photographs copyright Bill Munns)

AT LEFT AND BELOW: The placid waters of Halong Bay are crowded with more than a thousand towering limestone islands, which are riddled with fossil-bearing caves. A popular resort during the era of French colonialism, Halong Bay has more recently been a center of tourism to snowbirds from the Soviet bloc. *(Photographs by Jamie James)*

Morning mist rises over a farm in Ba Thuoc. *(Photograph by Russell Ciochon)*

On one of our last days in Ba Thuoc, we hiked to Dieu Rock Shelter. This limestone overhang was continuously inhabited by early man for over 10,000 years, beginning about 18,000 years ago. *(Photograph by Jamie James)*

such as Halong Bay. Afterward, we hoped to go to Cambodia
(which at that time still called itself Kampuchea), to visit some
paleontological and prehistoric archaeological sites there, as
well as the legendary Khmer monuments of Angkor. This time
we got the green light, and in May 1988 we set off again for
Vietnam.

Air Vietnam may not be the worst airline in the world, but
it is certainly the strangest. It is the only one we know (except
for its sister airline, Air Kampuchea) that offers standing-room
service. When we boarded the Soviet-made plane, we were
greeted by the loud blast of a Bee Gees tape, which seemed at
once anachronistic and absurdly inappropriate. Our seats were
by the emergency door; next to it was a long knotted rope,
coiled in a bucket, which was to be used in case of emergency.
A spider had spun an elaborate web in the NO SMOKING light
overhead, and everyone, flight staff included, chain-smoked
through the entire flight.

Our reception in Hanoi was bitterly disappointing. Binh
was very glad to see us, and greeted us with the friendly
warmth that we, on our side, were trying to project, but he was
the only one who did. Soon after our arrival, we were presented with an exceedingly dull itinerary, which was quite
long on entries like "Meeting with So-and-So, People's Committee on Such-and-Such," and "John Olsen delivers lecture,"
yet distressingly short on anything resembling active science.
They told us that it was only a rough draft, and that we could
make changes in the program, but we soon realized that that
was not the case: if it was not in the program, it was not going
to happen.

Our first ceremonial meeting at the Institute of Archaeology was a chilly one. Pham Huy Thong had been kicked
upstairs to be the head of a new government agency to develop
tourism for Vietnamese citizens who want to travel abroad, but
he was at the meeting to add his own touch of frost to the
proceedings. His French was perfect, and James, who speaks
some French, was able to converse with him directly. Our
friend Professor Hao, who had a very nervous and preoccu-
pied air, was also there, so Olsen was able to converse with him
in Chinese. The ability to speak directly with the principals was
of vital importance: we found out later that our translator was,

according to a Vietnamese informant, "pure secret police." That bit of information was not quite as sinister as it sounded; in fact, it would have been shocking if three Americans had come to visit and no one was there to listen. Her reports must have made dull reading.

Ciochon asked if he could examine the gibbon skull that had been found at Tham Khuyen, as he had requested in his letters. That, we were told, would be "very difficult to arrange," a maddening phrase we would hear often. The person who had the skull was in Berlin, and no one knew anything about the skull or where it might be. Perhaps it was in Berlin, perhaps not. That is a common custom in the socialist countries in Asia, which often thwarts visiting Western scientists: if a Vietnamese (or Chinese or Burmese) scientist finds something on an expedition, it becomes virtually his private property, to lock up in his desk drawer or use as a door stop. If he leaves the country for a year, then for a year none of his colleagues is able to examine the specimen. The practice has always seemed to us a strange one, not only unscientific but also un-Communist. Most Western scientists would accept the view that a specimen belongs not to the person who happens to find it but to the whole scientific community.

Then we asked about our request to visit Tham Khuyen, which was conspicuously absent from the program. That, too, was difficult to arrange. They told us that the Vietnamese-Chinese frontier was off limits for security reasons, even though there were no hostilities going on at the moment. Instead of going there we would go to the Ba Thuoc district, in western Thanh Hoa province, to see a site that had recently been discovered by Dang Huu Luu, a paleontologist on the institute staff. We asked about the site, and were given the bland assurance that it was quite interesting, which left us with the feeling that, in Ciochon's words, "the way things are going, if the site were any good they wouldn't let us go there."

After this disappointing meeting, we went to the Museum of History. This was quite an important visit for us, for we wanted to have another chance to examine Boriskovskii's controversial stone tools from Nui Do. In our letters, we had requested permission to examine them more closely and to take photographs for publication in a Western scholarly journal. However, when we arrived there, with Madame Nga and Binh, it was clear that no preparations had been made for our visit. We had to compete with a gaggle of teenaged soldiers to look into the cases; and when we asked about having a good look at the artifacts, Binh began sweating visibly. He smiled nervously and murmured, "Ah, very difficult to arrange." He was behaving in the edgy, embarrassed way he has when his hands are tied by a bureaucratic system he hates but has no control over. A few minutes later he said in a soft voice, "Oh, we forgot to tell you. Your request to visit Kampuchea has been denied."

At this point there was a new low in U.S.-Vietnamese relations. We were very disappointed, and could not understand what had gone wrong. Ciochon forgot about any niceties of cultural sensitivity and shouted, "What do you mean you forgot? How do you forget something like that?" Binh and Madam Nga began to giggle, the worst possible sign in a negotiation with Asian people. Ciochon, furious, almost said some things that he would not have been able to unsay, but James and Olsen, despite their own feelings of disappointment, managed to get him to back off. We broke off our visit to the museum, and went back to the hotel to bitch.

Next morning we left for Ba Thuoc. When we had mentioned our destination to a Vietnamese friend of ours, an official at the government press office named Mr. Dy, he had said, "Oh! the road to Ba Thuoc is not good." This turned out to be a laughable understatement—even the ox carts had a tough time of it. The drive was utterly miserable, even by the local standard, which leaves considerable scope for misery: nine of us in a Russian minivan that had no suspension worth mentioning, jouncing over a rutted road, in fierce, sweltering heat. It took us a solid twelve hours to travel a distance of about one hundred miles as the crow flies.

In the late afternoon, as we left the coastal plain and entered the jungle, we were surrounded by an eerily beautiful topography of karst towers, lusciously green, with tendrils of mist twining round their pinnacles. The soaring limestone towers were riddled everywhere with caverns and fissures. The sight of so many prospective fossil sites did much to lift our spirits.

At one place the road descended into a stream a bit wider than the others we had crossed, and while the driver waded into it to see if it was fordable, we took tea and coconut milk at a bamboo shack by the side of the road. Binh asked our host how much farther it was to Ba Thuoc and was told it was "two towels away." The towel is the local unit of distance measurement, Binh explained: people walking down the road cover their heads with a wet towel to alleviate the oppressive heat, and one towel is how long it takes for a wet cloth on a person's head to become completely dry. We were close.

Ba Thuoc, the westernmost district of Thanh Hoa province, just fourteen miles from the Laotian border, is about as isolated as a place on this earth can be. We stayed at the district headquarters, a cluster of moldy concrete bunkhouses surrounded by large stagnant tanks of water that seemed to have no purpose except to breed malarial mosquitoes, for the green water, teeming with life, was certainly not potable. The entire district of Ba Thuoc is unelectrified, but the headquarters does have a generator. Two hours after sundown it is turned off, and darkness and bats overtake the village.

A Banquet in Ba Thuoc

Our first night at Ba Thuoc proved to be the turning point in our relations with the Vietnamese. We were the guests of honor at a festive banquet. The food, like the road, was not good—chicken of preternatural toughness, eggs fried to a medium gray, gritty rice, and a stringy sort of ditch weed that is served at every meal in the summer in Vietnam—but it was clearly the best fare they could offer, and we were grateful to have it. The only beverages were warm, strong beer and the lethal local variety of white lightning, which was used for endless toast-making.

Ciochon and Binh, who were seated next to each other, were especially sedulous in their toasting, and by the time the dishes were cleared, they were in a very cheerful frame of mind. At last Ciochon's frustration and curiosity got the best of him, and he made bold to ask Binh why it was that everything that we wanted to do was so damn difficult to arrange. Why was it that our professional relationship, after having got off to such a warm start, should now be so cool? Binh replied, no less candidly, by asking what happened to all of the promises that we had made the last time we were there—what about the typewriter, the photocopying machine, the reference books?

Ciochon was stunned. "We *did* send them!" he bellowed. We had known that it might take some time for all these things to reach Vietnam, but surely fifteen months was time enough; and in any case the typewriter and books, we knew for a fact, had been delivered by our friend Judy Ladinsky. Ciochon explained all this to Binh, who listened in silence. Then Ciochon asked him why they had never answered any of his letters or cables, on which he had lavished so much time and care, not to mention money. Why had we never received a word in response?

Binh said, "What letters? What cables?"

As the two compared notes more carefully, and with increasing vehemence, the common thread in all these circumstances emerged: the photocopying machine, the typewriter, the books had all been shipped to Professor Pham Huy Thong, who had left the Institute of Archaeology very soon after our first visit. All of Ciochon's letters and cables, outlining what we hoped to accomplish on the trip, had been addressed to Thong personally, with the clear understanding that he would share them with his colleagues at the institute.

Then Binh explained how things had been perceived at the institute. After our visit in January 1987, more than nine months went by with nothing, no word from us. No sign of any of the gifts we had promised to send. Then all of a sudden a cable came, imperiously demanding to know if we were going to be allowed to come in January. There was no time to arrange a visit so quickly, so the negative reply had been sent.

This much, at least, was clear: Thong had kept Ciochon's letters to himself. All of a sudden everything made sense. Binh, for his part, was furious. No one could quite come out and say it, but it appeared very much as though Thong had made off with the goods we had sent to the institute. Pham Huy Thong was a member of the party and something of a revered father figure to the Vietnamese. His book of poetry *The Song of the Flute on the River O* is a widely read classic of Vietnamese literature. Someone as relatively powerless as Binh could never accuse a leader like Thong of uncomradely behavior. Interestingly, although Binh went off with Professor Hao and the other Vietnamese scientists to talk with them discreetly about this, nothing was ever said in the presence of the bureaucrat from the Social Sciences Committee, the official government representative there to make sure that we did not step out of line. James nicknamed Thong "Pham the Scam," and that was how he was known ever after.

After that night everything changed: once the Vietnamese realized that we had not been trifling with them, they became even warmer than before, and quite outdid themselves in their generous hospitality. Professor Hao, particularly, seemed very happy that his belief in our friendly intentions had been vindicated, and he immediately offered to have our visas extended so that we could take another field trip to Halong Bay, which had previously been declared "difficult to arrange." That was a major concession, for in Vietnam, as in any country, anything that involves the foreign office really is very difficult to arrange.

Most significant of all, we were now able to collaborate in earnest and get on with some serious digging. At daybreak the next morning, Dang Huu Luu led us to the site, which he had discovered two years earlier. It is a cave system, called Lang Trang after the tiny village it adjoins. We were escorted by a small detachment of unarmed adolescent soldiers, and by noon half the town was there to watch. Mr. Luu, a slender, soft-spoken man with perfect teeth, had repeatedly told us that there were many fossils, but we were not prepared for the wealth of material that we found there. The site consisted of two caves: the first cave actually contained two chambers, connected by a narrow natural arch; the second was much larger, and its mouth had been bricked up and fitted with a metal door. Throughout, the caverns are filled with fossiliferous breccia.

In the course of our brief excavation of Lang Trang on this first excursion, we found fossil specimens of artiodactyl (oxen, sheep, etc.), suid (pigs), and cervid (deer), all of which are common enough. We also turned up some rarer items: teeth of rhinoceros; a complete jaw of *Hystrix,* the porcupine; and fossil teeth of *Pongo,* the orangutan, which, as we have seen, has been extinct on the Asian mainland since the late Pleistocene.

When paleontologists are working in the field, they are often able to date a site roughly by the fossil groups that they find. Exactly the same process, albeit on a more restricted scale in terms of time, is at work when a classical archaeologist finds a shard of pottery and uses its distinctive style to date the human habitation he is excavating. The specimens that we found at Lang Trang on this first, exploratory dig belonged to the group known as *Stegodon-Ailuropoda* fauna, so called because *Stegodon,* the extinct elephant, and *Ailuropoda,* the giant panda, are typically represented in deposits from the period. That was of key importance, for *Gigantopithecus,* as we have seen, flourished in Southeast Asia during the same slice of evolutionary time as *Stegodon* and *Ailuropoda.*

There was considerable excitement in camp the day Mr. Luu found a fossil tooth of *Ailuropoda*: the giant panda is now extinct in this part of Asia, and its presence here in fossil form convinced us that Lang Trang was potentially a very promising site. Unfortunately, we were out of time. Mr. Luu's discovery of the giant panda fossil came literally as we were packing the van to leave Ba Thuoc.

It was clear that what we needed to do now was organize a return trip to Ba Thuoc for a protracted period of time, during which we would excavate the site in a systematic fashion. Spinning out our plans for our return to Ba Thuoc as we drove back to Hanoi, for the first time the Americans and the Vietnamese cohered as a real scientific expedition. Next time, there would be no communication breakdowns, no bureaucratic snafus. We would be able to address the scientific problems at hand, which are, after all, engrossing enough.

Two Surveys of Halong Bay

After this vital excursion to Thanh Hoa, we headed north for a few days at Halong Bay. When we arrived at our hotel, a sadly ruined resort, we had an unforgettable seafood dinner: mountainous piles of steamed crabs and shrimp, heavenly fried fish and squid, and a local delicacy the Vietnamese called blood snails, though they were actually tiny bivalves. Briny and delicious, blood snails get their sanguinary name from the little spurt of red juice they eject when they are opened.

In the morning we hired a ship to cruise through the bay in search of caverns suitable for exploration. As we had observed on our first trip, the limestone towers here are positively riddled with caves; almost every island appeared to have its own cave system. We were quite eager to get up to some of them to conduct a quick survey for fossils. After the previous night's dinner we were suddenly filled with the hope that Halong Bay might prove to be a possible contender as a site for a long-term excavation.

Our deep-drawing craft, however, would not let us get near enough to any of the towers. Then someone hit upon the brilliant expedient of hiring one of the local fishermen with his boat to ferry us between our ship and the islands. We hailed two old women trawling the bay in their *mung,* a simple pitch-bottom bamboo dinghy. For twenty thousand dong, the equivalent of four American dollars, they agreed to shuttle us about. This method worked perfectly well, yet the results were disappointing. In an admittedly cursory survey, we found nothing that approached Lang Trang cave in terms of the quantity or antiquity of fossils. Moreover, the principal problem continued to be access: although from our boat the caves appeared to be easily reachable, when we actually landed on an island, the climb up to the cave mouth invariably turned out to be beyond our modest rock-climbing skills.

At one of our island stops, the three of us and Binh came ashore at a particularly inviting spot. As usual, however, once we landed at the foot of the tower, the thirty-foot ascent looked pretty dangerous. Binh examined the rock face carefully, and declared that he was going to give it a try. Olsen agreed to join him, but Ciochon and James stayed behind. As the climbers slowly made their way up the rough rock cliff, which was covered with coarse brambles, they were soon lost to sight, but they kept a running commentary on their progress with their companions on the shore. At last they shouted down that they had made it to the cave. After perhaps an hour of digging, it proved to be hardly worth the effort. They had nothing to show for their trouble except a single jawbone of *Hystrix* and a few tiny foot bones—a rather disappointing payoff for so arduous a climb.

Then Olsen and Binh began the descent, proverbially the most dangerous part. Everything seemed to be going well, until James and Ciochon heard the horrible sound of loose, scraping gravel, a heart-stopping thud, and a muttered curse. Olsen had slipped into a bramble-filled crevice! Ciochon and James were literally hopping around on the shore, filled with an awful sense of powerlessness, but keeping up a cheerful line of talk to encourage Olsen. Like most Vietnamese men, Binh is small and wiry, but he is strong, and he was able to lever Olsen out. A few minutes later, the two of them emerged, scratched, bruised, and shaken. Olsen had received a deep, bleeding gash in his side, which took months to heal—and scar. That put an end to our survey of Halong Bay.

Months later, after our return to the U.S., Olsen happened across an interesting report in the *Bulletin of the Museum of Far Eastern Antiquities* in Stockholm, published in 1939, about an expedition to Halong Bay by J. Gunnar Andersson—the same scientist who had reported the first specimens of Peking Man at Zhoukoudian. He and a team of scientists had spent two and a half months in Halong Bay in early 1938, carrying out the first competent scientific reconnaissance of this remarkable region.

Andersson was at that time in the midst of an investigation of the karst towers of the Gulf of Tonkin, of which Halong Bay forms a part. Archaeological research carried out in the vicinity by the Ecole Française d'Extrême-Orient, which was based in Hanoi, had yielded material no earlier than the Song dynasties of China (A.D. 960–1279), so Andersson was able to declare that he was "entering a virgin field" in his search for materials dating from the region's prehistory.

Andersson's jumping-off point for his exploration of the karst islands of western Tonkin was a town called Honggai, directly across the bay from the resort community where we had stayed. Having engaged the services of a small flotilla that included a steam launch, *Le Touriste,* an open motor boat, and two sampans, Andersson and his colleagues cruised the island-studded waters near Honggai investigating both large caverns and small grottoes, the latter, he wrote, "often so difficult of access that we had to climb and descend by the aid of ropes." Olsen remarked later that he wished he had read that passage *before* he attempted his climb.

From Andersson's article and the descriptions of other late-nineteenth- and mid-twentieth-century travelers in the region, it is clear that Halong Bay and its environs were one of Southeast Asia's principal tourist attractions before the devastation of war in the 1960's and Vietnam's subsequent estrangement from much of the world community. The barren karst towers near Honggai, whose caverns we visited on this excursion, were known in Andersson's day by names such as l'île des Merveilles, l'île de la Surprise, and l'île de la Paix. While random graffiti, mostly names and dates in French, are still to be seen emblazoned on many cavern walls here, they clearly belong to a bygone era. The only traces of recent visitations we encountered were tattered copies of *Pravda* and Bulgarian cigarette packages left by the occasional Soviet sailor on his way to the deepwater port of Camranh Bay. After our recent visits to Halong Bay, which is now badly polluted and surrounded by bombed-out buildings covered with coal dust, it is strange to read Andersson's description, from 1939, of the same spot: "a charming little paradise."

In light of this comment, it is interesting to note that Honggai was a major target when American planes first bombed North Vietnam on August 5, 1964. This act set into motion the Gulf of Tonkin Resolution, beginning the American escalation of the Vietnam War. According to history books, American destroyers cruising the South China Sea off the Vietnamese coast were fired upon by Vietnamese naval vessels. In retaliation, President Lyndon Johnson ordered saturation bombing of the northern Vietnamese coast, which included all of Halong Bay. Honggai, with its heavy industrial base, was nearly wiped off the map on that August morning in 1964.

Andersson's scientific reconnaissance of the western Tonkin Gulf yielded two important contributions. First, thanks to his geological training, he was able to complete a thorough study of the processes by which the karst towers of Halong Bay were formed. Andersson's description of the erosional "life cycle" of karst peaks is the basis for our current understanding of these fascinating formations. When we returned here at the end of the year we were able to develop an even more detailed account of how these cavern-filled towers come into and pass out of existence.

Andersson's second major contribution has a more direct bearing on our own research in Vietnam. As an archaeologist, he sought evidence for the prehistoric occupation of these caves and grottoes. By correlating his discoveries with observations on changes in sea level that had affected the whole bay over thousands of years, Andersson arrived at a coherent interpretation of the site's artifacts, which remains substantially correct even though it was written a decade before the advent of radiocarbon or other means of direct dating. The artifacts Andersson found in the caves of Halong Bay—scraps of pottery, stone axes, antler and bone implements, as well as large middens containing shells of edible mollusks such as *Helix* and *Melania*—all suggest a late prehistoric, that is to say Neolithic, culture.

In addition to these cave sites, some prehistoric remains were also discovered in open-air sites on some of the larger islands. Andersson refers to these materials collectively as belonging to what he called the Danh Do La culture, after the island where he found the type site early in his investigations in Halong Bay. Andersson and his colleague, Madame Colani, at once recognized that important differences existed between the cave and the open-air sites. Their problem was the same one archaeologists commonly face today: Is the observed variability the result of actual cultural differences, or simply the result of a different pattern of preservation? While subsequent research conducted in Halong Bay by Vietnamese archaeologists allows us with some confidence to classify assemblages such as those Andersson discovered in 1938 as Neolithic, there nonetheless remains, as he himself wrote at the time, "a nice cluster of riddles still awaiting a solution!"

When we got back to Hanoi, we were plunged into the middle of what some wag called the Thong wars: Binh and our other friends at the institute were furious at their former director, blaming him for the mysterious disappearance of the goodies that we had sent them. Since they could not accuse him, they tried to enlist us as their advocates, but for obvious reasons we wanted to stay out of it altogether. Then, conveniently, Thong was called away to Moscow on important business. Just before he left, he gave James a letter, in French, which James was to translate into English for everyone else, and then Madam Nga would render his English translation into Vietnamese.

This letter, which purported to explain all, was in fact little more than a collection of dubious excuses. The fact that he could not bring himself to write a copy of it in Vietnamese looked suspiciously like buying time. Pham Huy Thong's story came to a tragic end just a few weeks after we left Vietnam: the old man died when someone, apparently a burglar, broke into his house in Hanoi. We were told that he died of a heart attack brought on by fear, but that does not sound much like the Thong we knew, who was fearless as a lion.

Our last days in Hanoi were devoted to hammering out an agreement with the Vietnamese, in effect a diplomatic protocol through which we could continue to work with the Vietnamese in an intensive excavation of the caves at Lang Trang. We signed the final document (which is printed as an appendix to this book) in a solemn ceremony at the Institute of Archaeology. Pots of tea were drunk, many photographs were taken, and both sides, behind their confident smiles, were wondering if they would be able to make good on all the promises they had just made.

CHAPTER 6

In Search
of the Giant Ape

The Hardest Science

In the first chapter, we made a point of how selective our view is of the fossil record of the early life of the planet. All the fossils ever collected represent only the tiniest sliver of what is out there, buried somewhere in the earth's crust. Yet the number of new fossil species waiting to be discovered has shrunk considerably. Typically, when we excavate a fossil site, what we find are large quantities of the remains of common animals and, with luck, one or two rarities.

The chances of coming across a new species nowadays are a fraction of what they were in the early part of this century, when paleontology first struggled into maturity as a science. Until scientists began looking for fossils systematically, very few were known—a few bones from extinct giant species had been turned up by farmers' plows, and were displayed as "unexplained natural curiosities." Once trained paleontologists began actively wielding their spades, they made a number of fabulous discoveries, and quickly filled up natural-history repositories such as the British Museum (Natural History), the Smithsonian Institution, and the American Museum of Natural History. The number of species that exists on the earth at any given moment is finite; that is just as true of the Pleistocene

Ralph von Koenigswald,
pictured here in Utrecht,
discovered the type specimen of
Gigantopithecus in a Hong Kong
apothecary shop. *(Courtesy Senckenburg
Museum of Natural History)*

epoch as it is of the present day. Thus, as the fossil record
soared from a millionth of one percent of all the fossils in
existence to a whopping one percent, or wherever it is that we
stand today, inevitably the number of new discoveries fell off
quickly and drastically.

It was not always so: when Ralph von Koenigswald discovered the first evidence of *Gigantopithecus* in the dusty drawer of
a Hong Kong pharmacy a little more than fifty years ago, it
was a golden age of fossil discoveries. Von K, as he is affectionately known, Franz Weidenreich, Davidson Black, and the other
paleontological pioneers in Asia were blazing a trail through
uncharted territory: everywhere they turned they found something that had never been seen before. The wonder is not that
they made so many discoveries. Rather, their contribution consists in the enormous amount of good sense they brought to
the task of analyzing all those specimens, drawing important
connections and conclusions among them. Out of this growing
aggregation of fossils, they constructed, stone by stone, as it
were, a coherent theoretical framework that attempted to make
sense of it all. As we shall see, they made many errors, but an
impressive proportion of their guesses proved to be right on
the money.

That really is what the science of paleoanthropology is,
making sense of fossilized bones, as opposed to the somewhat
tedious task of digging them up—precisely because we have a
limited sample of bones to work with, precisely because today's
impeccably logical theory can be tossed into the circular file by
tomorrow's find. In this sense, paleoanthropology is almost

more an art than a science, compared with such nicely predict-able disciplines as chemistry or physics. Build a bridge accord-ing to certain specifications, and you will know to the ounce how heavy a load it will support; combine two particular chem-icals, and you will always have the same compound and by-products as a result. In paleoanthropology, the scientist is almost in the position of a detective in a whodunit: we are much more sure about the things that we know *cannot* be true than we ever are about the things that *are* true. All our conclu-sions are provisional, since the fund of certain knowledge—our data, that is, the fossil record itself—is always in a state of flux, growing and subject to endless reclassification and revision.

Which is not to suggest that paleoanthropology is a "soft" science: far from it. Where the social sciences are fundamentally hampered, at least in terms of the relative "hardness" of their sciences, by the subjective nature of their data, our work is very much defined and limited by tooth bumps and sagittal crests, as well as by evolutionary theory. Rather, what we undertake to do might better be likened to that purest of sciences, cosmology. An astronomer must make sense of the endless numerical read-outs from satellites on a random course through the infinity of space, and try to bring order to the mind-numbing vastness of science's telescopic observation of the cosmos. Like us, they are prisoners of their data: to succeed in bringing order to them, they must keep their minds clear and listen to their instincts.

After the end of our first little exploratory season in Viet-nam, Olsen headed back to the States to gear up for his summer dig in the Taklamakan Desert, and Ciochon and James headed north to South China for what turned out to be a sort of Cook's tour of the World of Giganto. Our ultimate destina-tion was the Guangxi Zhuang Autonomous Region, where the pioneering major discoveries of Giganto had been made in the 1950's. The Guangxi region adjoins Vietnam on the north, and its capital, Nanning, lies scarcely two hundred miles from Hanoi—indeed, the two cities are connected by a major rail line and a highway. Yet because of the prevailing political winds, we had to go back to Bangkok and fly via Hong Kong to Kunming, in neighboring Yunnan province, where our *Giganto-pithecus* pilgrimage would begin.

Von K and the Dragon Bones

In every city we visited in China, the first stop we made was at
the traditional pharmacy. These establishments appear not to
have changed at all since Koenigswald discovered the first
remains of *Gigantopithecus*. Dusty display cases and oaken chests
are filled with substances that, tradition holds, have medicinal
uses. These include the efficacious—dried herbs and flowers,
and animal essences such as snake bile—and the bizarre. Desic-
cated lizards, skins of flying squirrels, spiny skeletons of sea
horses are offered for sale to cure every conceivable human
ailment.

Among such nostrums pride of place goes to dragon teeth
and dragon bones. For more than a thousand years the Chinese have ground fossils into powders and mixed them in
potions, believing that they have miraculous medicinal and
aphrodisiac powers. Following the lead of Schlosser and
Andersson, who had found *Homo erectus* teeth in Chinese pharmacies, Ralph von Koenigswald, fresh from his search for
Homo erectus in Java, scouted the traditional apothecary shops
in Java, Sumatra, Borneo, and Sulawesi. In 1935, on a trip to
the Philippines, he recovered in a Chinese pharmacy the first
fully fossilized orangutan teeth ever discovered. He enquired
where these dragon teeth had come from, and he was directed
to an apothecary in Hong Kong. In the first lot of teeth he
examined there—undoubtedly a deep dusty drawerful, such as
those we encountered in China fifty years later—Von K found
a very large lower third molar, which he realized belonged to a
species unknown to science. He named this new primate species *Gigantopithecus blacki*. The genus name is a coinage of
Greek roots meaning "gigantic ape"; the species name is in
honor of his friend and colleague Davidson Black, who had
died the year before.

Over the next four years Koenigswald searched the traditional pharmacies of Hong Kong and Guangzhou (formerly
Canton), and found some 1,500 fossil teeth of orangutans, but
only three more Giganto molars. The huge primate was apparently very rare. Noticing that yellow earth still clung to all four

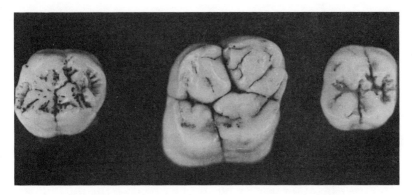

These molars of *(from left to right)* orangutan, Giganto, and *Homo erectus* show why the giant ape got its name. *(Photograph by David Gantt)*

of the molars he had found, especially in the pulp cavities, and that the roots had been gnawed away, as though by porcupines, he deduced that the teeth came from cave or fissure deposits. When he interrogated the pharmacists about the probable source of these particular dragon teeth, he was told they were most likely from Guangxi. The other notable remains mixed in with the Giganto and orangutan teeth—after eliminating the ubiquitous and very common bovid and suid teeth—were, in descending order of frequency, *Ailuropoda, Stegodon,* and the tapir. In other words, although the name had not yet been coined, Koenigswald's collection constituted an assemblage of *Stegodon-Ailuropoda* fauna. On this basis, he estimated that the teeth of *Gigantopithecus* came from middle-Pleistocene deposits dating from circa 125,000 to 700,000 years ago.

Von K returned to Java to continue his search for *Homo erectus,* but he was taken prisoner by the Japanese during World War II. His precious collection of *Gigantopithecus* teeth—at that point, the only known specimens of the fossil ape—spent the war years in a milk bottle, buried in a friend's backyard in Java. Meanwhile, Franz Weidenreich, who succeeded Davidson Black as the director of the Cenozoic Research Laboratory in Beijing, commenced a careful study of *Gigantopithecus* and its relationship to *Homo erectus* in Asia, using plaster casts of the four Giganto teeth that Koenigswald had sent him. Because of the unusually large size of the *Homo erectus* specimens from Java, Weidenreich came up with the notion that there was a period of gigantism in human evolution, and that modern man was the diminutive descendant of these giants—and that among them, *Gigantopithecus* was the most gigantic of them all.

In his book *Apes, Giants, and Man*, which is eminently readable even when it argues theories that have subsequently been disproved, Weidenreich argues that the four teeth are very manlike, and that Koenigswald misjudged the animal's affinities—in other words, its proper place is in the human family tree. Weidenreich gets a bit carried away in his theorizing, arguing that *Gigantopithecus blacki* was actually the ancestor of Koenigswald's *Meganthropus paleojavanicus* and declaring, "This primate was not a giant ape but a giant man and should, therefore, have been named *Gigantanthropus* and not *Gigantopithecus*." That fitted in perfectly with his idea that man arose in South China, modern Yunnan and Guangxi. Later, according to Weidenreich, there was a split and then migrations, southward to Java and northward to Zhoukoudian. By 1945, when *Apes, Giants, and Man* was published, Giganto, the cornerstone of Weidenreich's theory of hominid evolution in Asia, was generally regarded as a human ancestor of gigantic proportions.

After the war, Koenigswald came to the United States, bringing with him his valuable cargo of *Gigantopithecus* teeth and Javanese *Homo erectus* specimens. He was critical of Weidenreich's theory. On the basis of the reanalysis of the original four molars and studies of four more he had found afterward, he held that the *Gigantopithecus* teeth were much too specialized to be those of a direct human ancestor. Furthermore, in hominid evolution it is very rare for two species to live as contemporaries if one has given rise to the other. Rather, the ancestral form is usually outcompeted by the descendant species, and it dies off. Koenigswald believed, after his study of the faunal remains found in conjunction with *Gigantopithecus* and *Homo erectus*, that the two did live at the same time. (Now, of course, after the Vietnamese discovery at Tham Khuyen and the Chinese finds in Hubei and Sichuan provinces, we know that the two species lived side by side.) He therefore described

Gigantopithecus as a specialized anthropoid ape not related to *Homo erectus*—the view currently held by most paleoanthropologists, including ourselves.

During Koenigswald's wartime internment, however, Weidenreich's views had become widely accepted. To end the controversy that arose, more complete specimens of *Gigantopithecus* were needed, a task impossible at the time for anyone but the Chinese to undertake, for the Middle Kingdom was in one of its periodic phases of disarray, and was completely closed.

In the 1950's, with the establishment in Beijing of what is now called the Institute of Vertebrate Paleontology and Paleoanthropology (usually known by its English initials as the IVPP), Chinese paleontologists began to steer a completely independent course, and their work would ultimately have profound implications for world paleoanthropology. High on the IVPP's list of scientific priorities was to discover the source of *Gigantopithecus* fossils, in order to determine the species' age and relationship with its natural environment. In paleoanthropology, just as in archaeology, context is all: if you find a fossil by the side of the road—or in the drawer of a Chinese apothecary—it tells you almost nothing, really, except that such a thing exists. Only when you know where it came from, with what other animals it lived, what it ate, and the many other aspects of the animal's life that may be inferred from its context, are you doing science, as opposed to collecting.

A Visit with Jia

At the conclusion of our Chinese jaunt, James went to Beijing to visit the IVPP, where he met and talked with Jia Lanpo, one of the grand old men of Chinese prehistoric studies. When Jia was a young paleoanthropologist affiliated with the Cenozoic Research Laboratory, he was part of the team led by Davidson Black that discovered Peking Man at Zhoukoudian in 1929. He vividly recounted the original expedition mounted out of Beijing in search of *Gigantopithecus*. The IVPP organized a team—led by Pei Wenzhong, the man who actually made the discovery of the first skull of Peking Man, and with Jia himself as expedition vice director—that went to the warehouses that supplied all the apothecary shops in China with dragon bones and dragon teeth. They found vast quantities of fossils at the warehouses in Nanning, the capital of Guangxi Zhuang Autonomous Region. In Nanning, they divided into two teams. One, led by Pei, headed north, and the other led by Jia, went south.

Jia's paleontological detective work took him to southernmost Guangxi, to the town of Daxin, which the local people said was the source of all the fossils. At one point he was less than fifty miles from Vietnam. Conditions were very difficult: roads were impassable, there was no drinking water, the monsoon rains made progress on foot very slow. "We ate bitterness," says Jia. When they finally arrived at Daxin, an area characterized by karst-tower topography, and asked the local people where the dragon bones came from, they were referred to an old lady who had in her house a bamboo tray full of fossils. One of them was a *Gigantopithecus* tooth. She pointed out a very tall tower, described by Jia as "a hundred meters [over three hundred feet] straight up—almost falling over, it was so steep." The cave mouth was clearly visible behind a screen of brush.

At that time no one had yet discovered a fossil of *Gigantopithecus* in proper geological context; it was known only from the specimens from the apothecary shops and, now, from the tooth in the woman's bamboo tray. It was four in the afternoon and raining hard when they arrived at Daxin, but, Jia says, "We were young, and couldn't be restrained. We climbed straight up to that cave." Jia himself found the first *Gigantopithecus* tooth in situ, in a hard reddish matrix. According to Jia, *Gigantopithecus* teeth are easy to spot: they have a particularly thick enamel, and, he says, you can see it sparkle and glisten like gold. All together, Jia recovered three *Gigantopithecus* specimens, intermingled with other examples of *Stegodon-Ailuropoda* fauna.

Meanwhile, Pei was carrying on the search toward the north, playing Scott to Jia's Amundsen, as it were. It was near the city of Liuzhou, at a cave site called Liucheng, that Pei made the all-time great *Gigantopithecus* haul. Much has been written and published about Pei's discoveries at Liucheng, also sometimes called *Gigantopithecus* Cave, and most of it has been wholly or partly inaccurate. Ciochon and James (who admit that in the past they have unwittingly contributed to the perpetuation of some of these errors) visited Liucheng in the company of one of the men who assisted Pei's team from the IVPP; conversations with him and other eyewitness accounts allow us here to set forth for the first time an authoritative account of the discovery and excavation of *Gigantopithecus* Cave, one of the most important events in modern paleoanthropology.

In 1956, an old peasant named Qiu Xiuhuai, who mined dragon bones to supplement his impoverished living as a farmer, found an enormous jawbone while digging in the cave. He knew that he had found something quite valuable, and he sent his grandson to school to tell his teacher what he had found. The teacher came and had a look at it, proclaimed it to be a relic from a giant man, and told Mr. Qui that it was worth a lot of money. So the old man set off down the road toward the city to sell his treasure, when he happened to meet a bank clerk. He showed the jawbone to the bank clerk, who saw at once that it was something very valuable. Mr. Qiu offered to sell it to him, but the bank clerk convinced him that it would be bad luck to sell such a relic, and he asked the old man to give it to him instead.

The bank clerk took the fossil with him to Liuzhou, where he lived, and showed it to the local representative of the cultural bureau. That man made contact with the director of the provincial museum in Nanning, who turned the information over to the Institute of Vertebrate Paleontology and Paleoanthropology. By that circuitous yet functional process, which took nearly a year, Pei Wenzhong found out about the discovery of the giant jawbone. That was how he came to be in Liucheng in November 1956 with a team from the IVPP and the Guangxi provincial museum in Nanning, looking for the source of such an interesting object. When Pei saw the fossil, he was able to identify it at once as the jawbone of *Gigantopithecus*, the first one ever discovered. It had all but three of the teeth still attached to it, and their morphology was, of course, well known.

Qing Zhoufu, a peasant who assisted Pei in the excavations, told us this story over a lunch in the former home of Mr. Qiu, virtually in the shadow of the karst tower in which, 290 feet almost straight up, *Gigantopithecus* Cave is located. Then a nineteen-year-old lad, Qing was present when the team discovered the first *Gigantopithecus* jawbone to be found in situ. He recalls that the mandible came not from a breccia matrix but from a very hard deposit of a substance resembling red clay. The bamboo scaffolding up the face of the tower is no longer there, and the cave cannot be reached except by the extremely nimble—while we were there, little boys clambered up the sheer rock face as easily as monkeys—but Qing says that it is a very deep and extensive system, and that the jawbones came from the deepest part of the main cavern, perhaps a hundred feet into the tower.

Qiu Xiuhuai, who discovered the first jaw of *Gigantopithecus*, died in 1985. At his request he was buried at the foot of the Liucheng karst tower, in clear sight of the caves that yielded the three Giganto jaws and more than a thousand teeth. Mr. Qui's stone-covered tomb, because of its flat, horizontal surface on what is otherwise a steep incline leading up to the karst tower, makes a particularly good point from which to view the caves. During our visit to the site, a dozen small children from Qui Xiuhuai's village stood on top of the tomb laughing and shoving as they pointed to the exact location of the three caves.

Pei came to Liucheng three times over a seven-year period to excavate; it was on his second visit, in 1957, that Pei found a jawbone in situ. This second mandible was discovered by an eagle-eyed workman who spotted it protruding from a block of matrix that was being lowered in a bamboo basket down the

A rare photograph of Pei Wenzhong, the great Chinese paleontologist *(center)*, at the excavation of *Gigantopithecus* Cave, in South China, in 1957.

(Photograph by Huang Wanpo)

face of the tower. The matrix was so hard that Pei had to send the block to Beijing in order to extract the specimen with chemical preparations.

Qing told us that during this 1957 visit Pei held a series of public lectures in Liucheng. With the village schoolteachers and the local cultural bureaucrat who had originally reported the existence of the first mandible, Pei explained the significance of what they were doing. He hoped not only to win the local citizens' support for the dig but also to discourage them from mining the caves for dragon bones and teeth. At the end of the season, Professor Pei asked Qing what he would like as a reward for his part in the excavation. Qing says he told Pei that making a contribution to science was reward enough for him, but Pei gave him thirty feet of good cotton cloth anyway.

In addition to the three mandibles, Pei's group discovered over a thousand fossil teeth of *Gigantopithecus* and hundreds of other mammalian specimens, including some very unusual dwarf varieties. One of them was a dwarf species of giant panda (a seeming contradiction in terms, to say the least), called *Ailuropoda microta*. It was only half the size of the living giant panda, and had a number of primitive features, such as a very short muzzle, which would have given the head a rather spherical appearance. Chinese scientists have recently concluded that it is probably an ancestor of the modern giant panda.

There was nothing dwarfish, however, about the *Gigantopithecus* jaws. The discovery of the three Liucheng mandibles added weight, both literal and figurative, to the conjectured giant ape. Since Koenigswald's discoveries, no one had ever doubted that the creature existed; the fossil teeth had been definitive and incontrovertible evidence insofar as the description of the species was concerned. Yet the mammoth jawbones, the sheer heft of them, made an impression that far exceeded any dry description of the animal extrapolated from the limited data offered by the teeth. One jawbone in particular was quite extraordinarily large; it was suggested that it belonged to an adult male, and that the other two were from a female and a juvenile.

Western scientists learned about Pei's spectacular discovery through articles published in Chinese journals and from a popular account that appeared in the *Illustrated London News* in

1957. The most authoritative work about *Gigantopithecus* to date is the monumental monograph published by paleoanthropologist Wu Rukang, of the IVPP, in 1962. Pei's bonanza strike at Liucheng continues to be the subject of intensive study at the IVPP, where Wu keeps the Giganto mandibles locked up in his office drawer, readily at hand to show visitors.

Even the non-primate remains from Liucheng cave are still generating great interest. A newly released study by Pei Wenzhong (published posthumously), which documents the fossil mammals recovered from *Gigantopithecus* Cave, has led Chinese scientists to date this cave fauna to the early Pleistocene, about 1 million years B.P. At other cave sites *Gigantopithecus blacki* is associated with essentially modern-sized giant pandas, but at Liucheng the giant ape is found with a dwarf species of giant panda that is likely the direct ancestor of the modern species. Even though nearly 1,000 teeth of Giganto were found at Liucheng, there was not a single tooth of *Homo erectus* recovered. Clearly, the Liucheng cave site represents an earlier time period—the early Pleistocene, before *Homo erectus* entered eastern Asia.

One puzzling question about *Gigantopithecus* Cave, which no one has been able to answer satisfactorily, is how such an enormous cache of this animal's remains, so extremely rare everywhere else in its distribution, happened to be concentrated in this one locality. Some tantalizing possibilities present themselves—perhaps a group of the giant apes died together in an earthquake or some other natural disaster—but we have no evidence that could support any such hypothesis, and we shall doubtless never know the answer to the question.

The next discovery of *Gigantopithecus* in China after Liucheng cave came in 1965 at a site called Wuming, a few hours' drive north of Nanning, the capital of Guangxi. This was the last stop on our *Gigantopithecus* pilgrimage. Nanning is a vibrant, teeming city; paradoxically, it is much more of a "southern" city than Hanoi, two hundred miles to the southwest. Compared with the restrained hush of the streets of Hanoi, Nanning is a riot of activity, its arcaded streets streaming with humanity until midnight every night of the week. Our sojourn here commenced with a visit to the provincial museum, where the staff greeted us warmly. They showed us their collection of stone tools and fossils found throughout the Guangxi Zhuang Autonomous Region, including a quite impressive collection of human skulls from Bronze Age burials.

Then we were presented with the pièce de résistance, the museum's collection of twelve Giganto teeth. Strangely, these specimens came not from Wuming or Daxin, the *Gigantopithecus* sites situated quite nearby, but from Liucheng, via the IVPP in Beijing. The institute is the central clearing house of fossils in China, and the *Gigantopithecus* finds in Daxin and Wuming, consisting of a small number of individual specimens, were considered too important to be left in the provinces. In exchange for surrendering these important finds, the local museum was given a handful of *Gigantopithecus* teeth from the one thousand recovered at Liucheng—more, perhaps, as a sort of consolation prize than for study.

The next morning we headed for the Wuming site, which is located in a beautiful stretch of karst landscape, the rugged limestone topography that is typically full of caves. Wuming is near the top of a tower the local people call Bulali Mountain, just behind a picturesque village called Ganxu. Ganxu bears an uncanny resemblance to a Central American village, with an open brick marketplace erected in the middle of the town square. Men and dogs were napping, protected from the blistering noonday sun by shade trees hung with Spanish moss, while women did the laundry. The cave where the *Gigantopithecus* teeth had been found was a beauty; it was actually a tunnel, about two-thirds of the way up the tower, which went straight through the mountain. Eleven of the teeth were found in some hard, yellowish breccia in the principal cavern, on the side facing Ganxu; the twelfth was recovered in a chamber farther into the interior of the mountain.

The *Gigantopithecus* teeth from Wuming are significantly larger than their counterparts from Liucheng, and, most important of all, the other animal fossils found with them have led Chinese researchers to believe that the locality dates only to the middle Pleistocene, around 400,000 B.P., making it considerably younger than Liucheng. This suggests, first, that *Gigantopithecus* was around as a species for a longer period than was previously believed, and second, that the great ape may have increased in size as the species evolved, which follows a trend seen in other large Pleistocene mammals.

The Other
Gigantopithecus

The most striking confirmation of the latter hypothesis was the discovery of India's *Gigantopithecus giganteus,* which was found near the northern Indian city of Bilaspur in Himachael Pradesh province on March 17, 1968. Or at least that is when it became known to Western science, for on that day a peasant named Sunkha Ram took one piece of the Giganto jaw from the base of a mud fence, where he had buried it twenty-four years before, and sold it to Grant Meyer, a member of Elwyn Simons's Yale University India Primate Expedition. How the jaw of *Gigantopithecus giganteus* came to be buried in Sunkha Ram's mud fence is a tale straight out of pulp fiction.

In 1944, when Sunkha Ram was a boy of twelve, he often helped his father tend the fields of *gram,* a pealike vegetable that is cultivated throughout northern India. One day, as he was wandering through the fields right after the *gram* had been harvested, he found among the rubble three pieces of a huge jawbone. He took them home and asked his father what they might be. His father replied, "The bones of devils." Sunkha Ram asked his father what he should do with them, and his father told him to keep them, because "they might come in handy some day." So Sunkha Ram took the jawbone fragments back to the field where he had found them, and buried them in a mud-rock fence.

The specimens stayed in the fence until 1968, when Sunkha Ram heard about Simons's expedition, which was looking for fossils. On that March morning, he slipped one of the jawbone fragments into his pocket and went to his job, working on a road crew in the valley of Haritalyangar. Later in the day, he found paleoanthropologist Grant Meyer and showed him the specimen. Meyer immediately gave him some rupees for the "devil bone." In the evening, Meyer and other expedition members visited Sunkha Ram at his home in the village of Domera.

After much discussion and persuasion, they convinced Sunkha to sell them the other two pieces of the mandible, and at last the jaw was restored to its original, complete form. They asked Sunkha Ram to lead them to the spot where the mandible had been found and conducted extensive excavations in the *gram* field for a period of six weeks, but found no more evidence of Giganto.

Later in 1968, Elwyn Simons and an Indian colleague, S. R. K. Chopra, gave the name *Gigantopithecus "bilaspurensis"* ("giant ape of Bilaspur") to the specimen, but this later had to be changed to *Gigantopithecus giganteus* to follow the zoological rules of priority in the naming of new species. In 1915 paleontologist Guy Pilgrim from the Geological Survey of India in Calcutta had named a single lower second molar tooth collected near the village of Alipur in northern India *Dryopithecus giganteus*. Subsequent researchers compared this single tooth, now in the Calcutta Museum, with the second molar of the complete jaw discovered by Simons's team, and found them to be identical. Since the jaw clearly belonged to the genus *Gigantopithecus*, the priority for naming the species was to use Pilgrim's name of *giganteus*, proposed in 1915, instead of the later *"bilaspurensis."* Guy Pilgrim was actually the first paleontologist to discover the giant ape, but he was never aware of it.

Gigantopithecus giganteus was about half the size of *Gigantopithecus blacki*, but it had all of its characteristic features—a deep and robustly thick jaw, flattened canine teeth, peglike incisors, and large flat molars. Though the two species are morphologically similar, they are separated by about 5 million years of earth history. *Gigantopithecus giganteus* was found in sediments that date to the end of the Miocene epoch, about 6.3 million years ago. Clearly, the Indian species was adapted to a different environment, and likely had a different diet, yet it was unmistakably *Gigantopithecus*.

The emerging thesis that Giganto tended to grow larger and more robust as it evolved received additional support from some fossil finds of the ape made in the 1970's, once again in China, which are considerably larger than the Liucheng sample. In 1970 five such *Gigantopithecus* teeth were discovered at a site called Longgudong ("Dragon Bone Cave") in Jianshi county, Hubei province. Over two hundred more Giganto specimens were also collected from local apothecaries. Three years later, a single tooth was found in a cave in Bama county, western Guangxi. Both the Jianshi and the Bama finds, as well as the specimens from Wuming, are dated to the middle Pleistocene— that is, after Liucheng.

Yet undoubtedly the most fascinating and compelling revelation about *Gigantopithecus* in recent years has come from a series of finds that associate the giant ape with man. The first of them was the discovery of both Giganto and *Homo erectus* fossils at Tham Khuyen cave by Vietnamese paleoanthropologists. We ought to emphasize at this point that the Vietnamese and Chinese fields of exploration are not just adjoining regions, they are really the same place. Tham Khuyen and the sites in Guangxi where the significant Chinese discoveries have been made are topographically identical, and under normal conditions would be in direct communication. The next find that provides evidence of the coexistence of the giant ape and *Homo* was at Jianshi, where the five oversize *Gigantopithecus* teeth mentioned above were uncovered in situ in association with unquestioned remains of *Homo erectus*.

Then in 1987 came the discovery by Huang Wanpo, a paleoanthropologist at the IVPP (who is also a leading proponent of the existence of the *almas,* or Chinese wildman of specimens of *Gigantopithecus* in association with fossil remains of *Homo erectus* at a cave site in Sichuan province called Wushan. While some of the individual specimens are still rather controversial among his colleagues at the IVPP, there is no question at all that the two species are present at Wushan: on a recent visit to Beijing, Ciochon saw the fossils himself, and identified them as Giganto and *Homo*. Huang's *Gigantopithecus* find is particularly interesting, as it extends the animal's range farther north than was previously thought to be the case.

CHAPTER 7

The Dig

We Re-Up

As scientists, our principal work is conceptual: reading about the work of our colleagues, outlining objectives in preparation for fieldwork, thinking and writing about the questions that have puzzled prehistorians over the past hundred or so years. Yet there is something satisfying about the practical side of our profession, as well: we may never arrive at the airtight solutions to the great enigmas of paleoanthropology, but we can perfect the art of excavation. Planning an expedition, choosing the personnel and putting together the equipment, satisfies a deep-seated adolescent urge: scratch most paleoanthropologists and archaeologists, and you will discover a kid who loves to go camping, somebody with particular ideas about what makes a good pocketknife.

After our relations and communications with the Vietnamese were straightened out, we finally reached the stage of mounting and outfitting an expedition—and doing a bit of science. The Vietnamese expected us to arrive right after the new year in 1989 for a short winter season at Ba Thuoc. We had chosen winter to avoid the merciless heat of the last trip. Right after Christmas 1988 we rendezvoused in Bangkok, bringing with us from the States much of the excavation equipment we had promised the Institute of Archaeology: a powerful, gasoline-powered German rock saw, impressive in its bright orange sheet-metal locker; a heavy-duty electric drill; an elaborate electrical lighting system for use in the caves; and two 225-

pound gasoline-powered generators, packed in wooden crates, to power all of the preceding.

In Thailand we bought a vast amount of camp gear, including kerosene stoves and lamps, rope and chains, and every kind of tinned, powdered, freeze-dried, and shrink-wrapped foodstuff known to man. In the end, a couple of hotel rooms were piled to the ceiling with the stuff. Then, disaster struck: our negotiations with Thai Airways about excess baggage— obviously an essential priority, given the alpine heaps of gear we had—broke down. We were told flatly that we would be permitted to check one bag each, not to exceed twenty kilograms (forty-four pounds), and not one ounce of overweight. It seemed that *60 Minutes* was sending a team to Hanoi, and science would have to take a back seat to prime-time television.

Then Ciochon had one of his brilliant ideas. It seemed that Air Vietnam had a flight from Bangkok to Hanoi on the second of January. Our visas were not supposed to be valid until the fourth, but if one member of the expedition were allowed in early, it might be possible to bring in a large load. Air Vietnam has a dismal reputation, and so its resources, such as they are, are underutilized. They told us that even half a ton of overweight would present no problem. James was volunteered, Navy-style, for the task of ferrying it in. The only remaining obstacle was to get permission from the Vietnamese for him to go in early.

Our meeting at the Vietnamese embassy with Vu Dang Dzung, the cultural attaché, was an exercise in double-think absurdity. The interview began with an incident that perfectly illustrated the cultural gulf, à la Kipling, that will always divide us from the East. It was a lovely, cool morning, and the Vietnamese embassy compound in Bangkok is an eminently pleasant and breezy place. Yet the first thing Mr. Dzung did was to turn on two hurricane-force fans and a rumbling air conditioner. The result was that we all froze to death and could hardly make out a word that Dzung had to say, for he mumbled and had a maddening habit of covering his mouth with his hand while he spoke. Yet it would have been impolite to ask him to turn them off.

It was clear from the start that our request would be approved, but it was necessary that the appointment fill the hour, so Mr. Dzung delivered an interminable and inaudible political discourse. When the unnatural cold began to bring out goose-flesh on our arms, Olsen slipped surreptitiously over to the air conditioner and turned it off, and it was then possible to catch the drift of our host's remarks. Dzung's litany was obviously a memorized text, for whenever any one of us made a polite comment about something he had said, he would return to the beginning of his sentence, or even to the top of the paragraph, and repeat it all word for word.

Two days later, James went "over the top," taking with him twenty-one pieces of luggage that weighed in at 1,430 pounds. The changes in Hanoi in less than a year were amazing. Before, James and the others had been gawked and giggled at and followed by swarms of children chanting "Hello! hello!"; now he was able to walk down the street unmolested, almost unnoticed. Certainly many more foreigners of every stripe were to be seen in public places. Some new restaurants, and good ones at that, had opened up. And there was something else, more important: a palpable glimmer of hopefulness was in the air. The sense of isolation was still there, but now it was somehow less awful and oppressive.

Two days later we were all reunited in Hanoi: in addition to Ciochon, Olsen, and James, there were two more scientists, Olsen's wife, Mary Kay Gilliland Olsen, a cultural anthropologist who had done her fieldwork in Yugoslavia, and Katerina Semendeferi, a Greek geologist who had studied in Romania before coming to Iowa to study with Ciochon. Also, a four-person film team from National Geographic accompanied us to shoot a documentary film about the dig (it is being broadcast nationally on the National Geographic *Explorer* series). The team was led by producer Judith Moses, an old Asia hand who had been in Vietnam in 1984 to shoot a segment about American war veterans returning there for the television program *20/20*. In addition, *National Geographic* magazine sent still photographer Ken Garrett to shoot pictures for a feature story about the excavation. This was going to be one well-documented expedition.

Indeed, that was just the half of it, for the Vietnamese brought along a still photographer and a film team of their own. The latter were shooting 35mm film (albeit not sound-synch) with a battered, clunky Russian camera. That floored the National Geographic crew, who were using 16mm film: 16mm is half the size and a fraction of the cost of 35mm, which nowadays is generally reserved for shooting feature films. Everyone was very cheerful and careful about not treading on each other's professional toes, but it was still a bit of a circus at moments. On at least one occasion Ken Garrett was taking pictures of the Vietnamese film crew shooting the National Geographic film crew shooting the scientists.

Our first afternoon in Hanoi we met in formal conclave with our Vietnamese colleagues, supposedly to plan the expedition. In what was becoming a little tradition, this meeting proved to be a confused debacle: slowly we were becoming aware that in Vietnam, nothing gets decided at meetings; rather, important decisions are much more likely to be made in quiet, informal conversations. The institute had a new director, a party member who was more interested, it seemed to us, in demonstrating his power over the group than in accomplishing any scientific work. Binh, Professor Hao, and Dang Huu Luu—the scientists we were actually going to be working with—sat quietly, looking into their teacups, and once we caught the drift of things, we followed suit. The only thing we agreed on was that we were leaving first thing the following morning for Halong Bay.

A Karst Primer

By now, we knew Halong Bay well. Ciochon and Olsen had made three trips there, and James two. Yet none of the others had seen it, and we wanted to explore the area with Katerina Semendeferi, the team geologist; for Halong Bay, in addition to its considerable picturesque charms, is also a living textbook in limestone geology. Semendeferi was ecstatic when she saw the huge variety of karst formations on our cruise through the bay. Before we explain the process by which karst landscape is formed, and the different types of this topography, it is important to understand why paleoanthropologists and archaeologists working in Asia are so vitally interested in such things.

In a tropical or semitropical climate, such as that of Vietnam, the extreme dampness makes it nearly impossible for bones and most cultural artifacts to survive in the open. The vast majority of fossils and artifacts that we have from this part of the world were recovered from caves, sinkholes, and other features typical of karst topography. In prehistoric times animals fell into sinkholes, were washed into caves when rivers overflowed their banks, or were dragged into crevices or under crags by scavenging animals—or they were butchered and eaten by early *Homo* living in caves. These cave- or overhang-dwelling people made fires, cooked, performed burials, and carried out the other artifact-generating activities of our species. Over the intervening thousands of years, while humidity, heavy precipitation, and general jungle rot destroyed everything that was exposed, these objects were, to varying degrees, protected by their strategic location in the caves.

The irony is that it is exactly the fossil-and-artifact-destroying damp that creates karst geology. Karst—the name is taken from the Karst Plateau on the east coast of the Adriatic Sea, which is the type specimen, so to speak, of this sort of topography—may be defined as any geological formation created by the dissolving and accreting action of precipitation. Thus geological features ranging from the tiniest depression to the grandest underground cavern are all properly considered karst. Because of its high degree of solubility, limestone is the most common raw material of karst topography, though dolomites, gypsum, and other minerals may be shaped into the distinctive forms of karst geology.

There is considerable variety among the different processes of karst formation, and geologists are not in complete agreement on the precise relationships among the various morphologies, or types of formations, but the following generalized description of how a limestone cave system forms will provide a basic understanding of the topography of the area under discussion.

This region of South China and northern Vietnam is a continuous, two-mile-thick shelf of limestone, which was deposited here 250 million years ago when the area was covered by the sea. Once this vast limestone plateau became elevated above sea level, it became exposed to processes of erosion by wind and water. In the early stages of karst formation, precipitated water seeps through fractures and breaks in this great plane of limestone. The water works its way down to the water table, and then laterally toward surface streams. As the surface ages, the streams erode the valley floor, and the water table drops. Meanwhile, the strata of limestone carrying the surface water widen and enlarge, developing into a horizontal system of fissures. This downward trend continues as the river valley grows deeper, and new channels develop to carry precipitation down to the water table. As the inside of the limestone becomes increasingly honeycombed by the flow of seeping precipitation, the higher areas, hollowed out in earlier epochs, become exposed by the usual processes of erosion, and what were once interior channels for trickling groundwater become exposed crevices and chasms. It was in this latter stage of development that the fantastic natural architecture of Halong Bay was formed.

Katerina Semendeferi, who wrote her master's thesis for Ciochon about karst topography, pointed out the different types of formations, which were as plainly etched against the sky as line drawings in a geology textbook. The earliest stage of karst is known variously as cone karst, cockpit karst, and funnel karst, though none of these images is quite right. This morphology is characterized by a bumpy, softly rolling profile, rather like a melting ice cream sundae. These cone-like clusters of peaks are found throughout South China. Chinese geomorphologists, who call them *fengcong*, which means "crowded peaks," define this type of karst as a group of peaks with a common stony basement.

The majestic tower karst, the next stage of development, has steep, often near-vertical walls of limestone, which rise from a planed limestone floor. The Chinese thought that these tower karst groups resembled forests of big trees, so they called them *fenglin*, or "peak forest." The tower karst formations in Halong Bay are riddled with caves, some quite high (the oldest ones), some at water level, others underwater.

The third type of karst is called pinnacle karst, and while it is less in evidence in Halong Bay, there are a few good examples. In pinnacle karst landforms, the limestone is shaped by

Pinnacle karst takes some bizarre forms, as here, at the Shilin (Stone Forest), in Yunnan province, China. *(Photograph by Jamie James)*

deep, narrow fissures into many separate pinnacles. Most geomorphologists believe that pinnacle karst is the result of extremely rapid erosion, usually under conditions of massive monsoonal rainfall. Pinnacle karst formations come in strange, baroque shapes, as Ciochon and James learned on their trip to Yunnan province, China, in the summer of 1988, when they visited the Shilin (Stone Forest). This is one of the most bizarre natural formations in the world, more closely resembling a gallery of monumental modernist sculpture than anything one would expect to find in nature.

Upon our return to Hanoi, Ciochon and Olsen examined the *Gigantopithecus* teeth recovered from Tham Khuyen. Binh retrieved the specimens from their locked cases and set them out on tables in a cramped little room under a portrait of Ho Chi Minh. Scarcely an hour after Ciochon, Olsen, and the others had sat down to work, they were told to wind things up, because the young woman who was responsible for locking up the room wanted to go home. There seemed to be no appeal: Binh squirmed a bit when we complained, but generally when problematic rules are encountered, our Vietnamese friends just stoically observe them. No one asked if it was possible for someone else to lock up—or, if she could just wait until we were through. No, the woman with the key wanted to go home, and that was that. In Vietnam, winning the big battles is easy; the picayune things are what thwart you.

A Welcoming Ritual

We followed a different route to Ba Thuoc this time, so it took us a scant ten hours to traverse the hundred miles. It was nearly nine o'clock at night when our acid-green Soviet van finally pulled into camp. Our headquarters for the duration would be a deserted logging camp, a cluster of concrete bunkhouses. Open fretwork along the tops of the walls must have let in a cooling breeze in the summer, when the weather is scorchingly hot hereabouts, but in January it kept the place from ever being quite comfortable. A hand-painted wooden sign over our mess table proclaimed DANG CONG SAN VIET NAM QUANG VINH MUON NAM, which means "Long live the Communist Party of Vietnam!" On the lawn in front of the bunkhouse was the rusted metal casing, about a yard long, of a 500-pound bomb. We learned later that it had been dropped by an American F-4 jet fighter during the war, quite near Lang Trang cave. The loggers had stood it upright, nose-down in a truck wheel, to use as a dinner gong.

An advance team from Hanoi had arrived a couple of weeks before to prepare everything for our arrival. We arrived in Ba Thuoc just as the sixteenth district Communist Party congress was convening. Vietnamese flags fluttered from bamboo stakes placed along the roads, and inspirational slogans in bold Vietnamese calligraphy and portraits of Marx, Lenin, and Ho Chi Minh were painted onto blank walls. After the party congress was over, the flags came down, but the portraits remained, and they never ceased to seem incongruous in this Stone Age village.

In the afternoon we went to a cave called Buu Dien (which means post office, for it is right down the hill from one) to do a bit of preliminary prospecting. The cave lies opposite a densely forested ravine, about twenty yards up a steep limestone slope facing the Ma river valley. Here, Ciochon found a fossil mollusk shell, which was significant because it established that there had been a riverine environment here.

Breccia is the generic name for mineral deposits in caves. The matrix that contains fossils and cultural remains, breccia varies from soft, crumbly compositions of fine, red claylike earth to consolidated gritty pebble conglomerates to rock-hard cemented travertine, a crystallized form of calcium carbonate. It is found deposited in and around the limestone that actually constitutes the cave chamber. The usual scenario of breccia and fossil deposition is the following: after the caves have been formed by the process of groundwater erosion, subsequent alluvial flooding in the caves deposits the sedimentary rock and minerals that will become breccia. Mixed in with this effluvia are teeth and bones, which will petrify and become fossils, and occasionally stone tools and other durable cultural remains, which are either washed into the cave or brought there by human inhabitants. As the cave fills with sediment and other debris, the action of water dissolves limestone from the cave walls and ceiling which permeates this mix of sediment, bone, and other debris, crystallizing it into a consolidated breccia.

The final step is that archaeologists and paleoanthropologists like us arrive on the scene and do a little human erosion, removing the deposits with picks, hammers, and saws. If a fossil or artifact is found, then the remnants of breccia clinging to it must be removed. If it is soft enough, it can be knocked off with a pick or even scraped off with a dental pick or the fingernail. Ciochon has the dreadful habit of sucking on fossils and then rubbing them on his pants to remove the bits of breccia. The rest of us would reprimand him, but like a nail biter he could not seem to cure himself of this unhygienic practice. If, however, the breccia is quite hard, as was the case at Buu Dien cave, then mechanical or chemical ways must be found of softening the matrix in order to get at whatever fossils or artifacts are there. Ciochon tried soaking the breccia in water, which did not work; the gritty lump from Buu Dien sat in a teacup filled with water the whole time we were in Ba Thuoc, yet not so much as a grain came loose.

That afternoon, the people attending the party congress came to visit us for a traditional drinking ceremony of the Viet people, the ethnic majority in Vietnam. We asked Binh if there was going to be any singing or dancing, and he said cheerfully, "No, just drinking." Binh is a prodigiously hard-working archaeologist, but when the appropriate time for merrymaking arrives, he applies himself to that with scarcely less dedication. The ritual, called Lao-Lao, was very appealing: a large earthenware jug, perhaps a yard tall, was filled with rice wine, and twenty or thirty long drinking straws made of slender bamboo curved up from the rim. The ceremony consisted entirely of everyone crowding round and sucking on the straws—as they had said, it was just drinking. The liquor was not bad stuff, rather like hard cider with a tang of caraway seed. The whole affair was over in twenty minutes; then the Communists piled back into their flatbed truck and returned to district headquarters, singing and waving farewell.

The Caves of Lang Trang

On our visit to Thanh Hoa province in May 1988, we had conducted a survey of caves in the area, and Lang Trang was clearly the most promising, a conclusion supported by the experiences of Binh, Dang Huu Luu, and the others who had worked in the area. On the previous trip, we had found several dozen well-preserved fossils in the space of a few days, suggesting an unusually rich deposit of bone. Furthermore, they had been the "right" fossils—that is, they indicated that *Gigantopithecus* and *Homo erectus* might be present. As we have seen, the index fossils we recovered were of the group known as *Stegodon-Ailuropoda*, which is typical of the middle to late Pleistocene. The fossil tooth of *Ailuropoda* that Luu had found on the earlier expedition to Lang Trang had provided us with as close a temporal fix as we could get until we were able to take samples back to a laboratory in the States. We did do that later, and the results completely altered our interpretation of the site—and indeed revolutionized our thinking about Southeast Asian paleontology. But at the time we were in the field, we only had a rough sketch of a time line to work with.

The Lang Trang site (the name is taken from the village, hardly more than a dozen bamboo houses, where our camp was located) was about half a mile from camp. It is in fact a complex of caves situated at the foot of a karst tower near the road, up a slight slope of about five yards. Our first morning at Lang Trang we looked over the two adjoining caves that we had visited in May 1988. The first of these was a sort of minisystem, a large open overhang connected by a small tunnel to an upper chamber that narrowed as it climbed into a crevice. Cave two was just ten yards to the right of cave one, around the corner of the tower. Its mouth was bricked up with stone slabs, a fact which was not immediately apparent, and in this wall there was a metal grille door such as one finds on a jail cell, secured with a big padlock. Inside, the cave had been hollowed out. Luu explained that during the war, it had been fitted out to serve as an arms depot and air-raid shelter. By the end of our sojourn we learned that Ba Thuoc had been very heavily bombed during the war.

Katerina Semendeferi and Russell Ciochon explore the interior of cave two at Lang Trang. *(Photograph by Jamie James)*

The roof of the bomb shelter, or cave two, was literally studded with fossils. You could stand in any one place with a torch, and identify a dozen fossils within a few minutes. In order to excavate this cave we had brought the gasoline-powered rock saw and the generators, drill, and lighting systems. As we were leaving the cave, Binh asked us very casually if we would like to see the other caves. What other caves? we asked in amazement.

"Oh, we forgot to tell you about the other caves when we were here last time," said Binh with typical aplomb. (The phrase "Oh, we forgot to tell you . . ." became something of a byword among us; in most cases, the phrase preceded bad news, especially of the accounts-payable type, but in this case it was very good news.) We went straightaway to see them. The third cave was not really a cave at all but a fissure in the side of the tower, at ground level, which rose to a height of about thirty feet. At the top was a hole about one yard across, which opened into the rear of the "bomb shelter." This fissure was clogged with huge blocks of breccia, boulders really, that seemed to have been hurled out of the "rear window" in the bomb shelter. We later surmised that the North Vietnamese army (NVA) had cleared the second cave to transform it into a shelter and arms dump, and had thrown out these blocks of breccia. The local people who remembered those days later confirmed our supposition. These breccia blocks were filled with fossils: a casual inspection of them found a dozen fossils. Later, they were hauled back to camp, where our workmen cracked them into small pieces and chiseled them down. Many superb specimens were obtained by this method.

The fourth cave, about a hundred feet from the others, was exceptionally beautiful. Just fifteen feet above ground level, with a tall stand of bamboo screening the entrance, it appeared to be divided horizontally into two chambers, upper and lower. Across the middle of the cave's mouth was a natural arch, that had been formed when a big chunk of red breccia had fallen down. From a vantage directly in front of the entrance, the ground descended gently into the lower chamber. The main chamber was roughly twenty-three feet by sixteen. At its end the cave branched off into a deep rocky fissure straight ahead from the cave mouth, and off to the right a narrow tunnel meandered up and away into a steep chimney (that is, a vertical tunnel) deep inside the tower.

This cave we called Lang Trang IV, with Lang Trang I being the overhang and its connecting tunnel, Lang Trang II the bomb shelter, and Lang Trang III the crevice behind the bomb shelter. The latter is not a separate cave at all, but the Vietnamese called it one, so we adhered to their nomenclature for the sake of convenience.

On that first afternoon at Lang Trang, Semendeferi commenced mapping the cave system, an essential first step in any modern excavation. She began by establishing a central datum point. She and Olsen chose an arbitrary spot that was more or less central in cave one, and drilled a hole in the rock. There, Semendeferi planted a steel rod in concrete. This central datum functions like the middle point in a graph, where the X and Y axes intersect; it provides a point of reference for the map. Whenever a find is made, its exact location in space can be determined by describing its relationship, through compass points and elevation, to the central datum point. In modern archaeology, knowing exactly where an artifact or bone was found is almost as important as the thing itself; such a grid system enables us to keep track of find locations accurately and easily.

Across the River

In the afternoon, Ciochon, James, and Judith Moses walked down to the Ma River, which flowed right behind camp. We were escorted by Mr. Phong, the representative from the Social Sciences Committee, who was there as an all-purpose facilitator (and also, no doubt, to keep an eye on us). On sandbars in the middle of this wide river, rude bamboo huts had been erected, and twenty or thirty people, healthy, middle-aged men and women, were hanging around them, apparently idle in the middle of the day. It was a very strange sight, because Vietnamese peasants are *always* working. Mr. Phong talked to them and learned that they were panning for gold. The people told him that gold nuggets as big as your thumb had been discovered in the river—though that, after all, is what gold-panners always say.

Mr. Phong hired one of them to carry us across the Ma on his sampan. We sculled downstream to a point roughly due west from Lang Trang, seeking a modern river-level cave that might provide an analogy to our site. We did not find it; the nearest tower was too high to provide a useful comparison. Nonetheless, we disembarked on the opposite side of the river to do a little snooping. There, we found a Vietnamese grammar school in session—that is, it was in session until the children saw us coming. They came flying out the door and surrounded us in an instant. We had experienced several cases of heavy gawking, but these children seemed to be utterly mesmerized by us.

This bank of the river, the western side, was plainly more rustic, more isolated, than the excavation side. Men on the excavation side wore wristwatches, some of the boys had T-shirts with English-language legends (mostly advertising cigarettes and cars), and one occasionally saw women who were not wearing the tribal hand-loomed dress. Here the people had a more traditional appearance. Phong talked to the teacher, a very shy young woman wearing a brilliantly colored Muong costume of hand-loomed raw silk. She told him that we were the first white people to come to that side of the river. The school was a one-room whitewashed concrete house at the foot of a monumental karst tower. Nearby there was a ten-foot-tall termite hill. In the schoolhouse, what appeared to be a Vietnamese spelling lesson had been scrawled on the blackboard. The children tried to be friendly, but the novelty of the visitors was simply too much for them; they dissolved into hysterical cascades of laughter at our every move.

From the Vietnamese point of view we were in the Ba Thuoc district for a very long time, but actually, three weeks is not long for a modern archaeological dig. We moved quickly to set up the excavation. Caves one and two at that point were the principal objects of the dig, so we had our workmen build a bamboo scaffold in front of the overhang and inside the bomb shelter, in order that breccia might be removed from these inaccessible places with the rock saw. These structures, made of six-inch-thick bamboo logs lashed together with rattan, appeared to be somewhat rickety, but in fact they were just as solid as and probably more trustworthy than any pipe-and-plank construction; bamboo is not only strong but also very resilient.

Meanwhile, in the floor of cave four, Olsen and Binh, on a hunch, dug a test trench, the classic method for determining whether a site is worth excavating. An archaeologist chooses a likely spot and removes one square meter down to a depth where artifacts are no longer found. If he finds something interesting, then ... well, then it is interesting. If nothing turns up, most likely, a lot of time has been saved. Olsen and Binh picked a square adjacent to the cave wall, laid it out with string running on little bamboo stakes, and began to dig.

Just a few hours later, they sent Madame Lan, our translator on this trip, to bring the others back to cave four. They had found something: a Bronze Age hearth, wherein were buried eight flakes, flat slivers of stone that are the by-products of stone toolmaking. They knew it was a hearth because the earth was dark and hardened, the result of continuous fire making. A quantity of fossils also came to light, including teeth of *Sus* (pig), *Hystrix* (porcupine), a large bovid (cowlike mammal), a cervid (deer), and the fossilized remains of a freshwater crab and several freshwater snails and of a large mollusk. The latter were most likely the leavings of a Bronze Age meal. Olsen and Binh were elated: it was just time for lunch on the first full day in the field, and already they had raked in a major haul. Over a collation of peanut-butter sandwiches and instant soup, Olsen told us that the breccia in cave four was nearly ideal to dig in, soft and crumbly, yet the fossils were thoroughly mineralized.

Meanwhile, the reports from caves one and two were not as encouraging. The breccia was gritty and hard and difficult to remove. The rock saw worked as efficiently as we could have hoped; if it was not quite like a hot knife slicing through butter, it did its work of cutting through the sediment well enough. It was filthy work, however, instantly covering whoever wielded the saw with a thick layer of powdered breccia. We were not finding as many fossils there as we had hoped, and those we did find were difficult to extract. Ciochon set up a sort of assembly line with the Vietnamese workers: one man would cut out blocks of breccia with the saw (that, naturally, was the most coveted position), others loaded the blocks onto the vans and the jeep for transport to the camp, where workers spent the day chiseling down the blocks. Many good specimens were found this way, but some of them were fractured or chipped during the removal process.

The next day, Olsen and Binh abandoned their trench in Lang Trang IV long enough to examine a chimney that Semendeferi had found in the upper part of the same cave. While they were there, they did a little digging, and they made a major discovery: a cluster of cultural remains, which they later identified as a possible burial site. Located in the little tunnel that led back toward the chimney, the site yielded, among other things, a nice end chopper (in other words, a chopping tool fashioned from the longitudinal end of an elongated pebble, archaeospeak for a very small stone tool), possibly of the Sonvian period, approximately 30,000 years old. That afternoon, off to one side in the tunnel, Olsen and Binh found a tiny chamber that contained numerous stone tools typical of the Hoabinhian period, including some quartzite sumatraliths. Sumatraliths are an index fossil of the Hoabinhian culture, first identified, obviously, in Sumatra. These large tools might have been cores from which small cutting edges were flaked, and they themselves might have been used as percussive tools.

The most interesting object found here was a cowrie shell, perforated as though for stringing on a cord. The cowrie is a marine gastropod, and this specimen was definitely not a fossil; that means that it could not have been deposited here during an ancient marine period, and was almost certainly brought to this place by its human occupants. It is entirely possible that the shell was acquired by barter from residents of the sea coast, which at that time was much closer than it is now. The cowrie's presence so far inland can only be explained logically by its having had a ritualistic purpose. A burial is the most likely candidate, but the human remains have not yet been recovered, if they are indeed recoverable; it is certainly possible that whatever human remains there were might have been removed previously, perhaps for some magical purpose. In the same little chamber Olsen and Binh found another stone chopper, flaked on three sides, and a flaked quartzite pebble. The earth was dark and hardened, giving evidence of fire. They also found a Bronze Age pottery shard, which had somehow found its way into this Paleolithic site. Such anomalies are by no means rare, but they usually remain unexplained enigmas.

A Shift in Emphasis

Clearly, we were going to have to reevaluate our priorities. We had come, we thought, to excavate Lang Trang I and II, the overhang and the bomb shelter, but Lang Trang IV now appeared to be the most productive site. We held a serious pow-wow over a sumptuous dinner—instant noodle soup and sweet-and-sour shrimp à la Apollo Program, with a special ration of chocolate-covered macadamia nuts—and decided to shift the emphasis, at least tentatively, to Lang Trang IV, while continuing to remove breccia from caves one and two with the Vietnamese workmen.

The latter operation was grinding forward inexorably. The roar of the power saw and, more particularly, the sight of the large, hairy, pale-skinned people who had brought them, attracted larger and larger crowds every day. By the third day, there were over a hundred curious people standing silently in the road, watching us at work. It became a serious problem as they crept closer and closer to watch the saw—potentially a dangerous situation. We tried to enforce stringent security, and posted some of the soldiers as guards to keep the crowds away. That ploy worked—for about one hour. The guards proved to be just as curious as the villagers, and before long they were simply leading the way.

The little boys were the most dedicated idlers. One lad, wearing a Soviet helicopter pilot's helmet, asked Mr. Phong, "If they're Americans, why aren't they shooting at us?" Professor Hao told us that the boys he talked to thought that we were looking for gold, like the 'forty-niners in the Ma River, who were, after all, their parents and uncles and aunts. Once the boys learned what we were looking for, however strange it must have seemed to them, they joined the search. Little boys began bringing us fossil teeth that they had "found," many of

At Lang Trang IV, the excavation moves forward: in the upper chamber, the mapping team charts the cave's interior; below, archaeologists excavate under lights powered by an electric generator. *(Photograph by Russell Ciochon)*

them remarkably good, clean specimens. While this might seem to be a boon, and however much the boys' intentions were benign, as far as Ciochon was concerned it was a disaster. "If they're going to start bringing us specimens, we might as well pack up and go home," he gravely intoned.

He related the story of Ralph von Koenigswald's discovery of a *Homo erectus* skullcap in Java. It seems that the local collector who had discovered the skull had broken it into twenty pieces. Someone had told him that the crazy German was willing to pay for any piece of a hominid skull, and he wanted to maximize his take. While there was no such mercenary motive behind the boys' activities, their finds were scientifically very suspect. As a rule, there is minimal value in bone per se. One will make exceptions, obviously: if a little boy had brought us a skull of *Gigantopithecus,* we would have taken it. But the skull itself would convey to us little information beyond the fact that it probably came from somewhere in the Ba Thuoc vicinity; whereas, if we excavated it ourselves, it would yield up a world of insights about itself and the place we found it, and the other fossils and tools found with it.

Hao questioned one of the boys who was bringing in the specimens, who told him that they had found the fossils at an underground river inside the karst tower—which explained why the specimens were so clean. He was a tiny thing, probably no more than six years old, and he had shimmied through a little hole in cave one and crawled down a crevice to the stream. That meant that these specimens had already been removed, most likely by water erosion, from their original place of deposition. Furthermore, after the little boys showed Ciochon and Hao the tiny aperture he had crawled through to get the specimens, it was obvious that we would not get them any other way. At this, Ciochon relaxed a bit and altered his decree so that we could accept, but not pay for, specimens— not that anyone had asked for money.

Archaeology has been uncharitably defined as the systematic destruction of a place, and that description certainly fits what we accomplished at Lang Trang. At the same time that the breccia from cave one was removed, little by little, and exhaustively examined for fossils, Semendeferi and Luu continued to map the whole system, so that each discovery as it was made could be linked with its exact source in the cave. Meanwhile, the test trench in Lang Trang IV had become such a roaring success that the excavation was extended to the whole cave floor, as well as the chimneys and crevices higher up, where Olsen and Binh had discovered the cultural remains. We compared notes every night at dinner, over rice and beans, or occasionally fresh pork stew, tomato salad, beer and Bulgarian mineral water (sometimes preceded by a dram of Scotch whisky or a Tang Bang, vodka with instant orange juice powder). We discussed the day's discoveries while we cleaned the specimens and readied equipment for the next morning.

The Americans were much more boring campers than the Vietnamese. The highlight of our evening was when we tuned into the BBC or Voice of America news broadcasts on Ciochon's shortwave radio. Then we read our novels or played cards until lights-out, generally about nine o'clock. The Vietnamese, by contrast, were quite wild, staying up to drink *ruou,* the local white lightning, and play cards by the light of their oil lamps. Unlike our tame hands of hearts and canasta, however, they played for big stakes, and we could hear them carrying on some nights till well after midnight.

The fourth day of the dig, Friday the thirteenth, turned out to be a lucky one: while cutting blocks of breccia out of Lang Trang I, Ciochon found a lens-shaped vein (geologists call such a deposit a lens) of dark, sandy sediment running through the main deposit, which was unusually rich in fossils, including muntjak, a musk deer the size of a big dog; sambar, a large deer of the genus *Cervus (Rusa)*; more *Sus*; and, of much greater importance, *Ailuropoda,* our first find of giant panda on this expedition. We immediately set to work cutting out hunks of the lens, revealing a small chamber that we surmised was the source of all the fossils the children had been bringing us.

One softball-sized sample of this coarse, sandy lens was analyzed at the University of Iowa. As its sedimentary components were being studied under a binocular microscope, an even more important discovery was made. The sample was full of the small teeth and fragmentary limb bones of a diverse microfauna, including rodents, bats, reptiles, and fishes. This micromammal component, mostly teeth and small bones about the same size as the coarse sand particles that constitute the lens, probably washed into the cave during a violent monsoon that caused the Ma River to overflow its banks and flood the cave. This would have temporarily interrupted the normal process of breccia formation. After the waters receded, however, the slow process of breccia formation began again, sealing the sandy lens within the breccia of Lang Trang I until we uncovered it.

This was our only discovery of microfauna at the site. Precise identifications of these tiny creatures have not yet been made, but when completed, they will significantly increase the total number of species recovered from Lang Trang. Micromammals are also good indicators of prehistoric environmental conditions; eventually, we may know much more about the climate and habitat of Lang Trang at the time that *Homo erectus* was living there.

The "Orgy"

A small contretemps arose when the National Geographic film team went across the river to film the village that Ciochon, James, and Judith Moses had visited a few days earlier. The locals were up in arms when they found out that the foreigners had been shooting there without permission. There was talk of seizing the film. It was a classic shakedown; Moses had to eat a great deal of crow and paid 400,000 dong (the equivalent of eighty dollars) into the local treasury to pay for a feast-cum-folklore demonstration.

It was worth every dong. The feast proved to be one of the most moving and fascinating experiences of the trip; Moses called it "the orgy," and from a sociological point of view, that is just what it was. It was held in a large house elevated on pilings, constructed of a carved hardwood, beautifully finished, that resembled mahogany, from a tree the Vietnamese call *lim*. The two principal racial groups in the Ba Thuoc area are the Tai and the Muong; the house belonged to a Tai farmer, but the Muong had to be invited as well to ensure civic harmony. That meant that we, the honored foreign guests, had to go through the welcoming ritual twice. When we arrived, the sister of the house's owner, an old woman whose mouth and lips were dyed a deep, sanguineous scarlet from a lifetime of chewing betel, crooned a song of welcome and gave us shots of *ruou* and cigarettes. The latter were Vietnamese-made, but they were called, curiously, "No. 1 American Blend." We were expected to partake of these whether we wanted to or not. Almost all Vietnamese smoke and drink more or less in moderation (though mild-mannered Professor Hao is one of the exceptions).

The Tai musicians played beautiful music, a repetitive modular composition for gongs, drums, and bamboo percussion blocks. The latter were pounded by a group of young girls in traditional costume. The music was irresistibly rhythmic and somewhat eerie. It reminded us a bit of the Doors' music, which one associates with Vietnam in an altogether different context. The musicians, like everyone else, were drinking generous libations of *ruou*, and soon they were dancing and wending a serpentine path through the crowd as they played. This game of musical follow-the-leader was greatly impeded by the presence of two film teams and two professional still photographers; in addition to Ken Garrett, the National Geographic photographer, there was also the official photographer from the Institute of Archaeology.

The people were wonderfully warm and friendly, especially the women, who continually patted and cosseted Katerina Semendeferi, Mary Kay Olsen, and Judith Moses, and gave them innumerable gifts, including silk weavings and dried beans for them to take home with them to plant, "so they would never be hungry." In return, the American women gave them perfume samples. Everyone was a bit tipsy by the time the meal was served. The menu consisted of chicken soup, roast pork, the ubiquitous stringy greens, rice, and bananas. There was much weeping and wailing when we piled into the van to go back to camp. As a parting gift, Ciochon was presented by the house's owner with a fine boar's jaw with large, recurved tusks.

When we returned, we got some good news: the workmen charged with examining the blocks of breccia from cave three, the fissure adjoining the bomb shelter, had found, intermingled with fossil teeth of tapir and goat, a superb specimen of *Stegodon*. Of all the fossils we recovered at Lang Trang, this huge, ridged molar, weighing several pounds, was the most impressive to look at. The *Stegodon* specimen clarified the picture of what we were dealing with: it was a Pleistocene site, close in time to the confrontation between *Homo erectus* and *Gigantopithecus* that had brought us here in the first place. That night, as he sipped his Tang Bang, Ciochon observed that those two, *Homo* and Giganto, were the only specimens lacking in the fossil fauna we had recovered from Lang Trang.

The weather began to oppress us. The day we had arrived was a fine sunny day, but it was the last such day we would see the whole time we were in Ba Thuoc. While it was never extremely cold, it was never warm; temperatures hovered in the forties and fifties (Fahrenheit) day after day, with never a ray of sunshine, and our activities were curtailed. On our previous visit, in May, the weather had been so unbearably hot that we could scarcely move. Now we were chilled to the bone every day. The one good effect of the coolness was that the caves, supremely well insulated, were quite warm after the generator-powered electrical lamps had been burning for a while, which made us want to stay in the caves digging for as long as possible.

Binh got seriously ill with a respiratory disease in the second week we were there. None of us were doctors, but the symptoms were distressingly similar to those of pneumonia. We made him stay in camp—no easy task, for Binh is an indefatigable worker—and dosed him with some antibiotic pills we had brought with us for such an emergency. The Vietnamese, meantime, worked their own cure on him: they branded his back, along his spine and ribs. They accomplished this by burning his flesh with tiger balm administered with "French metal," which sounded mysterious enough; the burns were the size of large coins, so we hypothesized that the brand was an old French franc. The purpose, according to Binh, was to drive away "the bad winds." By week's end he was again in good health. He triumphantly claimed that his cure was a vindication of traditional Vietnamese medicine, but we noticed that he continued to take the antibiotics we had given him.

The National Geographic film crew left on January 16, but before they left, the Vietnamese film team got their chance to film the American crew shooting us. We had put it off for days, but finally submitted with good humor to their request. The scene they wanted seemed to us ridiculous: they had us walking up and down the riverbank in full spelunking regalia, with the National Geographic cinematographer, Scott Ransom, earnestly "shooting" away. Then we were made to clamber up the rocky crevice of cave three. Judith Moses lost her footing halfway up and fell into the arms of Jamie James, who, luckily, was standing at the foot of the crevice. In that scene, soundman Mark Roy was standing in front of us with his big boom microphone, but Ransom's camera was lying on a rock at the floor of the crevice, in plain view. We racked our brains trying to imagine how the film editor would make sense of the footage resulting from this shoot, but they seemed quite happy with it.

After the two film crews left, as we entered the last ten days of the expedition, there was a sense of getting down to serious work. By now, things were proceeding at a comfortable, workmanlike pace: blocks of breccia were steadily quarried from caves one and two with the gasoline-powered saw, which turned in yeoman service; the Vietnamese workers continued their methodical examination of the breccia, both the quarried blocks from caves one and two and the loose chunks from cave three; and, for the Americans, the main focus was the ongoing excavation of cave four. By now we had expanded far beyond Olsen and Binh's original square-meter trench and were digging up virtually the whole cave floor. We took turns wielding the trowel and finding the fossils, which occurred with remarkable frequency. Perhaps every ten or fifteen minutes, someone would utter a satisfied little gasp or groan of discovery, and hand over what they had found to the paleontologists, Ciochon and Le Trung Kha.

Kha is a wizened, wiry little man of about seventy years who has one of the best minds in Southeast Asia in the fields of archaeology and paleoanthropology. His range of interests is diverse: in addition to his extensive experience and knowledge in Pleistocene fauna, he has also written about contemporary fauna in Vietnam and the historical archaeology of the Cham (the civilization that dominated southern Vietnam, roughly from the Mekong River north to the area around the city of Hue, on the Perfume River, at the time the Khmer were ruling

Cambodia). Kha, a member of the team at Tham Khuyen that discovered *Gigantopithecus,* is now associated with the Institute of Social Sciences in Ho Chi Minh City (formerly Saigon).

Kha has a remarkable ability to identify fossil teeth, relying only on his experienced eye and a tattered set of photocopies from some reference books. Someone would hand him a fossil fresh from the earth, and he would ponder it for a moment and then intone his identification like a sibyl, in his delightful frenchified English. In the West, we are accustomed to working with a good comparative collection of type fossils, that is, identifying a new find by placing it alongside a known quantity, one that has been positively identified. Comparative identifications are particularly useful in the case of primate teeth, for teeth from some primates are remarkably similar. Identifications of *Homo,* especially when they are based solely upon fossil incisors, are always controversial. Kha has never had the luxury of a comparative anatomy collection, yet all the identifications he made at Lang Trang have held up.

He was one of the most popular members of the dig. He was also amazingly hard-working; nonetheless, he always found time to play a bit of soccer with men younger than his sons. The English-speaking Vietnamese called him Professor Rather Good, for that is what Kha means; for the same reason, they called Professor Hao Professor Very Good.

Semendeferi by this point had some rough sketches of her map for us to work with. Olsen was using them and his own geological observations to develop a theory about the formation of cave four. He hypothesized that the principal deposit of fossils was made sometime during the middle Pleistocene in the lower chamber. At that time cave four had two chambers, upper and lower. The back part of the floor of the upper chamber collapsed, perhaps in the late Pleistocene or early Holocene, falling down onto the floor of the lower chamber, creating the natural arch to be seen in the front part of the cave today. Subsequently, according to this theory, there was a Bronze Age occupation over this newly fallen breccia, which would explain the more recent depositions on the floor of the main chamber. While Olsen's theory is logical, and fits all the evidence, he is cautious about promoting it beyond the status of hypothesis.

CHAPTER 8

Ecce Homo

Encounter with an Ancestor

Sometimes after dinner, while Olsen was writing up his field notes, James and Ciochon would wander over to the Vietnamese part of the compound to visit Le Trung Kha. Although Kha stayed up till midnight most nights, working on the fossils by lamplight after the electricity had been turned off, he loved for us to come visit him. Kha's English was about as good as James's French—which is to say, bad—but we communicated well enough.

Professor Rather Good was a very good storyteller. He told us about studying in France in the forties, about trying to accomplish scientific work in Vietnam during the recent war with our country. As we sipped his warm, bitter tea, and the little room filled up with the pungent smoke of his cigarettes, inevitably these late-night conversations turned to speculation about the life of early man in these parts, and his encounter with the great ape which had prompted our visit to Kha's nation in the first place.

Ciochon had been studying Semendeferi's maps of the valley, which led him to the conclusion that the riverside vegetation in the middle Pleistocene was most likely a gallery forest, a very thick, lush jungle that overhangs the river so that the boughs almost touch. At that time, the Ma River meandered right alongside the karst tower that contains the Lang Trang cave system. These caves had most likely served as sites for human habitation ever since man first came to the valley.

James pointed out that our ancestors' evenings in Lang Trang in those days might not have been very different from ours: at day's end, they, too, must have huddled for companionship around the dying embers of a fire, perhaps sharing a bamboo cup of fresh water. We cannot know for sure whether or not they could talk with one another, but being human, they must have found solace in one another's company.

In the course of these late-night talks with Kha we first began to discuss the possibility that human hunting might have been responsible for the disappearance of some large mammals from this landscape. We knew about the discovery of burned and butchered orangutan bones at a site in northern Vietnam called Nguom Rock Shelter; Kha also told us about finds of giant panda fossils in Vietnam that appeared to have been hunted by man. Eventually, we would raise the possibility that *Gigantopithecus,* too, had been wiped out by human hunting, a question we shall go into at length in a later chapter. Kha did not object to this scenario, but he never could understand our fascination with the giant ape: for him, *Homo* was of infinitely greater importance. Clearly, as far as he was concerned, unless we found a human specimen at Lang Trang, this would end up being just another excavation, not terribly important.

Then, on January 18, Nguyen Van Hao made the key discovery: in the floor of cave four he found a premolar of *Homo.* Since it was an isolated tooth, it was difficult—impossible, really—to identify the species. When we were in the field we thought that the Lang Trang deposit was much younger than it has subsequently been proved to be; thanks to the electron-spin resonance dating of the site carried out by our colleague Henry Schwarcz, at McMaster University in Hamilton, Ontario, after our return to America (see Chapter Nine). With this relatively young time frame in mind, we thought that Professor Hao's specimen must come from *Homo sapiens.* However, given the range of 440,000 to 520,000 years established by Schwarcz, the specimen should be assigned to *Homo erectus.* Any other interpretation is unpersuasive, because the geological circumstances of the find argue against the possibility that later fossils of *Homo sapiens* got mixed in with the earlier fossil fauna.

We did not know at the time that we had found *Homo*

Nguyen Van Hao, the Vietnamese
leader of the expedition, made
the first discovery of *Homo*
at Lang Trang. *(Photograph by
Jamie James)*

erectus—and one of the oldest dated Pleistocene sites in Asia,
at that—but there was considerable rejoicing nonetheless. Human identifications are always made a bit more cautiously than
other identifications. If you make an erroneous claim about a
pig tooth, no one is likely to get too upset. But make a mistake
about your own genus, and watch out! Yet it was Kha himself
who proclaimed the specimen to be *Homo*, and no one was
about to quarrel with him. If anything, Professor Rather Good
tends more to take the conservative view than the hopeful one
in his identifications; in his words, that find alone made Lang
Trang an important site "not only for my country but for all
the world." How much more so when the actual antiquity of
the site was later established!

    If there were any lingering doubts about the *Homo* identifi-
cation, they were dispelled the next day, when Olsen found
another fossil of *Homo* in the roof of the lower tunnel of cave
four. At the right-hand end of the main chamber were two
tunnels, one level with the main floor, the other on the upper
level and parallel to the lower tunnel, which led back to the
chimney in the cavern's deepest recess. On a whim, John and
Mary Kay Olsen took the electric lanterns down the lower of
the two tandem tunnels, which no one had really examined, to

see if there were any fossils in evidence. There, embedded quite by itself in the breccia of the roof of the little passageway, he found a human incisor. In the remaining days of the expedition, three more specimens of *Homo* came to light from caves one and two, including one brought to us by a little boy from the stream bed under the tower. All together, five teeth of *Homo* have been recovered from caves one, two, and four.

One of our avowed aims when we came to Ba Thuoc was to find remains of *Gigantopithecus,* a goal we have not yet accomplished. Yet it ought to be pointed out that other paleoanthropologists would consider our find of *Homo* to be of infinitely greater consequence than simply digging up another Giganto tooth in an area where the great ape is already known to have flourished. Of course we realized our find was important from a number of points of view. In the first place, as we have suggested, our fascination with *Homo erectus* is largely due to the fact that it is "one of us," while *Gigantopithecus,* as interesting as it is, is a rather more shadowy figure, a dead-end on the fossil fringes of the hominoid family tree. In addition, the discovery of *Homo* at Lang Trang cave was important to us because it provided some tangible proof that we were on the right track: now we knew that we were very likely in an area near the site of that momentous first encounter between Giganto and our ancestors.

Nonscientists have the tendency to rate fossil finds as though they were songs on the Top 40, and often overemphasize the importance of a particular species. Yet of all species, generally nothing rates higher than *Homo.* Our discovery of *Homo erectus* in Lang Trang cave is particularly important, since it fills the gap between Zhoukoudian, in central China, and Java, some 2,500 miles to the south. It was a major find, and we recognized that immediately, but, strangely, it did not really make a deep impression right away—mainly because we did not yet know the date of the fossils. Also, we knew that it would take months and years of careful research and analysis to place the discovery in context. In modern science, even when there is that rare moment of an important discovery, often there is no great "Eureka!", no home-run rush. Context and analysis make good science, not the proverbial bold stroke.

Five Fossils

Altogether, we recovered 1,025 fossils, representing 36 mammalian species, an impressive collection by any standard. Now, how do we begin to sort through this pile of bones? We begin, literally, by sorting (see Appendix 2, the Excavation Fauna List). Of the 1,025 specimens, 213 came from Lang Trang I, 294 from Lang Trang II, 83 from Lang Trang III, and 435 from Lang Trang IV. The two most common species are the wild boar and the barking deer; and the two rarest, in terms of representation in the collection, are the Asiatic wild dog, *Cuon antiquus,* and the Asian golden cat, *Felis temmincki.* Members of our mammalian order, the primates, make up 13 percent of the total fauna, with at least six species accounted for: seventy-four specimens of two varieties of macaque monkey, forty-four of the orangutan, five of the langur monkey, two of the gibbon—and five of *Homo.*

How much can we really learn from these 1,025 specimens from this isolated cave system in the hinterland of northern Vietnam? A good deal more than one might expect. The study of isolated fossil teeth is meat and drink to a paleontologist; simply put, he must learn to identify all of the world's species of mammals on the basis of isolated teeth, which are often in poor condition. This ability is acquired by hours of comparative study of the mammalian skeletons and skulls housed in the world's natural history museums. Eventually, one reaches the point where the enormous variability and subtle distinctions among mammalian teeth are familiar and immediately recognizable, just as an art historian can instantly distinguish among the works of many artists working in the same general style. Let us illustrate the process by turning to five individual specimens from the Lang Trang excavation.

We can start with one of the common fossils, which is labeled LT III-38 (that is, number 38 from Lang Trang III), a complete lower third molar of the barking deer, *Muntiacus muntiak.* By the size and the medium amount of wear on the tooth, we can identify it as coming from a young adult; if it had been a canine, we would have known the animal's sex, because the male barking deer's canines are elongated into tusks. The species still roams the Ma River valley, and in fact we were able to buy a skull of a recently killed barking deer from a local man who had hunted it for food. By comparing the fossil tooth with one from the recent individual, it was easy to see that they were the same species; yet the fossil molar was much larger, which might indicate a decreasing trend in the animal's size since the middle Pleistocene. Barking deer are very small deer, averaging 20 to 22 inches in height at the shoulder, which inhabit the forests of India and Southeast Asia. The males have unusual antlers, set on top of bony pedestals protruding from the tops of their skulls. The animal's name derives from the deep barking sound it makes during breeding season and when alarmed by a predator.

By examining LT I-52, a lower premolar from the giant panda, *Ailuropoda melanoleuca,* we can tell a great deal about Ba Thuoc in the middle Pleistocene. Today, the giant panda is confined to the uplands of central China, in montane forests where dense stands of bamboo grow. From this distinctive premolar, we can say right away that the range of the giant panda circa 500,000 B.P. was significantly greater than it is today, in both the geographic and the ecological sense: Ba Thuoc is more than a thousand miles south of the current range of the giant panda, and it has a climate that is considerably more tropical. When we come to consider why and how *Gigantopithecus* may have become extinct, the giant panda will be discussed in detail.

From cave two, we recovered LT II-200, the enamel ridges of a partial lower molar of *Stegodon orientalis. Stegodon* is an extinct elephantlike creature that lived in Asia during the Pliocene and Pleistocene. *Stegodon* was somewhat larger than the living African elephant, and had large recurved tusks that could reach thirteen feet in length. Though it lived side by side with the ancestors of the surviving Asiatic elephant, it produced no living descendant species. A single tooth of *Stegodon* may have as many as fourteen ridges; the interstices are filled with cement. Looking down on the biting surface of the tooth, the ridges appear to be made of a series of cones of enamel. *Stegodon* teeth are so distinctive that a few ridges suffice to make the identification.

LT IV-132, a partial lower molar of the Malay tapir,

Tapirus indicus, was excavated from the soft breccia of the floor of cave four. The molar teeth of the tapir are identified by heavy cross-ridges, arranged in pairs. Tapirs are browsers and spend much of their time eating aquatic vegetation and the leaves, green shoots, and fruits of low-growing plants near water sources; thus their teeth are adapted for grinding. They have a very peculiar upper lip, which forms a short trunk with the nostrils located on the tip, making it especially well adapted for foraging for vegetation along the swampy river courses of southern Asia. Tapirs have short legs and heavy bodies, sometimes reaching a weight of nearly 700 pounds. Their closest living relative is the rhinoceros, but when they are submerged in water they behave much more like hippopotamuses. Today, Old World tapirs are found only in southern Burma and Thailand, the Malay peninsula, and the island of Sumatra. The presence of the tapir in Vietnam and South China in the Pleistocene, and its subsequent disappearance from the area, sounds remarkably similar to what happened to the giant panda.

In the softened breccia of the floor of cave four we also unearthed a large number of teeth of the orangutan, *Pongo pygmaeus.* One characteristic specimen is LT IV-335, a large upper third molar. Orangutan teeth are easy to identify; they are shaped like human teeth but are generally larger and have very crenulated (that is, minutely crenelated) enamel on the chewing surfaces. Because of the common occurrence of orangutan teeth throughout sites in Vietnam, Le Trung Kha has suggested that they might be useful for comparative dating purposes. Kha has found that orangutan molars gradually reduce in size and in the degree of enamel crenulation from the middle Pleistocene to the late Pleistocene. Orangutans, which are today found only on the uninhabited parts of the islands of Borneo and Sumatra, are the largest arboreal creatures in the world, weighing up to 200 pounds. They have developed unique hooklike hands and prehensile feet, allowing them to hang in trees tirelessly for hours, feeding on fruits, buds, and flowers. Even when they are frightened by predators, orangutans move very slowly through the forest canopy, making them easy prey for hunters. The changing patterns of distribution of the giant panda, the tapir, and the orangutan offer some tantalizing possibilities about what might have happened to *Gigantopithecus,* which we shall explore in a later chapter.

End of the Season

On January 20, we took our only field trip of the season, a twelve-mile hike to Dieu Rock Shelter, one of the most important prehistoric sites in Southeast Asia. It was a gray, misty day that continually threatened but never delivered rain. The route to Dieu Rock Shelter was on the far side of the Ma River, through a lushly beautiful valley, terraced for rice and tea cultivation. The shelter itself was a slightly overhanging cliff that served as a human habitation for thousands of years. In 1986, a joint excavation here was undertaken by a Bulgarian-Vietnamese team. Digging a trench to a depth of about twelve

Our last day at Lang Trang. Front row *(from left to right)*, Ken Garrett, Le Trung Kha, Jamie James, Pham Lan Huong, Nguyen Van Binh; standing, Ha Nguyen Diem, Dang Huu Luu, Katerina Semendeferi, John Olsen, Mary Kay Gilliland Olsen, Russell Ciochon, Nguyen Van Hao. *(Photograph by Jamie James)*

feet, they uncovered fourteen Hoabinhian burials and one possible Sonvian burial. Subsequent carbon-14 dating put the site at 18,000 to 9,000 B.P. In 1987 Vietnamese archaeologists from the Institute of Archaeology continued excavating there on their own.

We arrived at a rather bizarre cultural impasse on our way home. We stopped for lunch at the principal village near the rock shelter, where we went through the usual tea ceremony with the local chiefs. Then we were installed in a large house to eat the picnic lunch we had brought with us. We had just enough food for our whole party, but when we tried to share it with the Vietnamese, they nervously refused. Binh quietly asked us to save them some for later, for they were expected to share with the hosts. Thus we were made to feel terribly selfish for eating our ham and peanut butter and granola bars—after a hike of some seven or eight miles—because we had not brought enough to feed the entire village. Meanwhile, our Vietnamese friends and the local people shared a miserable-looking gruel.

On the drive back to Hanoi, we had our first serious disagreement with the Vietnamese, specifically with Professor Hao, which came close to undoing all that we had accomplished over three years of collaboration. It was a typical quarrel; the particulars sound ridiculous now, but at the time we were all convinced that there was a principle at stake worth fighting for. Hao had arranged for us to stay at the hotel in Thanh Hoa City that night, yet we wanted to go back to Hanoi so we could have a full schedule of work and meetings the next day. The hotel in Thanh Hoa City is a squalid, mildewy place, with no hot water, and the rates, owing to our status as "honored foreign guests," were laughably inflated. It was about a three-hour drive to Hanoi on the best road in north Vietnam; we would have made it back well before midnight.

Nonetheless, Hao had much to recommend his position driving in Vietnam at night is no doubt considered a highly eccentric practice—but instead of reasoning with us, he took the irritating attitude that he was the titular head of the expedition, and we must do as he said. The hotel had no guests, nor did it look as though it had had any for a long while. Perhaps Hao had promised the local authorities that he would bring them some dollars and would have lost face, that most precious of Asian commodities, if he had not come through. For whatever reason, Hao made it clear, as we all stood in the middle of the parking lot of the hotel, shouting and gesticulating at each other, that if we did not stay the night at this hotel, our collaboration was at an end. We stayed. Hao ended up paying for it himself, but he had won his victory. We were awakened at five-thirty A.M. by the blare of propaganda-cum-calisthenics over loudspeakers in the public square and were on the road before first light. In our last days in Vietnam we hammered out another agreement, which called for us to continue our joint excavation at Lang Trang and to scout other sites in Thanh Hoa province. In addition, Olsen and Ciochon promised to sponsor visits to their universities by Professors Hao and Kha. After a good night's sleep, everyone felt a bit sheepish about the scene in the parking lot, and apologies were made and accepted all round.

If there were any lingering traces of bitterness, they were banished the next day when a cable from Hong Kong arrived at the Institute of Archaeology announcing that a videocassette recorder and color television monitor were due to arrive later that week at Haiphong. An important part of our "baksheesh" package that year was the promise to the Vietnamese of a television and VCR, which Judith Moses had generously offered to supply out of her budget. It was an enormous hit, but perhaps not the best precedent; after that, we kept hearing hints about video cameras and personal computers and other items that were way out of line. We found ourselves in a typical American dilemma: we wanted to be seen as the lavish dispensers of manna, but resented it when our friends began to show evidence of the very materialism that we were inadvertently inculcating.

Five months later, when James and Ciochon returned to Hanoi for a brief visit, they made an interesting discovery. We arrived at the institute around ten o'clock in the morning, and the place seemed to be deserted: no one was in the library, no one was in the little office that served as the reception. When we walked round to the lecture hall, we saw a roomful of people watching a violent Hong Kong–made *kung-fu* movie on the VCR we had given the institute. We found Binh in his office, and asked him what was going on. He told us that the institute had set up a video theater in the lecture hall, charging admission to the public for showings of popular films. Among others, he said, they had tapes of *The Killing Fields* and *Platoon*. And that was just the half of it: the institute had also set up a copy shop with the photocopying machine that we had given them before, another little capitalist venture that was earning some much-needed cash. Somehow, one suspects that that was not exactly what Ho Chi Minh had in mind when he created the Institute of Archaeology! At first we were slightly scandalized, but on second thought it seemed quite enterprising of them. We were reminded of a joke told by Ken Garrett:

> Q: What is the new definition of communism?
> A: The long, hard road back to capitalism.

CHAPTER 9

The Date

Concepts of Time

The popular image of the archaeologist begins with colorful personalities like Heinrich Schliemann and Howard Carter, and comes down to us through a venerable tradition of Hollywood B movies and trashy dime novels, khakis and pith helmet intact. In the great moment of discovery, typically, the archaeologist forces his way into a dusty tomb, playing a dim torch over the fabulous treasure of some long-lost civilization; or, closer to our own field, while tramping through the Gobi Desert the intrepid explorer stumbles across a skeleton of a huge dinosaur in the cliffs of an ancient riverbed.

Such romantic discoveries still do take place occasionally, but these days scientists are more likely to make the real breakthroughs far from the field, while reviewing numerical readouts from a laboratory test, or while making an unusual comparative analysis of some disparate samples, or, most frequently, while simply *thinking*. In modern archaeology and paleoanthropology the interest lies not in the objects themselves but in the stories they tell, the information they contain, the answers they can provide to the questions that the archaeologist may be asking. One of the central questions an archaeologist will ask about a site, often the principal one, is "How old is it?" We have seen how index fossils can provide a very loose time frame for a locality: if you are coming up with *Tyrannosaurus rex,* you can bet the farm that you will not find

Homo erectus there (the Flintstones and Alley Oop notwith-standing). Yet index fossils can only provide a rough estimate of the date of a site. To get a more precise temporal fix on a site, you must subject a specimen from the locality to one of the sophisticated lab tests that are now at an archaeologist's disposal.

In these terms, our great discovery from Lang Trang, our equivalent of the golden treasure of Tutankhamen, is a hum-ble pig tooth from Lang Trang I. We brought it back from Vietnam and gave it to Henry Schwarcz of McMaster Univer-sity, in Hamilton, Ontario, who is one of the leading exponents of a new dating technique called electron-spin resonance (ESR). Subjecting that pig tooth, rather common and dull in itself, to ESR, Schwarcz was able to date it, and the Lang Trang site, to 440,000 to 520,000 B.P. The importance of this date cannot be overstressed: the antiquity of Lang Trang makes it one of the most important prehistoric sites in Asia.

Having gone to such pains in an earlier chapter to say that older is not necessarily better, we can still say that when some-thing turns out to be much older than one expects, as was the case at Lang Trang, then older is definitely more interesting. Now, how old is old? As usual, it is all relative. Our under-standing of the dates we can give to archaeological and paleoanthropological sites is only as good as our understanding of the dating techniques themselves, and of the concepts of time that underlie them.

In our ordinary lives, the only temporal concept we need is the conventional one, which views time as unwinding evenly and inexorably into the future, like a spool of ribbon, or a road that leads predictably ever onward. Yet archaeologists and paleoanthropologists generally think of time in two differ-ent ways: absolute, or chronometric, time, and relative time. The distinctions between them are important, since each per-forms a different function in archaeological interpretations. Examples of absolute time are dates generated by techniques derived from chemistry or physics, such as carbon-14, potassium-argon, and, in this case, by electron-spin resonance. They yield a specific point in time, albeit with a standard deviation that can range as high as hundreds of thousands of years. Like the date on a letter, they tell us how old something is in concrete and straightforward terms. Such a universal deter-

mination of age is important, because it helps to establish
global relationships.

Relative dating is a different approach, and is as old as
archaeology itself. It yields only statements like "This object is
older than [or not as old as] that object." Unlike absolute
dating, relative dating does not determine the actual age of
anything. Relative dating is useful, since it can establish se-
quences in the field, where chemical or isotopic laboratory
techniques cannot be applied. Relative dating is also the
basis for an approach such as seriation, or sequence dating,
which seeks to order like objects according to their degree of
similarity.

In most circumstances, archaeologists and paleoanthropologists employ both absolute and relative dating techniques.
One reason is that sophisticated lab methods such as electron-
spin resonance are very expensive, and can take months to
yield results. Usually, the question of an object's absolute age is
not terribly important; the establishment of temporal relationships among artifacts suffices. Also, one must be cautious when
dealing with dates ascribed by different scientists, using different techniques, working in different scientific fields and under
different circumstances.

The Asian Problem

That caveat is particularly applicable to research in Asia, where
fossil dates have been notoriously unreliable. The dating problem in Asia goes back to the very beginning of paleontology,
with the first discovery of *Homo erectus* in Java by Eugene
Dubois in the 1890's. Our difficulties began with the way in
which many such discoveries were made. Early collectors like
Dubois and Ralph von Koenigswald often relied on the local
people to find and collect hominid and other mammalian fossils, making it very difficult to determine the precise strati-
graphic position of the discoveries. In some cases, the native
workers would actually conceal the precise locality of discovery:
because they were being paid bonuses for every fossil they
found, it was in their economic interest to keep the informa-

tion to themselves, so they could secretly return to good sites in the hope of turning up more lucrative finds. Dubois and Koenigswald were able to collect vast numbers of fossils, but their proper associations and relationships were usually distorted or lost. Koenigswald attempted to remedy this inadequacy by dividing the fossils into three "time range" groups, called, from earliest to latest, Djetis fauna, Trinil fauna, and Ngandong fauna.

Context became even more problematic when Koenigswald began to purchase fossils from Chinese pharmacies, for in those cases localities and time ranges were completely unknown. He tried to estimate the antiquity of these dragon teeth collections on the basis of the percentage of surviving species represented. If one set of fossils contained a higher proportion of living species than another, which had more extinct species, it was adjudged to be younger; it would be labeled "late" Pleistocene, while the older one would be called "middle" Pleistocene, though at that point they were only words, assigned almost arbitrarily.

As more fossil mammalian faunas were discovered in India and China, it was necessary to develop a system for comparing them with the older discoveries made in Indonesia, in order to determine their relative ages and thus to identify what were called "faunal heartlands" of certain key species. Von K created two arbitrary faunal groupings: the Sino-Malayan, for species with Chinese affinities, and the Siva-Malayan, for species with Indian affinities. They were compared with the Djetis and Trinil faunas, as well as with other Asian faunas, in order to determine temporal relationships and possible migration routes for the key species.

Two basic flaws are immediately discernible in all these systems of faunal comparison in Asia. First, there was often imprecise control, or no control at all, over the type localities of the various sites, which meant that some of the faunal groups likely represented mixed assemblages. Second, all the dates that were given to named faunas and particular sites were relative dates. Of course, reliable absolute dating methods were not available until 1948, when carbon-14 was developed; then, in 1960, potassium-argon came along. Before these technologies, paleontologists all over the world faced the same problem: there was simply no other way to date fauna except relatively. Any attempt at absolute dating always resorted to the highly imprecise method of comparing the proportions of living species.

All that has changed since the introduction of the potassium/ argon (K/Ar) method, which has wrought a revolution in the field of archaeological and paleoanthropological dating. Carbon-14, while excellent for relatively late sites, was useless for dating a specimen older than about 50,000 years. Yet with K/Ar dating it was possible for the first time to get dates going far back in time, to the middle Pleistocene and beyond. Potassium/ argon dating determines age by measuring the amount of argon gas produced by the decay of radioactive potassium, which occurs whenever volcanic rock is formed.

Once a volcanic rock layer was dated, the fossil faunas recovered from immediately below that layer could be directly tied to the date: in other words, the great desideratum, an absolute date for fossil fauna, had been achieved. It is an excellent technique, and has produced some important results at the major hominid sites in eastern Africa, such as Olduvai Gorge, East Lake Turkana, and the Afar Depression. Donald Johanson used potassium-argon to date Lucy. However, the technique can only be used where there is volcanic rock, which happens to be plentiful in Ethiopia. Even in other places in Africa where volcanic rock was lacking, it was possible to date faunas relatively with pretty good results through direct comparisons with the fauna that had been absolutely dated.

The geologists who dated the important sites in Africa tried to apply the same methods to the famous hominid sites of Asia, but it did not work because of the scarcity of volcanic rock, the sine qua non of K/Ar technology. One *Homo erectus* site in Java, Modjokerto, was dated to the late Pliocene because it was thought to be located close to a volcanic pumice tuff that was K/Ar-dated to 1.9 million years B.P. But unlike horseshoes, close does not count in paleontology: for years, Asian paleoanthropologists tried to use the 1.9 million B.P. date to establish a very great antiquity for *Homo* in Asia, but in the end, it was discovered that the dated volcanic tuff was stratigraphically quite far removed from the *Homo erectus* site, which made any attempt to date the Java hominids on the basis of this K/Ar age determination totally unfounded. Throughout India, China, and Southeast Asia the same problem emerged: there simply were no hominid fossils in close association with datable volcanic rock. By comparison with the firmly dated African sites, Asian paleontology seemed so vague: the only thing anyone could ever say was that Fossil A is most likely older than Fossil B, which looks sort of like Fossil X, which we think is not quite as old as Fossil Z. All of which added up to the fact that no one knew how old *any* of the stuff really was. Clearly, what was needed was a reliable, accurate absolute dating method that did not require the presence of volcanic rock.

A New Technique

Enter electron-spin resonance. As pioneered by our colleague Henry Schwarcz, ESR uses as its primary material for analysis apatite, the stuff of fossil teeth. Teeth are ubiquitous in archaeological and paleoanthropological localities. It is safe to say that if you do not find any fossil teeth at a site, then you will not find anything, that you in fact do not have a site, for tooth enamel is the most durable substance in the bodies of most animals, including man, and it mineralizes readily into fossil. Furthermore, ESR is theoretically even more secure than other methods, for rather than dating the specimen's matrix, the soil or other depositional material surrounding it, as is the case with the potassium/argon technique, with ESR you are dating the thing itself.

Electron-spin resonance has actually been around for about thirty years, but it was not used for dating purposes until ten years ago, when Motoji Ikeya of Osaka University first adapted the technique for that purpose. Since then, it has become the hottest technique in the field. Henry Schwarcz and his associate, the German physicist Reiner Grün, who is now at Cambridge University, have revolutionized the field with their applications of ESR dating, and some of the dates they have gotten have been surprising enough to shake some basic assumptions of field researchers.

Electron-spin resonance depends upon the elementary principle that the best dating method is one that measures a process that begins precisely at the moment of deposition and halts at the moment of recovery by the excavator. That is just what ESR does, and the process it measures is the radioactive bombardment that an object undergoes when it is deposited in the earth. Henry Schwarcz, who is able to explain the somewhat arcane theoretical underpinnings of ESR technology with admirable clarity and eloquence, likens the process that the deposited object undergoes to what happens to the dosimeters worn by X-ray technicians and other laboratory technicians working in radioactive environments. A dosimeter is a device, usually in the form of a badge, that measures and displays the accumulated dosage of radioactivity to which the wearer has been exposed.

Any soil or sediment into which an object is deposited is weakly radioactive. The level of radioactivity is quite low, but it is always enough to build up a significant and measurable signal over the course of thousands of years. This radioactive bombardment is due primarily to the presence in the matrix of the three naturally occurring elements that produce radioactivity: uranium, potassium, and thorium. They are always present to some degree in any deposition; according to Schwarcz, one of the basic laws of geochemistry is "There's a little bit of everything in anything." The level of radioactivity in a sample can sometimes be substantially increased by cosmic ray bombardment, which complicates things considerably; however, fortunately for us, specimens deposited in caves are very well insulated from cosmic rays, and we may leave that factor aside.

Constant exposure to radioactivity causes "damage" at the atomic level, and that is what electron-spin resonance measures. There are two ways of measuring that damage: the first, called thermoluminescence, is a well-established method, but it does not work on teeth, so it is useless for sites like Lang Trang, where the great majority of the specimens recovered are, in fact, teeth. Yet teeth are exactly what ESR does date best. As radioactive bombardment takes place, electrons are knocked off their shells, and they become trapped in the crystals of apatite, the mineral that constitutes animal teeth. It happens that apatite is especially efficient at trapping those free electrons, which makes it a good "dosimeter" and thus an apt subject for ESR.

The formula that Henry Schwarcz uses to calculate the age of a specimen is T = AD/DR, where T is time, measured in years; AD is the accumulated dose, the amount of radiation in the tooth; and DR is the dose rate, the amount of radiation that the specimen receives in one year of deposition. To find the accumulated dose, Schwarcz takes a measurement of the radioactive signal in the tooth with the ESR spectrometer, at the Department of Geology at McMaster University. The terms of the result are purely arbitrary, says Schwarcz, usually the height in centimeters of the spectrometer's printout of the radioactive signal reading. By itself it means nothing except that some amount of radioactivity is present.

Then, using the cobalt-60 radiation source of the university's nuclear reactor, Schwarz subjects the tooth to a massive, carefully controlled dose of radioactivity, generally several hundred thousand rads. (The rad is the unit of energy used to measure radiation; one rad equals one hundred ergs per gram of irradiated material.) The radioactive signal of the tooth is then measured a second time, and after measuring the increase in radioactivity created by the control dose, Schwarcz is able to calculate algebraically the power in rads of the original level of radioactivity—the accumulated dose created during the period of deposition.

The dosage rate is determined by an analysis of the matrix. The best and the easiest way—some say the only way, but Schwarcz disagrees with them—is to measure the radioactivity in the matrix at the site, as the specimen is recovered. The alternative method, used for dating our pig tooth from Lang Trang, is to perform a spectrographic analysis on a matrix sample to determine the concentrations of uranium, potassium, and thorium. Schwarcz maintains that the dosage rate can be determined with a high degree of precision by this method.

The great advantage of ESR, as we have seen, is that it can be applied to virtually all archaeological and paleoanthropological sites. The disadvantage is the somewhat greater degree of uncertainty of the date. That is not to say that the date might be wrong, only that the precision of the date, the extent to which it must be modified by the terms of a standard deviation, may not be as sharp as in other dating methods. Schwarcz has not yet ascertained the standard deviation at our site, but at his other ESR-dated sites, standard deviations typically range from ±5 percent to ±15 percent. That may not seem terribly high, but carbon-14 dating, by comparison, routinely achieves results with a ±1 percent standard deviation, although the carbon-14 method is not applicable to a site of the antiquity of Lang Trang.

Of course, we did not know that in the beginning. Prior to the dating of the sample from Lang Trang I by electron-spin resonance, we gave some tooth samples from Lang Trang to the carbon-14 laboratory at the University of Arizona, where they were subjected to nitrogen and glycerine analyses, which determined that less than one percent of the original protein remained. This was much too low to date, even by this highly advanced carbon-14 laboratory. That chemical analysis was our first indication that the fauna from Lang Trang might be quite old. Since carbon-14 dates can go back as far as 50,000 years on bone samples, we knew that our sample was much older than that—and the ESR method now confirms an age ten times the span measurable by carbon-14 dating.

To have a meaningful understanding of what an ESR date means, one must have a precise understanding of the concept of standard deviation. If we say that the date of a specimen is 500,000 years, ±10 percent, that does not mean that there is a 90 percent chance that the object is 500,000 years old; nor does it mean that it is between 450,000 and 550,000 years old (although either of those statements might turn out to be true). Standard deviation is the term used in statistics to express the chances of error, and it is derived from a geometric, rather than an arithmetical, analysis of the probabilities. That means, in our hypothetical case, there is a 67 percent chance that the date falls within one standard deviation of the mean, i.e. between 450,000 and 550,000, and a 95 percent chance that it falls within two standard deviations of the mean, between 400,000 and 600,000 years. The greater the number of dated samples from a site, generally, the smaller the standard deviation.

Schwarcz and Grün (they jokingly call themselves the Black and Green Team) have come up with several dates that were profound shocks to the field researchers who had sought their aid. Among the sites that have had to be substantially rethought after being dated by electron-spin resonance is Qafzeh, an important *Homo sapiens sapiens* locality in Israel, just down the hill from Nazareth. A skull from Qafzeh, thought to be the earliest known specimen of anatomically modern *Homo sapiens,* had been relatively dated to 50,000 B.P. Throughout the 1980's most human evolution textbooks accepted that date and the Qafzeh skull as the earliest evidence of modern man. Yet ESR dating puts the skull's age at nearly 100,000 years. Clearly, this doubly ancient date has profound implications for our thinking about the timing of human evolution, which are still being evaluated and interpreted.

Another site where electron-spin resonance has come up with a date radically different from what was expected is Bilzingsleben, an early hominid site in Germany. The age of the site had been thought to be about 200,000 years B.P.; again, ESR doubled the age, to 400,000 years. Lest anyone get the idea that the method always tends to push the date back into greater antiquity, Schwarcz cites Monte Circeo, a famous Neanderthal burial site in Italy, where remains previously thought to be 100,000 years old have been redated by ESR to about 60,000 years.

The importance of all this is still being sorted out. We must be cautious, yet we must also be logical. The theoretical underpinnings of electron-spin resonance are secure, and Schwarcz's dates are as close to a verifiable absolute date as we are able to find in any quarter. If the dates we get from ESR shake up our preconceived notions, so be it. Sometimes a good shaking up is just what science needs.

In our own case, the ESR date on Lang Trang has had a profound influence on our interpretation of the locality. For the first time in Asia, a Pleistocene fauna group including hominids has been absolutely dated. Before our expedition to Ba Thuoc, the known sites of *Homo erectus* in Asia were those in China (at Zhoukoudian and some other sites, including Lantian, in Shaanxi province; Hexian, Anhui province; and Yuanmou, Yunnan), and various localities in Java, including Eugene Dubois's original discovery at Trinil and Koenigswald's finds at Sangiran (see map in front matter of this book). Positioned where it is, midway beyond the two established zones of *Homo erectus* discoveries, Lang Trang offers an important link in our knowledge of the first migration of man into Asia. The antiquity of Lang Trang also makes an immense amount of sense if one accepts the African genesis, as virtually everyone does, for Southeast Asia lies directly in the path of an eastward human migration from Africa; having reached the vicinity of Lang Trang, our ancestors might then have migrated north, to Zhoukoudian, and south, to Java. And even beyond the fact that Lang Trang now has the oldest dated hominids in Southeast Asia, its thirty-odd mammalian species will likely become benchmarks for relative comparisons of other undated cave faunas throughout Asia.

Remember our metaphor for the pursuit of the prehistoric past as an attempt to reconstruct a mosaic where most of the tiles are missing, and we do not know the design we are ultimately trying to put together. Our goal is to make connections between the sites that we do know, and to generalize from that limited knowledge. An excavator, however intrepid and hard-working, can only do a finite amount of digging in a lifetime, and one must hope for some luck.

By all appearances, we have had a bit of luck: we may have found the piece that fits right into the center of the human mosaic.

CHAPTER 10

"Fingerprinting" Giganto

A Good Question

The other important investigative tool besides ESR that we have applied to our work in Vietnam started out very much as a side issue. A principal difficulty confronting paleoanthropologists in their efforts to explain how a species such as *Gigantopithecus* adapted and the process by which it became extinct, is the lack of solid evidence about the diets of fossil animals. Evolutionary biologists are in general agreement that one of the principal reasons, if not the main one, for a species to become extinct is the lack in the environment of enough of the right foods to support the animal's population. Certainly there are other possible causes, such as disease, drought, and, as we shall see, being hunted, and thus *becoming* food.

Yet regardless of what sort of theoretical model one is developing, a major question to be asked and answered is, What did the animal eat? When one is dealing with a contemporary species, it is easy enough to answer: field observations can be made of wild animals on their daily rounds, and the contents of the stomach of a dead specimen may be analyzed and a rather exact picture drawn of the diet. However, when a species exists only as a fossil form, it has always been assumed that no primary evidence exists to form the basis of a dietary profile. (Strictly speaking, that is not really true, since there have been a few isolated cases, mostly fishes, in which the fossilized remains of meals, undigested at the time of death,

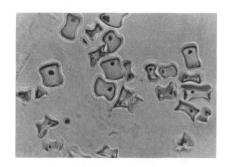

Bamboo phytoliths seen through a light microscope at a magnification of 400×.
(Photograph by Bob Thompson)

have been found in the digestive tract. Yet nothing of the kind has ever been found among mammals in a tropical climate.) Now, because of our work with phytoliths, paleontologists are able to detect first hand what fossil animals ate.

Phytoliths are microscopic pieces of silica—that is, silicon dioxide, SiO_2—that enter a plant by absorption through its root system and, for reasons that remain largely unknown, solidify inside and between the cells of the stems, leaves, and fruits. The phytolith thus takes on the shape of the plant cell by forming a silica impression of it. The existence of phytoliths has been known since the early nineteenth century. It was long believed that only certain plants, such as grasses, had phytoliths, but we now know that many sorts of plants contain them, including ferns, trees, and fruits. Phytoliths in some parts of the plant are different in appearance in every species in which they exist, just as the cells of different plant species are distinct from one another. They might be described as the fingerprints, on a cellular scale, of plant species. Phytolith studies have grown tremendously over the past twenty years or so, and we can now use the phytolith record to identify many plants.

As far as we know, no one had ever suggested applying the phytolith record to fossils until one wintry afternoon at the University of Iowa, when Russell Ciochon was lecturing about the evolution of *Gigantopithecus*. Among the many points covered in his lecture was his working assumption that Giganto's diet had consisted primarily of bamboo. He had arrived at this conclusion on the basis of the massiveness of the ape's jaw and the unusual wear patterns exhibited by its front teeth, and by the logical assumption that such large animals would have needed to consume a great quantity of *something*, and bamboo was the something in the greatest abundance in Giganto's environment. Yet that was only an assumption, a theory built up from a tissue of second-hand inferences and analogy to fill in the dietary blank of a fossil animal. After the lecture, one of the graduate students in the audience, an enthusiastic, long-haired Minnesotan interested in New World archaeology named Bob Thompson, came up to Ciochon and asked an interesting question:

"Professor Ciochon, since bamboo is known to have a high phytolith content, isn't it possible that some of them might be found adhering to the teeth of *Gigantopithecus*, if the animal was eating bamboo?"

It was a very good question. Like every scientific advance, this one started as a question, startlingly simple and direct, containing an original idea. One of the problems in the modern academic community is the extent to which the sciences have become compartmentalized: in a modern university, there are people who study fossils, and people who study phytoliths. Even if their offices are next door to each other, as scientists they are miles apart. Sometimes it takes a student, not yet indoctrinated into the esoteric workings of the academic machine, to make the ingenious connections that are required to advance science, as opposed to merely keep it drifting along.

The phytolith literature had already been applied quite successfully to stone tools: it is not quite a standard practice, but many archaeologists have examined the cutting surfaces of Paleolithic tools with the scanning-electron microscope, in search of phytoliths and the distinctive polishes they inflict on tools. If you found oak phytoliths on the edge of a stone ax, then you knew you were dealing with a tool that had been used to cut oak. No one had thought of trying the technique on fossil teeth, yet there was no reason why exactly the same principle might not be applied to the thousand-plus fossil teeth of Giganto, in order to see what those particular apes had dined upon in their final meal.

A Botanical "Fingerprint"

Phytoliths come into being because nearly all plants, everywhere, absorb silica in the groundwater that supplies them with the nutrients that keep them alive. The silica they absorb comes in the form of monosilicic acid, a ubiquitous, soluble form of the mineral created by the weathering of feldspar. The monosilicic acid comes through the roots and is carried upward by the plant's vascular system to the so-called aerial organs—leaves, stems, branches, and flowers. Some of the monosilicic acid solidifies in the cells: the results are called phytoliths.

The word was coined in 1846 by Christian Ehrenberg, a German scientist specializing in microscopy, and throughout the rest of the nineteenth century his countrymen continued to expand the identification of phytolith types particular to various plant species. Yet it had remained something of a hidden literature, scarcely known at all outside Germany until fairly recently. Many questions are still completely without answers. Why do certain plants produce phytoliths, while others do not? One hypothesis is that it is a defense mechanism. Plants that produce many phytoliths, particularly grasses, are less attractive as foods to many animals because of the mineral quality of the silicate particles: for example, phytoliths are what cause a blade of grass to cut the skin when a finger is brushed against it.

As the promise of applying the phytolith literature to fossil teeth became apparent, in 1988 we sought out the help of Dolores Piperno, a paleoecologist who has studied in Central America at the Smithsonian Tropical Research Institute in Panama for many years. Piperno, an outspoken and articulate archaeologist who spent ten years of preparatory work staring at phytoliths through a microscope, now studies the effect of the tropical environment upon human adaptations in prehistoric and early historic populations. Her interest in phytoliths originated in her attempts to find them in soils and sediments. She chose to look for phytoliths principally, she says, because they were something good to look for. As a rule, their state of preservation is remarkable: being pure mineral, they are the most durable, and thus the most widespread, plant fossil of all the botanical elements that one might seek out. The things are practically indestructible.

Piperno was intrigued by the possibility of finding phytoliths on the fossil teeth of *Gigantopithecus,* and brought her expertise to bear on the subject. The four teeth chosen for study—upper incisor, lower canine, lower premolar, and lower molar—were borrowed from the British Museum (Natural History) in London and the Forschungsinstitut Senckenberg, a research institute and natural history museum in Frankfurt. Because of his interest in the project, Bob Thompson was sent to London and Frankfurt in February 1988 to begin the phytolith study of *Gigantopithecus.* His enthusiastic description of the project was enough to convince the museum curators in Europe to let him borrow the teeth for further study at the University of Iowa, where there is a center for electron-microscopy research that has state-of-the-art scanning-electron microscopes (SEM). As a control, the teeth of other mammalian species, both extinct and surviving, were also analyzed for the presence of phytoliths.

Before the SEM study could be carried out, the teeth were thoroughly cleaned, to ensure that what we found was definitely part of the fossil and not something that came along and adhered to the teeth at a later date. First, they were immersed in a solution of Alconox, a laboratory cleaning agent, for twenty-four hours. The second step was to soak the fossils in 3 percent dilute solution of hydrochloric acid for two hours, to remove carbonate-bonded particles and any other residual surface materials. Then they were rinsed with distilled (and hence mineral-free) water, and kept in a container that had itself been cleaned by the same processes.

Each *Gigantopithecus* tooth was then mounted on an SEM stub, the device used to position a specimen in the vacuum chamber of the microscope, and blown clean with canned air immediately before insertion. The instrument we used was a Hitachi S-570, which is mostly used for analysis of the microcellular structure of tissue samples from the university medical school hospital. The advantage of this particular model is that it can examine specimens at very low energy levels, without one having to coat them with gold and palladium, as is sometimes required for SEM examination. When this coating is removed, it can sometimes take a bit of the enamel surface from the sample with it—far too grave a risk for specimens as fragile and rare as the *Gigantopithecus* teeth.

The whole tooth was scanned at low magnifications, from $60\times$ to $500\times$. Phytoliths first became visible at around $350\times$; then higher magnifications were used, up to $5,000\times$, to enlarge the phytolith images and photograph them. When we found a phytolith, we noted its position on the tooth, so that we could relocate it on subsequent observations. To establish that the images we found were indeed phytoliths, we used X-ray microanalysis to determine the elemental composition of the structures, and a silica dot map to illustrate on a black photographic plate the elemental shapes of each one. What we were doing, in essence, was creating an elemental atlas of the teeth and mapping on them the positions of the phytoliths.

What Did Giganto Eat?

At least thirty structures that were indisputably phytoliths were found on the Giganto teeth, most of them on the molar from the British Museum (Natural History). The phytoliths we found were from two kinds of plants, and also from different plant organs: first, the vegetative parts of grasses, and second, the fruits and seeds of dicotyledons. Grass phytoliths are for the most part long and needlelike; we found a group of them on the British molar. Another type of grass phytolith is the bulliform-cell phytolith. "Bulliform" means puckered, and these structures somewhat resemble cooked ravioli. Unfortunately, these particular grass phytoliths can only be identified to the family level. While this finding is consistent with Ciochon's hypothesis that *Gigantopithecus* subsisted on a diet of bamboo (which is, of course, a grass), it cannot be adduced as a proof in its support, for bamboo is a particular subfamily of grasses.

The whole issue of the shape and variety of phytolith structures is a problematic one, much more loaded with questions than answers. In the first place, there is no satisfactory (or, for that matter, unsatisfactory) explanation of why certain plants produce phytoliths while others do not. Then there is the matter of why it is that phytoliths take the shapes that they do. Sometimes they take forms that echo the shapes of the cells, as in the case of some of the grass phytoliths, which are long and thin like their "hosts." In other cases phytoliths bear little physical resemblance to the "host" cell, yet are still uniformly identifiable. As phytolith studies continue to grow, it will be possible to make more precise identifications.

The study of phytoliths is still a relatively new field, and the literature is growing at an exponential rate. One problem is the dearth of plant samples to use as type specimens, especially from isolated places such as Vietnam. Whenever we were driving in the countryside, Ciochon was continually stopping the car to snip leaves and stems from plants on the side of the road, which he stuffed into plastic bags to bring back to Dolores Piperno to use for phytolith typing. The chambermaids at our hotels in Hanoi and Bangkok were always laying siege to the faintly stinking collection of drying fruits and husks that he had spread out on his dresser.

The other group of phytoliths found in our analysis of the Giganto specimens was described by Piperno as being conical-to-hat shaped. These, she believes, come from dicotyledons, perhaps from the fruits of trees. Phytoliths from dicotyledons show enormous variety and seem to be assignable to individual genera and even to species. Piperno has surveyed the phytolith literature—some 1,300 tropical plants have now been catalogued—and has come up with some close analogues to the Giganto dicotyledons. She now tentatively identifies them as fruits from a tree of the family Moraceae.

These fruits are quite possibly durians, or jack-fruit, which are common throughout tropical Southeast Asia. On a visit to Cambodia in the summer of 1989, James and Ciochon visited a durian plantation in the southern port town of Kampot. The fruit of the tree is a woody pod more than a foot in length, covered in coarse spines. The edible part of the durian is a sticky white flesh that surrounds the seeds. The fruit gives off a powerful odor that most people find disgusting; it is clearly an acquired taste. Our hosts at the plantation in Kampot took great delight in presenting us with freshly-cut durian, knowing full well that we would not be able to stomach it. James refused

to touch it, saying it smelled like gasoline; Ciochon pretended
to like it and ate it for as long as he could bear. Even our
Vietnamese friends from Hanoi consider the fruit to be quite
strange, if not revolting. Yet Cambodians and some other Asians
consider durian a delicacy, and they are willing to pay high
prices for it, as are overseas Chinese and Thai people. Since this
large, smelly tropical fruit is difficult to ship, a single durian in
New York's Chinatown or the Thai markets of Los Angeles can
fetch as much as a hundred dollars. Durians clearly could not
have been the principal food source for Giganto, since there
are no more than three or four ounces of edible flesh per large
fruit. In any case, this evidence of possible durian sampling
among *Gigantopithecus* means that the animal's diet was more
varied than we had previously thought.

Now, the question arises as to why the phytoliths adhered
to the enamel surface. Indeed, can we be sure that they came
from something that the ape ate? In fact, the phytolith structure is firmly embedded in the enamel surface, almost as though
it is glued there, in much the same way that phytoliths stick to
the cutting surfaces of stone tools. A theory that has gained
some acceptance is that phytoliths become physically bonded to
the edges of stone tools by the combined action of friction and
moisture. An analogous process must be at work in the phytolith–
fossil tooth bond, by which the silicate structure is impressed
into the enamel as the plant is chewed. (The inorganic silica
composition of the phytolith is much harder than the tooth
enamel.)

Among the more fascinating images that we found as we
made our SEM tour of the tooth surface were several wear
striations. Silicon dioxide is a chemical compound that is
much harder than tooth enamel, and so as *Gigantopithecus*
masticated the phytolith-bearing plants, the silicate structure
scratched tiny tracks in the tooth surface. In one case, we
found the phytolith sitting astride the end of the track it had
just ploughed into the tooth—like a sled stopped in its path in
the snow.

An alternative scenario for explaining how phytoliths adhere to the tooth is that they may become lodged in the
depressions and fissures of the enamel surface of the tooth.
Since Giganto's dental hygiene was presumably not the best,

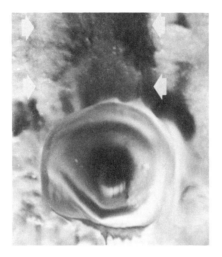

A phytolith from the Moraceae family on the surface of a Giganto tooth, photographed by a scanning-electron microscope, in the same place it has occupied for hundreds of thousands of years. The magnification is 5000 ×. The arrows indicate the track the phytolith has etched into the tooth's enamel surface. This phytolith might have come from the durian, a foul-smelling fruit of Southeast Asia. *(Photograph by Russell Ciochon and Dolores Piperno)*

they might have remained there for extended periods of time, which would have permitted them to bond with the enamel by a more gradual chemical process. In any case, the careful cleaning of the fossil teeth prior to SEM analysis, the direct association of wear striations with phytoliths, and this evidence for bonding all indicate that the phytoliths we found on the teeth of *Gigantopithecus* were from plants consumed during the lifetime of the animal from whose jaw the teeth came.

We were somewhat surprised by the result of our phytolith analysis. We had built a good case, by analogy and inference, that *Gigantopithecus* lived on a solid diet of bamboo. It is dangerous for a scientist to anticipate the results of his tests—if you are too firmly convinced of what you *ought* to find, then you will never be able to carry out a truly scientific study. Indeed, that sort of prejudgment is almost the definition of nonscientific method. Nonetheless, one must operate within the parameters of what is known, and any new data must conform to them. Among the parameters that apply in the present case is the fact that the other known megaherbivores, as they are called, all tend to eat a single plant or other type of food, a species abundantly available in their environment. Giganto's massive jaw morphology, particularly, would lead us to believe that the ape was adapted to the massive consumption of coarse plants. What follows is the line of thinking we were pursuing before the results of the phytolith analysis:

A comparison of recovered *Gigantopithecus* jaws and teeth with the jaws and teeth of other large mammals indicates certain similarities that help to enlarge the picture of the ape's diet. The molar teeth of Giganto are low-crowned and flat, with very thick enamel caps. The premolars are molarized: that is, they have become broad and flattened, and thus resemble molars. The canine teeth are not sharp and pointed, but are rather broad and flat, more like what one would expect premolars to be; the incisors are small, peglike, and closely packed. These observations, combined with the massive jaw morphology, make it really an inevitable conclusion that the animal was adapted to the consumption of tough fibrous foods by cutting, crushing, and grinding them.

Parallels with the Giant Panda

It is instructive to compare *Gigantopithecus*'s jaw morphology with that of one of the most well-known specialized herbivores in the world, the giant panda. The mandibles of Giganto and the giant panda, on the one hand, if set side by side with the jawbones of, say, the gorilla and the grizzly bear, appear much more thick, deep, and massive, while the latter have thinner, shallower, lighter jaws. That circumstance reflects the much more general diet of the gorilla and the grizzly, compared with the specialized one of the panda and, by inference, of Giganto, as well.

Another similarity between *Gigantopithecus* and the giant panda is the high incidence of tooth cavities. Wu Rukang, in his encyclopaedic survey of the sample of *Gigantopithecus* teeth in China, found cavities present in 11 percent of the teeth—an unusually high rate for an ape, but more or less equivalent to the rate of dental cavities in the fossil remains of the giant panda.

A Chinese researcher named Zhang Yinyun, who has studied a large sample of six hundred or so *Gigantopithecus* teeth at the Institute of Vertebrate Paleontology and Paleoanthropology in Beijing, has reported that he finds in them a high incidence of hypoplasia—arrested development of a particular part of the body. In teeth, hypoplasia is manifested by small, uneven pits in the enamel surface or as shallow grooves extending transversely around the tooth, indicating a period where growth was arrested. Zhang had suggested that this hypothesized hypoplasia might have resulted from food shortages and malnutrition, a view that dovetails neatly with the bamboo diet proposed for *Gigantopithecus*. As we shall see in a chapter devoted to bamboo, the great grass is subject to periodic die-offs, which produce food shortages that wreak havoc on the life of the giant panda.

Writing in 1988, before the phytolith analysis was undertaken, Ciochon hypothesized in an article in *Animal Kingdom,* a magazine published by the New York Zoological Society, "Judging from these similarities, it is possible that *Gigantopithecus* occupied a pandalike niche." That is a conveniently (and appropriately) vague formulation, evading as it does the basic question of what sort of a niche we are talking about, for the excellent reason that we cannot know precisely what sort of analogy would be correct. Ciochon, in his *Animal Kingdom* article (to which the journal's editors gave the colorful title "Gigantopithecus: The King of All the Apes"), carries his analogy with the giant panda a step further:

> Perhaps *Gigantopithecus* was also a bamboo eater. This would explain its great jaws and massive teeth as adaptations that enabled it to efficiently utilize bamboo as a food source. It also might explain the large number of cavities seen in *Gigantopithecus,* since the silica in bamboo may have caused abrasions on the teeth, which made them more prone to decay. This pattern of wear has been noted on the teeth of *Gigantopithecus* as well as on fossil and living giant panda teeth. Ultimately, however, concrete answers to the mysteries surrounding the lifeways of *Gigantopithecus* must wait until more and different fossils are unearthed.

Or, he might have added, until a new technological application, such as phytolith analysis, is applied to the fossils already collected, something which occurred a short time afterward.

Now the phytoliths have spoken, and we cannot overlook what they have to say, or simply try to explain it away. In the first place, the bamboo hypothesis remains very much alive; for, as we have seen, grass phytoliths were found that could very likely have come from bamboo. The primary shift in our thinking brought about by the phytolith analysis was to identify Giganto as less specialized in his diet than we had supposed. Clearly, the ape ate something other than bamboo, since we found phytoliths tentatively identified as being from the fruits of the Moraceae embedded in its tooth enamel.

Actually, no animal species has an exclusively specialized diet. Even the giant panda, whose vast consumption of bamboo makes it a classic case of an animal with an overwhelmingly specialized diet, sometimes eats other foods as well, as we shall see in the chapter devoted to the animal; if a bite of meat is readily available, the big bear will eat it. Conversely, even the most hardcore carnivores, such as the big cats, will occasionally have a munch of herbiage. In trying to establish the relative proportions of these disparate elements of an animal's diet, there is a real peril in generalizing from a small sample. After our first round of phytolith analysis, the isolated Moraceae specimen necessarily occupies an important role in our conclusions. However, if we subject an additional hundred *Gigantopithecus* teeth to microscopic analysis without finding another phytolith characteristic of the Moraceae, the original find will dwindle to statistical insignificance—not that we are making a forecast one way or the other. We must base our conclusions on the data we have at hand, and revise them as we go. In the meantime, limited sample or not, we now know considerably more about how Giganto adapted and survived than we did before.

Dolores Piperno makes the point that the leaves, seeds, and fruits of many nongrassy plants possess high phytolith contents, and would therefore constitute a tough diet—one that would require a large jaw and produce heavy wear on the teeth, technically described as a robust masticatory morphology. It is therefore difficult to estimate the relative roles of grasses and fruits in the diet of Giganto. However, it is reasonable to look to studies of the teeth of living primates, whose diets are known, for some guidelines in evaluating the relationship and frequency of dental phytoliths to the quantities and proportions of plants consumed. Even when we have primary data such as phytoliths, we must still rely upon analogy and inference in order to evaluate them. One of the great question marks remaining in the still-developing phytolith field is whether certain phytoliths have a greater tendency to adhere to tooth surfaces, and thus to show up in microscopic analysis. It is important to find the answer to that question if we are to determine the actual diet of an extinct animal such as *Gigantopithecus*.

Phytolith analysis has exciting possibilities up and down the whole field of paleoanthropology. One application that comes to mind immediately is the opportunity to test empirically the so-called "dietary hypothesis" in early hominids, which states that the robust australopithecines (*Australopithecus robustus*) were committed herbivores, while the more gracile species (*Australopithecus africanus*) had an eclectic, omnivorous diet. This hypothesis, which was based upon a comparison of the jaw morphology and the size and shape of the teeth of the two species, ought to be susceptible to an empirical test through phytolith analysis. Subjecting early human fossil teeth to phytolith analysis might also settle a lot of other old dietary arguments. For where the condition of the fossil teeth permits, scientists now have the potential to obtain direct primary data of the vegetable component of an extinct animal's diet, a tool they did not have before. That capability proved to be of key importance to us when we set ourselves to the task of building a reconstruction of *Gigantopithecus*. For that one cluster of hard data about the giant ape opened a window directly onto life in Asia during the Pleistocene—when our direct ancestor *Homo erectus* first arrived on the scene.

CHAPTER 11

The Fourth Great Ape: A Portrait

A Reconstruction of Giganto

To arrive at some reasonable conjectures as to why *Gigantopithecus* adapted the way it did, and to hypothesize about why this, the largest primate that ever lived, became extinct, we determined first to draw as complete and convincing a portrait of the beast as we could. Reconstructing fossil animals, putting some flesh on those mineralized bones, is one of the most fascinating—and treacherous—of scientific pastimes. To do so, we must temporarily suspend our habitual caution as scientists, and give our imaginations more of a free rein than they are accustomed to.

The challenge of reconstruction is almost entirely a conceptual one. If we want to know about the appearance, physiology, and habits of a living animal, we can go to the zoo or lie in wait for it in the wild. We can readily see its diet, its means of locomotion, and the color of its plumage or pelage. With a fossil animal, however, conjecture is all there is. Indeed, the reconstruction of a fossil animal is almost more art than science, for many of the determinations that must be made are entirely subjective, and the results cannot be tested in any meaningful sense of the term. While every decision is based on scientific fact, the resulting composite will be only one of many possible portraits of *Gigantopithecus*, all equally plausible and equally valid.

Nonetheless, having marshaled together what we believe to be every known shred of factual evidence regarding this fascinating fossil ape, we wanted to try our collective hand at limning a portrait of it. To do so, we have drawn upon the talents not of another scientist but of an artist: a former Hollywood makeup artist named Bill Munns. When our research into *Gigantopithecus* first began to attract attention in the national press, Munns sought us out. It may seem slightly unusual for scientists to entrust the sensitive task of creating a serious reconstruction to someone whose résumé includes such assignments as designing the special makeup effects for *Swamp Thing* and *The Beastmaster,* and creating the monster for *Blackenstein.* However, since his days of apprenticeship in the Grade B movie mills of Hollywood, Munns has become something of an expert on giving concrete, three-dimensional life to the fossil bones of extinct animals.

When our partnership with him began, Munns was engaged in the business of creating highly realistic, life-sized models of existing endangered primates—gorillas, orangs, the Chinese golden monkey (*Rhinopithecus*)—for zoos and educational institutions. The great selling point of Munns's models is that they are in no way taxidermic; that is, they do not require killing a living specimen, which is not an option in the case of endangered species. His "apes" are made from metal, latex and other synthetics, and that most renewable of resources—human hair. At the time he learned of our study of *Gigantopithecus,* he had begun to try his hand at reconstructing extinct hominids, such as the australopithecines and *Homo erectus.*

Ciochon supervised the operation, providing the paleontological data, while Munns, in collaboration with biological illustrator Stephen Nash, slowly evolved the life-sized, three-dimensional image of the beast from that information. The first step was to render the great ape in drawings. They had only teeth and three mandibles to work with, so they began, obviously, with the skull. Using the proportions of the skulls of existing great apes, they conjectured a skull that measured eighteen inches from the bottom of the jaw to the highest point of the sagittal crest. Munns relied on the Asian great ape, the orang, more than the gorilla, adapting the former's more subdued, dish-shaped face, and rising cranial vault to the proposed Giganto skull.

The next step was to project a hypothetical skeleton from the hypothetical skull. For this purpose Munns used two references, one modern, the gorilla, and one from the fossil record, an extinct giant baboon called *Theropithecus oswaldi*. After Giganto, they are the two largest primates known. *Theropithecus*, the male of which was roughly the same size as a female gorilla, around 250 pounds, is known from a 650,000-year-old site in Kenya called Olorgesailie, where dozens of skeletons of the primate were found, perhaps the leavings of a hunt by a group of *Homo erectus*. The decision to base the model on the gorilla and *Theropithecus*, rather than the orangutan, was made because they were both ground-dwelling, like *Gigantopithecus*, while the orang is arboreal, which dictates an entirely different set of skeletal proportions.

In order to determine the overall size of Giganto, we had to settle on a ratio of the head to the whole skeleton. In humans, the head is ordinarily about one-seventh of the total stature. The reconstruction of "Lucy," *Australopithecus afarensis*, which Munns built, is based upon a 1:8 ratio. Even a tiny difference in the head-to-body ratio can be crucial, for if the head shrinks even slightly in relation to the body, since the skull size is fixed, it can only mean that the body must grow. In his initial sketch, Munns put the ratio for Giganto at 1:7, but Nash objected that it made *Gigantopithecus* look a little too microcephalic; in the final design the ratio is about 1:6.5.

The size relationships among the limbs was the next issue. The variable at question here is called the intermembral index, which refers to the ratio of the length of the forelimbs to that of the hind limbs in living primates. To obtain the intermembral index, you add the lengths of the humerus (upper arm) and radius (forearm), and divide by the sum of the lengths of the femur (thighbone) and the tibia (shinbone). The ratio is usually expressed in multiples of one hundred; thus if the fore and hind limbs are of equal length, the intermembral index is 100. In *Homo sapiens*, the figure is 70, signifying that the arms are 70 percent the length of the legs. The orangutan is a brachiating primate, meaning that it moves about by swinging its arms, so its index is a whopping 134, clearly far too high for the terrestrial *Gigantopithecus*. To arrive at a good estimate of Giganto's intermembral index, Munns split the difference between the knuckle-walking gorilla, with 120, and *Theropithecus*, with an estimated 95, yielding 108.

Now he was ready to translate the numbers into three dimensions. The results were really startling; we knew that Giganto was big, but we had no idea *how* big. When you move into three dimensions, the volumetric expansion increases geometrically rather than arithmetically. In other words, if you compare the mass of a man who is six feet tall with a similarly proportioned three-foot-tall person, the tall man is not twice as massive, he is nearly four times the size of the little guy. (The actual factor is 3.75, according to Munns.) Based upon a comparison of the projected skull size of Giganto, Munns postulates that the ape was a bit more than one and a half times as tall as the modern gorilla. Even though *Gigantopithecus*'s "skull" is eighteen inches high, as opposed to ten inches for the gorilla, it was necessary to scale back a bit, because of Giganto's extraordinarily deep mandible, which was no doubt necessary for the massive consumption of coarse vegetation required to fuel the ape. Given that the average male silverback gorilla is about six feet tall, with a fighting weight of 400 pounds, Munns was able to calculate that *Gigantopithecus* was over ten feet tall and weighed as much as 1,200 pounds!

We were shocked by the projection, and there was a natural tendency to shrink and slim him down. But the figures are reliable, to the extent that they may be used accurately to "predict" the appearance of existing species from portions of their skeletons. If anything, says Munns, he was operating on the conservative side of the variables. And the phytolith evidence strongly supported the thesis that Giganto was a grass-eating omnivore; as we shall see, a body of zoological evidence exists to support the model of extremely large land mammals subsisting on a diet of low-nutrition grasses.

The first model Munns made was a stationary sculpture covered with longish human hair in golden shades, based on two Asian primates that were contemporaries of Giganto's, the orangutan and *Rhinopithecus,* the Chinese golden monkey. The hair on Giganto's back is a bit grayer, while the arms take on a reddish, auburn cast. This model was on exhibit at the San Diego Museum of Man in the spring of 1989. Then Munns became more venturesome, and proposed a computerized, motor-driven *Gigantopithecus* along the lines of the mechanical dinosaurs created by the Dynamation firm. The motile Giganto, which was completed in 1989, is covered with synthetic body hair. The change was dictated not by economics—surprisingly, human hair is cheaper than fake fur—but by necessity: the synthetic stuff can be sewn into Spandex fabric, which allows the skin to move over the armature of the model.

The mechanical *Gigantopithecus* is capable of sixty-eight movements, from pelvis bends and torso twists to wrist and elbow rotations and even eyeblinks. Individual finger movements are now being introduced. The model also vocalizes, a custom-made recording of grunts and roars that, Munns concedes, is closer to theater than natural history. Every public appearance of this remarkable creation is programmed by computer, by a process of building up movements that Munns likens to the computerized mixing of music.

The cost of the model, which was an undertaking of the privately owned model-making company for which Munns works, was $150,000. They hope to recoup their investment by mounting a traveling museum show comprising several extinct Pleistocene animals. In addition to *Gigantopithecus,* the exhibit's mammals will include *Platybelodon,* a shovel-tusked pachyderm; *Sivatherium,* a huge North American mooselike animal; and *Glyptodon,* which Munns describes as a "Volkswagen-sized armadillo." The exhibit will also include such fossil monsters as the 1,000-pound Madagascar elephant bird, the prehistoric condor, which had a 24-foot wingspan, and a 50-foot-long crocodilian from Mesozoic Texas. In addition to its obvious popular appeal, the exhibit will serve the important educational purpose of demonstrating that gigantism is not a phenomenon that died out with the dinosaurs in the great Cretaceous extinction, 65 million years ago; the Ice Age, too, had a penchant for the enormous. Taken in this context, it is clear that *Gigantopithecus* was no freakish monstrosity, but simply the primate exemplar of a planetwide phenomenon.

A Hindgut Fermentator

Bill Munns built *Gigantopithecus* from the inside out, so to speak, yet by a parallel process, relying upon the fossil record and reasoning by analogy, we may reconstruct the innards of the beast. One of the important contributions in recent mammalian zoology has been R. Norman Owen-Smith's studies of what he calls megaherbivores, the land mammals weighing more than a ton. *Gigantopithecus,* even by our heftiest estimates, was never close to that weight. Nor was the ape, taxonomically speaking, a herbivore; like the other apes and like *Homo,* it was an omnivore. Nonetheless, we can apply some of the principles underlying Owen-Smith's criteria to the ape.

One of the basic lessons learned from the analysis of megaherbivores is that the larger the animal, the lower its metabolic requirements, as expressed in terms per unit of body mass. Owen-Smith's vivid example is to contrast the metabolic rate of an elephant weighing 10,000 pounds with those of a 10-pound dikdik: while the elephant weighs a thousand times as much as the tiny antelope, its energy-maintenance requirements are only 180 times as great.

However, since the sheer mass of food required is necessarily much greater for the megaherbivores, their requirements in terms of the quality of their food is reduced proportionately, though to a lesser extent than the differential of basal metabolism to body mass. There are exceptions, notably the white rhinoceros and the hippopotamus, which prefer diets of a nutritional quality more or less equivalent to the diets of the bovids; but as a rule the megaherbivores subsist on diets of coarse, woody plants low in nutritional value, which typically are available in very large quantities. (Bamboo fits this profile precisely.) To return to the elephant and dikdik: if our 10-pound dikdik requires a diet of plants that are 80 percent digestible, applying Owen-Smith's algebraic functions, the elephant ought to be able to accept a diet that is only 10 percent digestible.

All of this bears directly on the soft anatomy of *Gigantopithecus,* which cannot be divined from the fossil record. Two principal adaptations among the herbivores allow them to extract a sufficient amount of nutrients from coarse food plants: first, the evolution of a foregut, and second, the ability to ferment the ingesta in the stomach. The foregut, which is found in herbivores such as the horse and the hare, can hold grasses and other plants high in cellulose for long periods of time, which permits a greater quantity of nutritionally useful substances to be absorbed. Alternatively, as in the case of the ruminants, such as the deer, the cellulose in their food is broken down by microbes in the animal's stomach, which in effect "precooks" the fibrous material during the digestive process. These animals are referred to by zoologists as hindgut fermentators.

We believe that *Gigantopithecus* must have been a hindgut fermentator, principally because, being an omnivore, it is quite unlikely that it could have evolved so highly specialized an anatomical adaptation as the foregut, which would have taken many millions of years to develop. Yet it is reasonable to assume that Giganto could have made the intermediate adaptation in the direction of herbivorousness by developing the capacity to ferment digesta in its gut.

In hindgut fermentators the process of fermentation occurs in the caecum, or large intestine, which in these animals, is generally much longer than in other animals, making it possible to take in more food, and to digest it more fully. Thus, for example, while carnivores generally have intestines about four to eight times as long as their bodies, a hindgut fermentator such as the deer has an intestine about fifteen times as long as its body, and the sheep twenty-five times.

One of the useful features of hindgut fermentation is that it is well adapted to a mixed diet. While unnutritious foods high in cellulose are packed into the folds of the caecum being fermented, if the animal should ingest some more high-quality food such as fruit or the occasional bite of red meat, then this can shoot right through the middle of the intestine and be digested quickly without disturbing the process of fermentation going on around it. The evolutionary advantage of this feature is obvious: it permits the animal to feed on whatever food is available. In times of stress, *Gigantopithecus* would have been able to maximize its potential food supply. It also fits in nicely with the phytolith record of Giganto's diet, which contains evidence of fruit as well as grass consumption.

We may even make some conjectures about the behavior of *Gigantopithecus* on the basis of this information. One of the most outstanding characteristics of the megaherbivores is their extreme slowness. In the first place, they have no particular need of speed: their enormous size and thick skins protect them from being hunted, and of course their feeding habits require no more of them than that they move from place to place as they systematically denude the landscape of vegetation. Furthermore, they are usually stuffed full of heavy, bulky food, which tends to produce a certain inertia.

Most important, physical activity burns calories, and calories are what the megaherbivores must guard most jealously: to provide the energy for a few minutes on the hoof, the animal must spend an hour feeding. Thus we may state almost without any doubt that *Gigantopithecus* was a slow, deliberately moving creature. To our eyes it would probably have had a phlegmatic, clumsy, and perhaps even comical appearance. It passed its days stuffing its face, most likely using its huge hands in the same way that an elephant uses its trunk—to shovel food down in bulk. Time not spent eating was devoted to resting and sleeping. Nothing about *Gigantopithecus* would have reminded us of an acrobatic monkey or a playful chimpanzee. No doubt the ape was capable of menacing and even ferocious behavior when required. Yet in its daily life, it played the part of the greedy, indolent pasha of the jungle.

The Social Behavior of Giganto

It is very difficult to draw conclusions about the social behavior of an extinct animal like *Gigantopithecus* with only three jaws and about 1,000 teeth to go on. However, since this sample of teeth is rather large, and since it comes from a single locality, Liucheng Cave, we can estimate the difference in body size between the males and females of the species—that is, the degree of sexual dimorphism—through a comparison of tooth size, which in turn can give us important clues about the social behavior of the giant ape. In his book *Fossils, Teeth, and Sex*, Australian anatomist Charles Oxnard statistically analyzed 735 teeth of Giganto that were complete enough to be measured accurately. Oxnard found that no matter what configuration of the teeth he studied (from first incisors through third molars), the same pattern emerged: each sample was neatly divided into two size groups of equal number, which Oxnard interpreted to

Looking out of the mouth of Lang Trang IV, the cave where we made many of the expedition's important fossil discoveries. *(Photograph by Jamie James)*

ABOVE: At Lang Trang I, we constructed a bamboo scaffolding to facilitate the removal of blocks of fossil-bearing sediment. *(Photograph by Russell Ciochon)*

RIGHT: Lang Trang III: when the North Vietnamese Army converted the cave behind this fissure into an air-raid shelter and arms depot, they filled it up with huge chunks of fossiliferous rock. *(Photograph by Jamie James)*

Russell Ciochon wields a gasoline-powered rock saw to remove blocks of breccia, the sediment that contains fossils in most cave deposits. *(Photograph by Jamie James)*

Viewed from above, John Olsen and his Vietnamese colleague Nguyen Van Binh painstakingly dig a trench in the floor of Lang Trang IV. *(Photograph by Russell Ciochon)*

It was in a Chinese pharmacy like this one in 1935 that German paleoanthropologist Ralph von Koenigswald discovered the type specimen of *Gigantopithecus*. The apothecary is weighing out fossils—known to the Chinese as "dragon bones"—to be used to concoct a medicinal potion. *(Photograph by Russell Ciochon)*

Ciochon and Olsen and Vietnamese colleagues examine a test excavation at the Paleolithic site of Nui Nuong, in eastern Thanh Hoa province.

ABOVE: These stone tools are typical artifacts of the Sonvian period of Vietnamese prehistory, which flourished between 20,000 and 15,000 years ago.

RIGHT: This river stone, excavated from Lang Trang IV, was used by prehistoric toolmakers as a source of raw material.

BELOW: A fossilized jaw of *Gigantopithecus* next to a modern human jaw, and four pairs of teeth juxtaposing specimens from Giganto and modern man, give some idea of the extinct ape's enormous size.

(All photographs by Russell Ciochon)

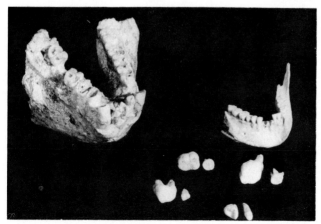

Our Vietnamese colleague Nguyen Van Binh is an astute archaeologist—and an excellent climber. Above, he nimbly explores a limestone cave near our excavation in Ba Thuoc; at right, he shows the fossilized jaw of an extinct pig, which he has just removed from the roof of Lang Trang II. *(Photograph [top] by Russell Ciochon; photograph [right] by Jamie James)*

be the male and female groups of this Giganto population. The size difference separating these sex groups of *Gigantopithecus* was enormous: the degree of sexual dimorphism in the teeth of Giganto is greater than that seen in any living primate species, including the gorilla and the orangutan, in both of which the male of the species is substantially bigger than the female.

If we survey living mammal species, including primates, in which the male is larger than the female, we find a social system where there is strong competition among males for mates, with most males having multiple female mates. Given this high degree of sexual dimorphism in Giganto, this behavioral model certainly could be applied hypothetically to the giant ape. However, Oxnard notes that the exactly equal number of males and females in the Giganto sample tends to disprove that hypothesis, because one would expect to find a much higher proportion of females to males (in the model, each male has several female mates). He argues that a large primate such as *Gigantopithecus,* if subjected to harsh environmental stress, could evolve a social system in which significant sexual dimorphism existed without competition among males. In such a system, matings could result between any and all receptive adults. The survivability of such a population would depend on the contin-ual production of offspring. Oxnard states, "The resultant increased proportion of females pregnant at any one time under such a system (perhaps almost all of them), together with harsh environmental conditions, including fierce predator pressure, could combine to produce small inter- or intra-sexual selection but strong sex-role differences and therefore strong sexual dimorphism." From our previous discussion of Giganto's dietary preferences and from its high incidence of dental hypo-plasia (pitting of the enamel), which is certain evidence of environmental stress, we can begin to form a picture of the paleobehavior of the giant ape that shows a species gradually evolving into an evolutionary cul-de-sac.

With this physiological and paleobehavioral background in place, we are approaching the point where we may conjecture about the answer to the perplexing and inevitable question that arises when one ponders an extinct fossil animal: Why, and how, did the species pass into oblivion? In the case of modern animal species, there is, regrettably, little suspense, as a rule: the answer is almost always that extinction is the direct result of human agency. As we shall see, early man may have played a pivotal role in the extinction of the fourth great ape, too—a fascinating possibility that would give *Gigantopithecus* the dubious honor of being among the very first animals to be annihilated by man. Yet the world in the middle Pleistocene populated by *Homo erectus* was an altogether different place from the one we know. The natural world and man's place in it were holistic in a way that we can scarcely conceive of today. Thus, before we address ourselves to the question of how Giganto became extinct, let us briefly examine the natural world that the ape inhabited, beginning with the plant that continues to be the dominant living force in Asia.

CHAPTER 12

The Bamboo Connection

A Hardy Tribe

Nowhere else in the world has a single plant had as dominant an impact on the evolution of life and human development as bamboo has had in East Asia: the grass blankets the whole region in luxuriant profusion, and provides the key not only to the adaptation of *Gigantopithecus* but also to the flowering of human culture in that part of the world. If the cultivation of rice made civilization possible here, without bamboo the early Asians' cultural yearnings would have taken a radically different direction. A supremely durable and versatile plant, bamboo's influence on life here is not restricted to the practical, subsistence level; its graceful, nobly rising profile, fringed with delicate feathery boughs, seems almost to have entered into the Asian soul. The musical instruments of Asia are made from bamboo, and the continent's exquisite paintings are made with bamboo brushes.

Bamboo makes Southeast Asia ecologically unique. As *Homo erectus* migrated out of Africa into Asia, he encountered this supremely useful plant for the first time, and it became the foundation for our ancestors' cultural adaptations in this part of the world. *Gigantopithecus*, meanwhile, had been evolving in this bamboo-rich environment for at least 5 million years, and was a part of the welcoming committee. *Homo erectus* had to develop new tools, some of them made from bamboo, as he learned to adapt to a unique and entirely new fauna—

Gigantopithecus munching on a stalk of bamboo, likely the ape's principal food. *(Drawing by Stephen Nash and Russell Ciochon)*

including the giant ape, which no human creature had ever seen before. *Homo erectus* did adapt successfully to both, thanks in large measure to his mastery of the unique properties of bamboo.

When we talk of bamboo, we are lumping together approximately 1,200 species of the family Gramineae, most of which constitute the genus *Bambusa,* though there are other genera that comprise grasses we would call bamboos, including *Arundinaria* and *Dendrocalamus*; taken all together, the bamboos form a tribe, a sort of subfamily in modern botanical classification, called the Bambuseae. Some botanists believe that there are species in Southeast Asia that still have not been identified. The bamboos, to attempt an all-purpose definition, are long-lived, evergreen, woody grasses; in size they vary tremendously, from the giant varieties, which tower to heights of nearly a hundred feet, to the dwarfs, which Japanese bonsai artists cultivate in elegant ceramic dishes. There are even a few climbing varieties.

Bamboo's distribution throughout southern and eastern Asia approaches a state of continuous cover. Even in the Himalayas, up to an altitude of nearly 11,500 feet, alpine species of bamboo are to be found, though the giant varieties thrive only to about 2,500 feet above sea level. As a group, the bamboos are almost absurdly hardy. One tends to forget that it is an evergreen; while that is hardly an issue in the hot and wet tropical climate of southern Indochina, in the uplands of the peninsula the winters are chilly enough to threaten less sturdy species. Yet in any climate where people can live, throughout most of China and all of Southeast Asia, bamboo thrives like the weed that it is.

The one peculiarity of the Bambuseae, which makes it something of a treacherous ally in the evolutionary process, is its penchant for mass failure. At varying intervals, anywhere from twenty to sixty years, vast bamboo forests simply die off. The cause of these failures is not clearly understood. One school of thought explains the phenomenon as the result of droughts, which is logical enough but fails to account for the periodical nature of the die-offs. Another, more likely, theory attributes die-offs to the plant's flowering cycle, which would seem to exhaust the vitality of the bamboo forest and thus provoke the mass failure. This thesis is lacking in experimental evidence, but the time intervals between documented periods of florescence fits in well with what we know about the die-offs.

Despite this weakness, if it may be called that, the near-ubiquitous plant has been a linchpin in the ecology of Southeast Asia for millions of years, and provides a key connection between *Gigantopithecus* and *Homo erectus*. While it is not absolutely certain that bamboo was the principal food of Giganto, this idea finds at least inferential support from the phytolith analysis, and logic argues strongly in favor of the hypothesis. Considerable populations of such an enormous animal must have relied upon a very large, steady food supply, and bamboo is simply the only candidate to fill the role. The plant was equally essential to the life of our ancestors. As with the question of the diet of *Gigantopithecus,* we shall never arrive at a state of certitude on this question, for the simple and inescapable reason that any bamboo used by *Homo erectus* rotted away many thousands of years ago.

Our conjectures about the use of bamboo by human ancestors must rely upon inferences and analogies, and chief among them is the premise that prehistoric uses of bamboo may be hypothesized from historical uses and present-day practices.

Many areas of Asia are still at a quite primitive level of civilization—among them the Ba Thuoc district of Thanh Hoa, Vietnam, where our excavation is taking place. Aside from the fact that much of the people's clothing is machine-made, and the presence of the occasional wristwatch, life in Ba Thuoc has not changed enormously from early historic times. Thus, to form an idea of how profoundly bamboo influenced the life of early man in this part of the world, we must seek an understanding of its importance in modern Asia.

A Key to Asian Culture

In their elegant book about bamboo, Robert Austin and Koichiro Ueda make a sweeping statement: "It is the most universally useful plant known to man. For over half the human race, life would be completely different without it." That is no exaggeration. Throughout the whole area of the world that is covered with the tribe Bambuseae, all realms of life are dependent on bamboo. From sophisticated Japanese cities, where every home from the Imperial Palace down to the most humble rural dwelling is floored in bamboo mats, to the poorest villages of Southeast Asia, where most houses are made entirely of bamboo, it is literally the stuff of life. Weathered bamboo is a major source of fuel throughout Asia. The science of papermaking, essential to the development of writing and art, could never have flourished as it did in Asia without bamboo as an abundant raw material.

The words of a Victorian traveler, Colonel Barrington de Fonblaque, although somewhat gloomy and perhaps not up to the most enlightened standards of the latter twentieth century, are nonetheless still for the most part apt as a description of Asian life: "What would a poor Chinaman do without the bamboo? Independently of its use as food, it provides him with the thatch that covers his house, the mat on which he sleeps, the cup from which he drinks, and the chopsticks with which he eats. He irrigates his field by means of a bamboo pipe; his harvest is gathered in with a bamboo rake; his grain is sifted through a bamboo sieve, and carried away in a bamboo basket.

The mast of his junk is of bamboo; so is the pole of his cart. He is flogged with a bamboo cane, tortured with bamboo stakes, and finally strangled with a bamboo rope."

Entire industries—notably shipping—could never have developed in Asia, at least not in their present form, without bamboo. The very design of most common Asian boats derives from bamboo. Whereas in the West the first watergoing vessels were dugout logs, the basic concept that underlies all subsequent Western shipbuilding, in Asia it is generally believed that the first boats were designed using bamboo as a conceptual model, with a boxlike profile and watertight compartments. Virtually every element of a junk except its sails is made from bamboo.

Bamboo is a major recurrent theme in Chinese literature. In the sixth century A.D., a treatise about bamboo by one Dai Kaizhi was published, which enumerated sixty-one different sorts of bamboo. Some of Dai's nomenclature is still in use as the common names for species of the plant: square bamboo, filial bamboo, gold and jade bamboo, phoenix-tail bamboo, etc. In the eleventh century, the famous scholar-scientist Shen Gua (A.D. 1030–1095) wrote tantalizingly of finding fossil bamboo in the district of Yan Zhou. In his *Meng Xi Bi Tan [Writings from a Dream Stream]*, Shen tells that when he was the prefect of the district, the bank of a river collapsed, and in the rubble he discovered more than a hundred fossils of bamboo shoots, recovered at a depth of a few dozen feet.

With its genius for analogy, Asian civilization found in bamboo the perfect model for ideal human behavior: securely rooted in the soil and growing strong and upright, bamboo is the standard metaphor for the righteous citizen. The poet and political theorist Wang Anshi (A.D. 1021–1086) wrote the following paean to bamboo, elaborating its fine moral lessons for mankind (the translation comes from *Bamboos of China*, by Wang Dajun and Shen Shaojin):

Ascending the winding path through bamboo groves
brings the coolness of the hall.
Your slanting shadow and whistling sound linger long
with meaning.
We admire your uprightness, yet are filled with
compassion for your leanness.

Of your great wisdom becoming more resolute with age we
are all aware.
You, like the weeds, ask nothing from people but rain
and dew.
You follow the example of conifers, defying the bitter
frost and ice.
Please take care of your roots, for you have a long way
to go.
From your stems phoenix pipes beyond price will ring
through the land.

The final verse refers to a prehistoric legend about the establishment of the musical scale. The story goes that Huang Di,
called the Yellow Emperor, who ruled circa 2700 B.C., ordered
a musician of the court, one Ling Lun, to settle once and for all
the question of the temperament of the musical scale. Ling
constructed twelve chimes of bamboo to serve as the standard
for the twelve tones of the scale: six of them imitated the song
of the female phoenix, and the other six mimicked the sono-
rous voice of the male. According to Wang and Shen, the myth
is too sophisticated to have been created, as they put it, "by the
simple culture of the ancients"; they believe that the legend
originated around a thousand years later.

Bamboo and the
Rise of *Homo erectus*

Just as bamboo likely performed a key function in the adaptation of *Gigantopithecus,* so it surely played a basic role in the
success of *Homo erectus* in Southeast Asia. We cannot state with
absolute certainty that bamboo played the same essential part
in the culture of *Homo erectus* as it does in the life of modern
man in Asia. However, what might be described as the circumstantial evidence is almost overwhelming; if the burden of
proof were on those who would dispute the bamboo hypothesis
(which it is not), they would be hard put to persuade even the
most hardened skeptic against the importance of the plant in
the development of human culture in Southeast Asia.

In chapter three, we examined the work of the Harvard archaeologist Hallam Movius, Jr., who first noticed that the Paleolithic cultures of the Far East were lacking in the symmetrical, well-finished hand axes that are ubiquitous in the toolmaking cultures of Europe and Africa. In China and South Asia, one finds smaller, cruder tools, such as the choppers we found at Ba Thuoc. The Western tool kit, called the Acheulean after the type site in France, Saint Acheul, has always been considered to be more advanced, more "civilized" than that of Asia. Movius propounded the view that the Far East was a region of "cultural retardation," and followers of his such as Carleton Coon carried it a step further, suggesting that the Asian races were isolated and backward. Coon drew a line through the map of Asia, to divide the Acheulean tool–producing cultures of the West from the presumably "retarded" peoples of the East. The line extended diagonally down the northern edge of China to the Himalayas, then southeasterly along that mountain range toward Indochina, and finally embraced all of Southeast Asia.

The infamous Movius Line has long been reviled by Asian archaeologists and their liberal-thinking colleagues in the West; in recent decades, scholars have discarded the notion of cultural retardation *a priori*. However, we are now in a position to explain empirically, or at least logically, why the heavy-duty, more "advanced" tools of the Acheulean assemblage are scarce (though not entirely lacking) in Asia: Asian ancestors must have used bamboo tools in their place.

As far as we know, this idea was first put forward by the Russian archaeologist P. I. Boriskovskii, in *Vietnam in Primeval Times,* his landmark work on Vietnamese archaeology, which was published in translation, piecemeal, from 1968 to 1970 in the Soviet academy's English-language journal *Soviet Anthropology and Archaeology*. In the opening chapter of his book Boriskovskii writes: "The wide use of bamboo and shells sharply distinguishes the Stone Age of Vietnam from those of Europe and Siberia. The fact that the assemblage of primeval stone implements found in Vietnam is very distinctive, limited in variety, and sparse, and that certain groups of stone implements, such as arrowheads, are entirely lacking, is doubtless associated with this in considerable measure."

Boriskovskii catalogues the qualities of bamboo that made it so eminently useful for such a variety of purposes to Hoabinhian man. He attributes the plant's strength and durability to its high silica content—thus coming tantalizingly close to anticipating our recent breakthrough of phytolith analysis. He writes, "Bamboo splinters and strips supplemented the massive chopping and cutting [tools] made of river-borne cobbles of igneous rocks and, for particular purposes, replaced the sharp chips and flakes elsewhere made of flint." He never explains precisely how he arrives with such certainty at his conclusion that the Hoabinhian culture used bamboo tools to fill the needs that were met by the stone tools of the much earlier Acheulean assemblage; logically, it is an impeccable conclusion, but most modern scholars, at least in the West, would feel more hampered by the lack of primary evidence than Boriskovskii seems to be. Obviously, no Paleolithic bamboo tools could have survived, so their absence in the archaeological record is meaningless.

Boriskovskii turns rather to the many uses of bamboo in present-day Vietnam. For example, he notes that some of the ethnic minorities in Vietnam, such as the Tai and Meo, still use bamboo arrows in the hunt. "These arrows are not tipped with iron, stone, or bone, but are merely sharpened bamboo sticks with a vane at the base consisting of a piece of palm leaf. Nonetheless they are very sharp and hard and constitute a dangerous and indispensable weapon." While we were in Ba Thuoc (where, it will be remembered, Tai people are one of the minority groups), one of the local boys came around to show us his crossbow, which he had constructed himself of heavy bamboo, with an ingenious trigger mechanism made of inlaid bone. The projectiles he used with the bow were bamboo arrows of exactly the type described by Boriskovskii. The crossbow propels these bamboo arrows with terrifying speed and strength; there is no doubt that they could bring down a large mammal, especially if the dart were enhanced with an organic poison.

Indeed, bamboo remains the single most important raw material in the life of the people of Ba Thuoc; only rice is conceivably more crucial to their existence, and even it probably finishes in a dead heat with bamboo. While we were in the district, a family's house burned down. We naturally assumed that it was a terrible tragedy, and were surprised at the non-chalance of the townspeople. One of our interpreters talked with them, and he explained it to us: "It is a simple matter to build a new house from bamboo," he told us. "The whole village will help, and it will only take a few days." Once we began to look for it, we saw the plant everywhere in Ba Thuoc, performing every conceivable agricultural use, from harnesses and ploughing apparatuses to little lozenge-shaped baskets for carrying piglets to market. We became a part of the bamboo culture ourselves: when we wanted to erect a scaffold to allow us to mine breccia high up in cave one, naturally we built it from bamboo.

Farther along in his book, Boriskovskii finds additional evidence for the primacy of bamboo as the raw material of choice for Hoabinhian man from a rather surprising source: the few stone tools that have been recovered from the sites. He describes a microscopic analysis of Hoabinhian stone tools he carried out at Hanoi University. The results were quite revealing: examined at approximately forty-power magnification, the tools exhibited very little wear. In a key passage in *Vietnam in Primeval Times*, Boriskovskii asserts that the reason they received only light wear is the same reason there are so few stone tools in the first place: "Stone tools were not very intensively used both because the principal tools were of bamboo, wood, and shell, and because people had available many river pebbles which could be worked with comparative ease and were in a position, when they had worked just a little with one tool, to throw it away and chip themselves another stone, which in turn would also be worked with for a short time."

The Hoabinhian culture may perhaps be characterized as the first "disposable society"; far from being less civilized than their Stone Age contemporaries in Europe and Africa, the Hoabinhians might be regarded as actually more sophisticated in their approach, at least from such a modern perspective. *Homo* everywhere was adapting to the complex of raw materials that were available to them. In Europe and North Asia, that meant, principally, stone and, to a lesser extent, wood. In South Asia, Paleolithic cultures were able to fill a significant number of their technological needs with a single type of plant: the Bambuseae.

Why would an intelligent creature such as *Homo erectus* bother with heavy stone tools, the manufacture of which is itself an awkward and occasionally painful business (try chipping and flaking flint or other hard stone, and you will see what we mean—even callused hands take a beating), when there existed everywhere around him in great abundance a light, portable plant that was actually better suited to the purpose? Obviously, for certain tasks, such as the culling and crushing of grains and the extraction of marrow from long animal bones, *Homo erectus* would have needed a basic stone tool kit. However, for the great majority of the tasks connected with the processing of vegetables or the preparation of animal skins, bamboo tools would have been quite sufficient. Just compare the ease of manufacture and efficiency of a sharpened bamboo pick or needle for punching holes in an animal skin with a similar tool made from stone.

More recently, Geoffrey Pope, an American paleoanthropologist who has worked extensively in northern Thailand, advanced the same theory in an article in *Natural History* magazine. Pope's article makes the point about the prehistoric uses of bamboo with a striking graphic representation: the distribution of bamboo is represented on a map of Asia; superposed upon that is the Movius Line—which corresponds exactly to the curve delineated by bamboo distribution. Thus throughout the part of Asia that Hallam Movius branded a region of "cultural retardation," bamboo was the plant that dominated the landscape. (See the map on page 43.)

Pope, incidentally, makes an ingenious observation about the presence of basalt cobbles at Paleolithic hearths he has excavated in Thailand, which correspond to similar discoveries at Hoabinhian hearths in Vietnam. He had wondered why early ancestors bothered to move such heavy, cumbersome stones to their campsites; the answer came after he and his colleagues used the locally available limestone for their own cooking fire. The heat of the fire reduced some of the limestone to quicklime, which powdered and caused skin rashes and a burning sensation in the lungs. They replaced the limestone hearth with basaltic rock, and the complaints disappeared. Early man no doubt made the same discovery, and that accounts for the presence of heavy stones at Hoabinhian hearth sites.

A final note about Hallam Movius: we ought not go overboard in castigating him. He had a lot of good ideas, and the imputation of racism to his writings is largely the result of imposing the standards of a later era on a pioneer in the field. However, this misstep of his is a classic example of fuzzy archaeological thinking. Often, we burn up so many brain cells in thinking about the archaeological record, in puzzling over the objects we have unearthed, that we forget to take into account what is *not* in the archaeological record. Of course, as scientists we are trained not to base our formal arguments on negative evidence. Nonetheless, as in the Sherlock Holmes story where the master sleuth's solution is prompted by the fact that the dog did not bark, sometimes the gaps in the record can prod us to make a theoretical breakthrough.

CHAPTER 13

The Panda Hypothesis

Raccoon or Bear?

No other animal is so closely identified with Asia as the giant panda. The huge roly-poly mammal with the whimsical black spots outlining its eyes against a round, furry white face is immediately recognizable from a thousand representations on T-shirts, toys, and tourist souvenirs. When mainland China and the United States ended a long-standing rift in diplomatic relations, the pact was sealed by China's donation to the National Zoo in Washington of a pair of giant pandas. When one of the handful of pandas held in captivity gives birth, it is a news story of great moment throughout the world.

Our interest in the giant panda does not, however, derive from its cuddlesome cuteness, which is universally acknowledged, nor from its symbolic geopolitical significance, but rather from its central role in the drama of evolutionary adaptation and survival that transpired in Southeast Asia between *Homo* and *Gigantopithecus*. Sometime during the last Ice Age, the giant panda became extinct in peninsular Southeast Asia at roughly the same time that the great ape *Gigantopithecus* became extinct in the same area. Thus we place a high priority on coming to an understanding of how the giant panda adapted—and ultimately failed to adapt.

Our interest in the giant panda, what we perceive to be its theoretical connection with human-Giganto interaction, revolves around two central evolutionary questions. In the first place, the diet of the giant panda is overwhelmingly based on the massive consumption of bamboo, the plant that played such an important role in the growth of human culture and that hypothetically was also the significant constituent of the diet of *Gigantopithecus*. The giant panda's diet is a unique adaptation: the panda is the only member of the order Carnivora that has a nearly exclusive (99 percent, to be exact) herbivorous diet. And in the second place, the circumstances of the extinction of the giant panda in Southeast Asia, as reconstructed by recent archaeological evidence, lead us to believe that early *Homo* played a key role in that development.

The panda has a very limited range at the present time, compared with its territory in prehistory; besides the known sites in Vietnam and South China, giant panda fossils have also been recovered in upper Burma, at Mogok Cave, and in northern Thailand, at a site called Thum Wiman Nakin (or the Cave of Paradise of the Serpent Naka), and from Tam Hang cave in upper Laos. Since the animal is no longer to be found in these localities, and since it became extinct at just the time that *Homo* began to flourish in this part of the world, it is logical to make a connection. We may reasonably hypothesize that man brought about, or at least hastened, the demise of the giant panda in Southeast Asia in one of two ways, or a combination of both.

The first possible cause of the panda's extinction in Southeast Asia is human hunting: it is pertinent to point out that the animal is still being hunted for food in the present day, despite the best efforts of the Chinese government to discourage the practice. It is also hunted for its pelt: two peasants in Sichuan province were recently executed for selling one panda hide each. The second possibility is that *Homo* outcompeted the giant panda, and destroyed its habitat. As we have seen, our early ancestors most likely used a prodigious amount of bamboo themselves; and as early man developed agriculture, large stands of bamboo were doubtless felled to make way for fields and pastures. Further complicating matters is the possibility that the other great herbivorous mammal in the area, *Gigantopithecus*, was also competing for the same finite food supply— very possibly for precisely the same tribe of plants. Inevitably, as we flesh out these scenarios, we are compelled to pile one hypothesis upon another, and draw comparisons between the

fate of the panda in peninsular Southeast Asia and that of its
giant primate contemporary.

It is difficult to get a good grasp of the evolutionary and
zoological identity of the giant panda, for its actual taxonomic
classification remains less than fully settled. The basic question
about the panda among zoologists today remains what it was
when the animal was first discovered by European naturalists
over a hundred years ago: Is it a bear or a raccoon?

In 1869 the giant panda was given its first scientific name,
Ursus melanoleucus, meaning black-and-white bear, by Père Armand David, the first Westerner to clap eyes on the beast. He
assumed that it was a member of the Ursidae, the bear family.
The following year, a French zoologist named Alphonse Milne-
Edwards reviewed the good father's work and concluded that
the panda's bones were certainly not those of a bear but rather
belonged to the Procyonidae, the family that includes the raccoons. A few months later another French naturalist, Paul
Gervaise, studied the animal's braincase and asserted that it
was that of a bear. In 1885 St. George Mivart declared the
animal to be a raccoon; in 1913 K. S. Bardenfleth proclaimed
it to be a bear. Henry Raven examined a specimen in 1936 and
found that it was similar to those of the Procyonidae, and
concluded that any resemblance to the bears was "an expression of convergence in size and food habits." Convergence is
the term zoologists use to describe the appearance of similarities between animals that are due not to true evolutionary
kinship but rather to the fact that unrelated groups of animals
living in similar but separate environments can often develop
similar adaptive traits. The features that develop by convergence are often referred to as analogous features, whereas
those that develop from a common evolutionary ancestry are
called homologous features. A classic example of convergence
are fishes and the aquatic mammals: the porpoise and the
shark look very much alike, but the porpoise is biologically
closer to the elephant, the domestic cat, or indeed people, its
fellow mammals, than it is to the shark.

In 1964, Dwight Davis carried out an extensive comparative
analysis of the giant panda, which was by then firmly known to
science as *Ailuropoda melanoleuca,* and declared momentously,
"Every morphological feature examined indicated that the giant

panda is nothing more than a highly specialized bear . . . of this there can be no reasonable doubt." Although some modern naturalists do entertain just such doubts and, furthermore, cast aspersions on Davis's methods, most zoologists nowadays do consider the giant panda to be an ursid. Still, no less an authority than George Schaller, the director of Wildlife Conservation International and one of the world's leading experts on the giant panda, from whose writings the foregoing account of this game of zoological Ping-Pong was drawn, believes that *Ailuropoda* ought to be given its own family. In his definitive study of the animal, *The Giant Pandas of Wolong*, written in collaboration with Hu Jinchu, Pan Wenshi, and Zhu Jing, Schaller concludes: "It is obvious that traditional systematics based on gross anatomical structures cannot decide the affinities of the giant panda; in any case, the animal cannot be forcefully relegated either to the raccoons or to the bears."

The controversy surrounding the taxonomic position of the giant panda is in large measure due to its perceived kinship with the other panda, the red panda. It is because of the red (or lesser) panda's existence that the giant panda was originally described as "giant," to distinguish it from the smaller animal. For fifty years, before the discovery of its fellow mammal, the red panda occupied the spotlight alone as one of the most beautiful of the strange beasts from exotic places that were being brought to the attention of a European public that was just beginning to turn its attention to natural history.

In 1985 a biomolecular solution to the riddle of the giant panda's position within the Carnivora was proposed by a research team headed by Stephen O'Brien of the U.S. National Cancer Institute. Using four independent molecular and genetic measures—comparisons of DNA, soluble proteins, blood immunology, and chromosomal structure among living bear species and raccoon species—the team was able to prove that the giant panda was, without doubt, a member of the bear family. The biomolecular evidence also confirmed that the giant panda was quite far removed from the lesser panda and all of the other raccoon species. In 1989, these results were reinforced by the discovery of a new genus of giant panda from the late Miocene of South China. At the seven-million-year-old site of Lufeng in Yunnan province, Chinese paleontologists reported they had found the "missing link" in panda ancestry, which established that the giant panda had indeed evolved from a primitive bear ancestor. Paleobotanical evidence shows that this late Miocene panda lived in a subtropical marshland with a wide variety of food resources. Chinese paleontologists are now speculating that the specialized bamboo diet of the living giant panda evolved rather recently in panda evolution, perhaps at the end of the Pliocene.

Discovery of the "Famous White-and-Black Bear"

The lesser panda was first identified in 1825, by Frédéric Cuvier, son of Georges Cuvier. The animal had just been discovered by amateur naturalists in the Himalaya Mountains; on the basis of their descriptions and a pelt and a few scraps of bone, the younger Cuvier gave it its scientific name, *Ailurus fulgens*, which means "shining cat," on account of its fiery-red coat. Not until 1869 (the same year that Père David discovered the giant panda) was a specimen of the beautiful little mammal brought back alive to Europe. The first captive red panda was shipped from Darjeeling to the London Zoo, where the zoo's superintendent, an immensely energetic man named Abraham Bartlett, took it into his private garden. This poor creature died less than a year after it reached London, and its carcass was dissected by a zoologist named William Henry Flower, who decided that the panda was sufficiently distinctive in its anatomy to merit its own family in the order Carnivora—thereby setting in motion a taxonomic debate that is only now beginning to be settled. The red panda is now firmly identified as a procyonid, that is, a member of the raccoon family. The only reason the animal was ever considered to be related to the giant panda, it would appear, is because of the superficial similarity in their face markings and because they were both discovered in China.

Strangely, the ancient Chinese authorities did not seem to take a very great interest in either the red or the giant panda. While there are references in the ancient chronicles to the *bei-shun* (*baixiong* in current orthography), a traditional Chinese name for the giant panda, which means "white bear," they are relatively sparse. The explanation for that is undoubtedly that the populations of the animal have themselves always been so sparse. The pelt of the giant panda was a trophy of great value, worthy of being offered as a gift to foreign kings. In fact, in an anticipation of the modern practice, there appears to have been an instance of live pandas being sent out of China as diplomatic gifts: in a Tang chronicle written in A.D. 621, it is recorded that the emperor gave two live *bei-shun* to the ruler of Japan. Yet for the most part, throughout Chinese art, literature, and science until the modern era, the giant panda is remarkable more for the rarity of its appearances than for what little information one can glean about it.

The giant panda enters the literature thanks to the intrepidity of the Catholic missionary and passionate amateur natural historian Père Armand David, who for more than twelve years wandered throughout East Asia in search of new animal species. In his journal Père David recorded his first encounter, in 1869, with the giant panda while traveling through the wilderness of Sichuan province in southwestern China:

"On returning from our excursion we are invited to rest at the home of a certain Li, the principal landowner of the valley, who entertains us with tea and sweets. At the pagan's home, I see a fine skin of the famous white-and-black bear, which appears to be rather large. It is a very remarkable species, and I rejoice when I hear my hunters say that I shall certainly obtain the animal within a short time. They tell me that they will go out as early as tomorrow to kill this carnivore, which it seems must constitute an interesting new discovery for science."

Not until 1936 was a giant panda captured and brought back alive, by an expedition sponsored by the Bronx Zoo, which originated in Shanghai. The group was headed by an American explorer named William Harvest Harkness, Jr., who had been the first person to capture Komodo dragons, the spectacular giant monitor lizards that live in what were then known as the Dutch East Indies. Harkness joined forces with an Englishman with the colorful name of Floyd Tangier Smith, who was known by the even more colorful nickname of "Zoology Jones." Thirteen months after setting out, William Harkness died of a mysterious disease. His wife, Ruth, a socialite and fashion designer, decided to go to China and take over the expedition, to the amazement of her friends in New York. "Zoology Jones," meanwhile, headed off on his own panda quest.

The Harkness Expedition, with the services of an ancient Sichuan scout called Lao Tsang and a Chinese-American crack shot named Quentin Young, found what they were seeking near the village of Tsaopo, in the ancient Kingdom of Wassu. Old Tsang saw a fully grown giant panda, and, despite Mrs. Harkness's explicit order forbidding it, fired his ancient blunderbuss musket at it. He plunged into the thicket after his quarry, leaving Mrs. Harkness and Quentin behind. She recounted what happened next in her book, *The Lady and the Panda:* "We listened for a moment, and went on a few yards farther, where the bamboo thinned slightly, giving way to a few big trees. Quentin stopped so short that I almost fell over him. He listened intently for a split second, and then went ploughing on so rapidly I couldn't keep up with him. Dimly through the waving wet branches I saw him near a huge rotting tree. I stumbled on blindly, brushing the water from my face and eyes. Then I too stopped, frozen in my tracks. From the old dead tree came a baby's whimper. I must have been momentarily paralyzed, for I didn't move until Quentin came toward me and held out his arms. There in the palms of his hands was a squirming baby *bei-shun.*"

That baby panda, named Su-Lin (after Quentin Young's mother), was carefully nursed; its mother had been killed in the capture. Su-Lin was brought back alive to the Bronx Zoo, the first such specimen of the giant panda to be exhibited in the Western world. Later, it was revealed that "Zoology Jones" had actually been the first to capture a giant panda. He had smuggled his specimen through the vigilant Chinese customs by dyeing its fur brown and passing it off as a brown bear! However, the panda captured by Smith-"Jones" died at sea on its way to the London Zoo.

In the years since Su-Lin gave the species its Western debut, the giant panda has become perhaps the most popular animal in the world. Scholarly works have been written about why we find them so extraordinarily appealing. And as we have observed, the animal has even taken on a certain political significance. In recent years, as the official emblem of the World Wildlife Fund, the giant panda has become a symbol of the endangered species of the world. Strangely, the principal reason that the giant panda's survival is imperiled has a direct bearing on the issues surrounding our enquiry into the adaptation of *Gigantopithecus*.

A Model for *Gigantopithecus*

In the previous chapter, dealing with bamboo, we asserted that in wilderness the Bambuseae have long covered most of south and east Asia in prodigious profusion, and that is certainly true—as far as it goes. However, it is well known that everywhere throughout the world the wilderness is shrinking, and that is as true in China as it is in tropical South America or the American West. And one of the principal victims of industrialization and modern agriculture in China is the thick cover of bamboo that has enabled the giant panda to survive to the present day. Bamboo is a very unnutritious food, and vast quantities must be consumed in order to support the life of a huge mammal such as the giant panda—or, hypothetically, the giant ape *Gigantopithecus*. We shall propose here that the effect on the giant panda of a shrinking bamboo supply, whether caused by human deforestation or by the plant's periodic die-offs, might function as a model for the similar impact on *Gigantopithecus* of a decreasing food supply during the last Ice Age, when the great ape became extinct.

First, look at the modern panda's diet. Since the endangered status of the animal became known, about thirty years ago, several extensive studies of its behavior, especially its diet, have been made. Its predilection for bamboo is one of the stranger dietary adaptations known to science. It is also rather a bad choice, for the giant panda, as a member of the order Carnivora—which it certainly is, whether it be bear or raccoon—is not a true herbivore at all, and therefore lacks the specialized adaptations of herbivores, such as the foregut and the fermenting hindgut, for extracting the maximum amount of nutrition from relatively unnutritious plants.

The panda, however, has none of these specialized adaptations. The giant panda might be likened to a vegetarian person in a meat-eating society, for in both cases the individual has assumed a diet that is essentially "unnatural" for it. In order to survive, the panda must spend as much of its time as possible stuffing bamboo into its face; to that end it evolved its famous "thumb," an enlarged wrist bone which functions as a sixth digit opposing its forepaws. Schaller found that giant pandas in the wild ate anywhere from twenty to forty pounds daily of the stems, leaves, and shoots of *Sinarundinaria*, a variety of bamboo especially beloved of the creature. That works out to 8,000 to 14,400 pounds yearly per animal. It does not take much arithmetic to see that a very steady and extensive supply of bamboo is required to support a sizable population of *Ailuropoda*. Particularly significant in terms of projecting supply over a long period of time is the fact that the panda's favorite food is the new growth of the plant, the shoots, which it always eats in preference to old leaves and stems. Thus the shoots, which would ordinarily form the basis of the following year's bamboo crop, are precisely the part of the plant in greatest danger from the animal's voracity.

In other words, long before human deforestation came to Asia, there was ailuropodean deforestation. Nor is the giant panda alone: other mammals that eat bamboo include various ungulates; the golden monkey; the red panda, which seems to be almost as fond of bamboo as the giant panda (though being omnivorous, and a fraction of the latter's size, it eats a much more modest amount of the plant); and the bamboo rat, which is the only creature that competes with *Ailuropoda* for bamboo shoots (excluding, that is, man). Clearly, widespread populations of giant panda in Southeast Asia would have had a tremendous impact on the supply of bamboo, which we know was vital to the growth of human civilization, and which we suspect was essential to the success of *Gigantopithecus*.

However, as we have seen, bamboo possesses one fatal flaw: its tendency to die off periodically. Animals that adapt to a diet of the Bambuseae must be prepared for hard times at least once or twice a century. In the last great bamboo die-off, in the mid-1970's, which was particularly severe because three different species of the plant had their periodic declines at the same time, giant pandas in the Min Mountains of Sichuan turned to a variety of other plants for food. The great mammal is now known to eat at least twenty-five species in addition to the Bambuseae. Moreover, ample evidence exists that the giant panda occasionally eats meat: the Great Panda Expedition, mounted in 1974 by the Academia Sinica (the Chinese Academy of Sciences, which is one of the central authorities for all educational and intellectual activities in the country), found small rodents in the stomachs of giant pandas in the wild. George Schaller has also recorded instances where the animal ate bamboo rats, golden monkeys, and musk deer when the opportunity presented itself. Yet despite these anomalies, bamboo makes up 99 percent of the giant panda's diet.

Another important aspect of the panda's adaptation to this extraordinary megabulk, miniprotein diet is that the animal must expend as little energy as possible in order to lower its daily input quota of food. To this end, it moves as little as possible, spending hours feeding while stretched out on its back, propped up just enough to reach out for more bamboo. The giant panda spends more than 40 percent of its day at rest; it will never be caught running, or even loping, when a leisurely crawl will suffice. One of the strange aspects of its present distribution is the fact that it now lives in the cold upland regions of Sichuan province. Staying warm in winter is, of course, one of the major calorie-consuming necessities of life, and while the panda's thick fur provides excellent insulation against the elements, one would have expected an animal with the giant panda's fuel requirements to have survived in a warm, moist climate rather than the relatively cold environment of its present range.

The possible explanation for that is intimately connected with what originally attracted us to study the giant panda in the first place: namely, that the shrinking distribution of *Ailuropoda* might well be caused—one would almost like to say must have been caused—by the spread of human civilization in this part of the world. The fossil record shows us that in the Pleistocene, the giant panda flourished throughout virtually all of East Asia, at least as far south as Ba Thuoc and as far north

as Beijing. Even more revealing is the historical record, which
shows that within the last 2,000 years, the giant panda ranged
in Henan, Hubei, Hunan, Guizhou, and Yunnan, all provinces
from which the animal has since vanished.

Even as recently as 1850, pandas were still to be found in
western Hubei and Hunan and in eastern Sichuan. Thus, in
140 years its distribution has been more than halved. The
cause for this ever narrowing range, as Schaller writes, "must
be ascribed not to changing climate but to the growth of
human population. Forests were cut for timber, and land was
converted to fields and pastures. And pandas were hunted.
The animal's pelt was much sought as a sleeping mat, for
aside from being springy, it was said to predict the future (a
peaceful sleep indicated good fortune), and it kept away ghosts."

Much the same combination of factors could explain the
failure of *Gigantopithecus,* particularly when one takes into account that the giant panda and Giganto would have been
competing for the same food supply, which was constantly
shrinking as their common enemy, man, spread through the
area.

Loss of habitat and competition for a limited food supply
may not have been the giant panda's only problems. Our
Vietnamese colleague Le Trung Kha believes that the intrusion
of man into the habitat of *Gigantopithecus* and *Ailuropoda* brought
about the extinction of the animals in Southeast Asia, but not,
principally, because our ancestors were peaceably clearing land:
Kha asserts that the main reason these great mammals died out
in his country was because early man hunted them down and
killed them to the point of extinction.

CHAPTER 14

Why Did Giganto
Become Extinct?

The definitive answer to this question will lie, like the fruits of Tantalus, forever just beyond our grasp. Disentangling the precise combination of factors, biological and environmental, that led to the disappearance of any species in the prehistoric era is a complex and frustrating business. While experimental laboratory procedures continue to grow ever more sophisticated, enabling us to get more and more information from the specimens we do have, the paleontological record is just too inherently limited in what it can tell us. Yet as we assemble more data, and as other sciences begin to fill in fresh perspectives on the prehistoric world, there is always scope for intelligent conjecture.

A Brief Defense of the Dodo

To begin with, we would like to add our voices to the chorus of evolutionary scientists who seek to rehabilitate somewhat the reputation of extinction as a biological process. There is nothing shameful, in the evolutionary scheme of things, about extinction. The dodo was a large flightless bird of the island of Mauritius, which European settlers had hunted to extinction by 1681. Now, in the vernacular of our language, "dodo" has come to mean a simple-minded person who has let the times pass him by. The word "dinosaur" is used to describe anything that is too absurdly big and awkward to have a useful existence—approximately synonymous with a "white elephant," another

195

case of undeserved zoological slander. Yet all of these animals had a span of successful adaptation far longer than man has any right to expect, given our present course of heedless ecological despoliation.

The often-cited example of the cockroach is perhaps instructive: here is a creature that predated the dinosaurs and, so goes the proverbial wisdom, will outlive us. Yet we have not elevated the cockroach to a position of eminence just because of its specific longevity. It is a particularly human frailty to conceive of evolution as a beauty contest, with extinction the equivalent of losing, the ultimate humiliation. As the evolutionary biologist Stephen Jay Gould points out, without extinctions there is no place for new species, and that process of renewal is exactly what evolution is.

The fact that *Gigantopithecus* became extinct does not signify that the giant ape was either a dinosaur or a dodo, some ridiculous, oversized monstrosity that lumbered ignominiously into well-deserved oblivion. The animal's size may well have been a contributing factor to its ultimate demise, but the reasons that species receive the evolutionary pink slip are manifold; and being "too small" is just as likely to contribute to a species' downfall as being "too big," though such value judgments are misleading and irrelevant. While the paleontological record is still too spotty to form a completely secure concept of Giganto's life span as a species, we may safely say that the animal flourished for at least six million years, quite a respectable figure. Furthermore, *Gigantopithecus* became extinct in the company of a great many species of every shape and size. Perhaps significantly, Giganto was the only ape to perish in the Pleistocene, for that was the epoch when a newcomer on the scene, *Homo erectus,* our ancestor, was gaining ascendancy throughout Asia.

Paul Martin, a colleague of John Olsen's at the University of Arizona who specializes in paleoecology, has painstakingly documented a remarkable correlation between the arrival of large human populations and the extinction of most species of large animals, the so-called megafauna. During the Ice Age, the first great cultural era of *Homo,* giant animals such as the woolly mammoth, the mastodon, the giant ground sloth, *Gigantopithecus,* and many others became extinct. Of course establishing the contemporaneity of these events with the growth of human culture is a far cry from saying that the latter caused those extinctions. Yet by drawing parallels with well-documented modern extinctions, particularly some closely analogous instances from preindustrial quarters of the world, we may discern two primary ways in which early man most likely contributed to the extinction of megafauna in the Ice Age: by hunting, and by competitive exclusion, i.e., the head-to-head competition for territory and resources, which man almost always seems to win.

Extinction and Extirpation

First, we need to clarify what is involved in the actual process of extinction. Contrary to what you might expect, it is not necessary to script a scenario in which Stone Age hunters track down and kill every last male, female, and child of *Gigantopithecus* in order for the species to become extinct. Rather, extinction occurs when the breeding populations of an animal are reduced to the point that they are no longer viable, when they no longer have sufficient individuals or genetic material to perpetuate the line. Since new species often arise from geographically isolated populations of a species that is going extinct, it is also possible that man played an occasional role in the process of speciation (the creation of new species), through indirect and unintentional tampering with the gene pool.

Critical to our understanding of how man may have influenced the eventual demise of *Gigantopithecus* and other Southeast Asian megafauna is the concept of extirpation. Unlike extinction, the sister concept with which it is usually compared, extirpation does not require the complete loss of the species from the biosphere. Rather, it pertains to the localized and selective removal of a species from an environment, while some members of the same species survive elsewhere as relict populations. The term "selective" means that particular, identifiable factors have contributed to the extirpation, such as hunting or competitive exclusion, though they are only two of many possible contributors to the process.

The Chinese giant panda and orangutan of Southeast Asia provide excellent examples of the process of extirpation at

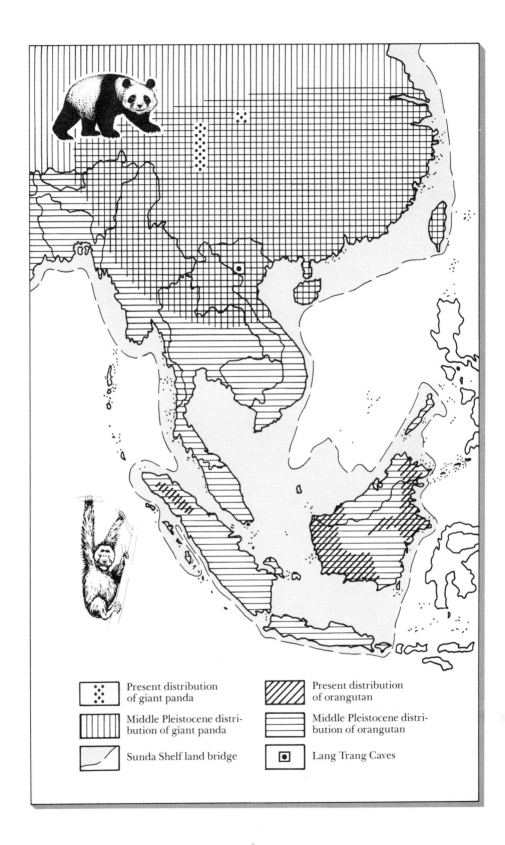

Present distribution
of giant panda

Middle Pleistocene distribution of giant panda

Sunda Shelf land bridge

Present distribution
of orangutan

Middle Pleistocene distribution of orangutan

Lang Trang Caves

work. We have found fossils of both animals in relative abundance in our excavation at the Lang Trang cave system, which is hundreds of miles from the present distribution of either animal. Thus we may say that the orangutan has been extirpated from the mainland of Asia, but survives in relict populations on the islands of Borneo and Sumatra. Likewise, the giant panda has been extirpated throughout most of its former distribution; and the very limited areas of Sichuan province in which it has survived as a relict might be profitably thought of as biological islands in the continental ocean.

In both cases extirpation occurred long before the present era of industrialized timber cutting and superintensive agriculture. In fact, the fossils of *Ailuropoda* and *Pongo* from Lang Trang are among the very youngest exemplars of these animals yet recovered outside their current ranges. Thus while neither the panda nor the orang is extinct, they were extirpated from large tracts of Asia several hundred thousand years ago—in the same areas and at the same time that *Gigantopithecus* underwent its existential crisis. The interesting question is, What are the factors that precipitated the crisis? Why did Giganto become extinct?

Until ten or fifteen years ago, archaeology would have had few scruples about saying that human hunting must have played a crucial role. Our thinking has undergone a complete change, for reasons that pertain directly to our understanding of our own kind.

The Dawn of the Hunt

For the past quarter century, since Robert Ardrey's writings popularized the notion that modern man is descended from "killer apes," archaeologists and other anthropologists have made a concerted effort to trace the origins of hunting, which

---

FACING PAGE: The current distribution of the giant panda and the orangutan, as opposed to their probable range in the Pleistocene, several hundred thousand years ago: human hunting and habitat destruction were the principal reasons for the decline of these animals. Was a similar scenario responsible for the extinction of *Gigantopithecus*?

we may define as the strategic pursuit, capture, and consumption of game animals, and assess its impact on the emergence of that complex of characteristics we define as "human." Definitions of humanness are based on a wide range of criteria, which run the intellectual and philosophical gamut. For example, a biologist might identify a specific set of morphological or physical traits as the basis for a definition of the term. On the other hand, an archaeologist might focus on aspects of behavior, such as toolmaking or social relationships, to distinguish man from his near relatives in the animal kingdom. Both points of view, as well as some others, are equally "correct," yet neither paints a holistic picture of what it means to be human.

Hunting is crucial in putting together the profile of dawn man, for it combines two essential aspects of life: the omnivorous diet and social behavior. Man has probably always been an omnivore, and the remains of his early career as a meat eater are in evidence nearly everywhere that archaeologists have found fossil human remains. The earliest record of human culture consists of some scatters of chipped stone tools, approximately 2.5 million years old, found at several locations in East Africa, some of which also contain fossilized animal bones. It is there that the question of hunting begins.

In the past, whenever stone artifacts were found in association with the broken and occasionally charred bones of game animals, it was usually assumed that the site represented the aftermath of a hunt. In recent years, however, some anthropologists, led by archaeologist Lewis Binford of the University of New Mexico and paleoanthropologist Richard Potts of the Smithsonian Institution, have propounded the view that such associations do not *necessarily* mean that man's earliest Pleistocene ancestors were the mighty hunters of myth and legend. In fact, some scholars have gone so far as to impugn the hunting capabilities of all fossil hominids, holding that until the emergence of *Homo sapiens,* some 200,000 years ago, there was no human hunting whatsoever going on.

Technologically, our studies of prehistory are becoming ever more detailed, which makes possible sharper interpretations of the archaeological record. For example, microscopic examination of the fractures on fossil bones now permit us to say whether they are the result of being broken (whether a break occurs accidentally or by the hand of man is impossible to say), or of being butchered with stone tools. Stone tools leave a distinctive mark on bones when they are used to cut them. Yet even when it can be proved that the animal speci-men was butchered by *Homo*, as appealing as it would be to make the logical leap that the animal must have been hunted by the butcher, nowadays archaeologists are more likely to look before they make that leap. A logical instrument called Occam's razor is often used to determine how far one may stretch the data.

William of Occam, the great Franciscan scholastic, known as the *Doctor Singularis et Invincibilis*, born in 1349 in Surrey, advanced the logical imperative—the eponymous razor—that all unnecessary aspects of a case under examination ought to be discarded until they are necessary. His Latin tag express-ing this thought goes: *Entia non sunt multiplicanda praeter necessitatem*, "Entities ought not to be multiplied except from necessity." In the present case, the application of Occam's razor would compel us to consider first stone tools, and then broken, charred animal bones, but not to make any "logical" assumption that the former were responsible for the condition of the latter.

In considering the very earliest epoch of human hunting, even the most basic questions must go unanswered, because of the paucity of hard—and, for that matter, soft—evidence. For example, when does the first evidence of human hunting ap-pear in the archaeological record? Twenty years ago, the con-sensus was in favor of linking the earliest stone artifacts with hunting behavior. From Olduvai Gorge in East Africa to Zhoukoudian in North China, conventional anthropological wisdom held that the early and middle Pleistocene association of tools and game animals constituted an irrefutable proof that hunting played a crucial role in the human genesis. Since these assemblages seemed to be associated with fossils of every early member of our genus (for example, *Homo habilis* in East Africa and *Homo erectus* in China), it was even suggested that there was a causal relationship. Hunting, in other words, was consid-ered to be a uniquely and definitively human adaptation: if it was human, it hunted; and if it did not hunt, it was not human. However, conventional wisdom in anthropology does not have a better batting average than it does in any other field, and that sweeping approach has now been widely discounted. After all, certain technologically primitive forms of human hunting that persist to the present day in preindustrial societies—for example, catching rodents with the bare hands—are not essentially different from what your household tabby cat does to a mouse.

So, setting aside any such tantalizing association between chipped stone tools and broken game-animal fossils, what unequivocal evidence is there that early man engaged in subsistence hunting? Precious little, until the appearance on the scene of *Homo sapiens,* in the late Pleistocene. Does that mean that pre-*sapiens Homo* did not hunt? Of course not, only that we must be more critical of the archaeological record with regard to the significance of clusters of chipped and broken stones and bones than have many previous researchers.

One of the major changes in recent archaeological thinking is that we no longer see meat consumption and subsistence hunting as being synonymous. The archaeological record is maddeningly ambiguous about the processes by which our ancestors acquired wild food animals. Some of the earliest archaeological sites in East Africa where simple chipped stone tools are found in conjunction with remains of game such as gazelle and hippopotamus are now thought to represent hominid scavenging of kills made by lions and other carnivores, rather than the results of their own hunting. Again, microscopic proofs of human butchery settle nothing. Early tool-using *Homo* might just as easily have used his stone flakes and choppers to carve up the carcasses of animals killed by other savannah-dwelling predators as for the purpose of dispatching the prey in the first place.

The image of "man the scavenger" as opposed to the traditional "man the hunter" does not sit well with some, who infer—and prefer—a more active role for our ancestors in the quest for fat and protein. One archaeologist afflicted with this romantic view of prehistory has gone so far as to write in a recent scholarly article, "The common depiction of the . . . hunting party throwing rocks and spears at a mammoth trapped in a bog is erroneous. True hunters would be offended deeply if they were accused of resorting to this kind of hunting strategy." This perspective conveniently overlooks the difference between sport hunting and the exigencies of life dictated by the simple need to stave off starvation; nor is it precisely a concern of the archaeologist whether "true hunters" are offended or not.

The relevance of all this to our story is that inferring the role that early man might have played in the process of the extinction of *Gigantopithecus* requires us to confront the issue of whether or not *Homo erectus* was actually capable of killing a creature the size of Giganto, even if he had a mind to. Contrary to what one might expect, the crucial question does not turn on the issue of the technological competence of *Homo erectus,* whether or not he had the tools for the job, but rather upon a somewhat more complex paleoanthropological question: Did early man have the "mental muscle" to reason through the sophisticated strategies and tactics of hunting behavior, and the social organization to carry them out? Since these issues of mental and social organization are the most difficult to observe from the archaeological record, we are inevitably left with more questions than answers—and more controversy than secure scenarios.

One of the factors contributing to the difficulties in analyzing the archaeological record is that in many famous early Paleolithic sites, that is, dated to before 100,000 B.P., in Africa and Asia, we are not exactly sure how the stone tools and animal bones came to be deposited together. With few exceptions, most of the known early Paleolithic sites are spring-, stream-, or lakeside localities. Owing to the nature of the geological processes responsible for the formation of the sites, it is generally impossible to make clear-cut distinctions between human agency and natural sedimentation as the cause for the juxtaposition of stone and bone.

The famous fissures of Zhoukoudian near Beijing, the source of Peking Man, do provide a somewhat clearer picture. Here, human cultural remains and the fossils of butchered animals have been collected together in the caverns and eroded pockets of a limestone massif through a wide variety of human and natural agencies. At Locality 1, a deposit of sediments nearly 130 feet thick preserves about 230,000 years of human biological and cultural evolution, spanning the era from roughly

460,000 to 230,000 B.P. Zhoukoudian had always been considered the indisputably "safe" site for hunting advocates. While there is no doubt that cultural remains such as hearths and stone tools, as well as the broken and burned bones of various game animals, are associated with the fossils of *Homo erectus* at Zhoukoudian, the group of scholars led by Lewis Binford have cast doubt on the classic interpretations of the site for being too hopeful and "clean." In other words, the data can be explained by nonhunting scenarios.

For Occam's razor is a double-edged blade, or it ought to be: just because the data do not incontrovertibly support the thesis that, for example, the remains of Zhoukoudian constitute the aftermath of a hunt, nor do they eliminate the possibility. If one only applies the exclusive edge of Occam's razor, science is hogtied and left with the insipid task of stating and restating the obvious. Between the necessary and the impossible lies the vast gray area that constitutes our intellectual playground.

This is particularly true in anthropology: whereas in chemistry or physics, the results of an experiment are clear-cut and infinitely reproducible, in our science most of the really important questions will never receive definitive, logically necessary answers. The fact is that we shall never know for certain if *Homo erectus* hunted or not, because the data are just too scarce and problematical. Yet that does not mean we cannot make logical arguments in support of one view or another. The mere fact of the juxtaposition of tool and bone at a site like Zhoukoudian does not necessarily mean that Peking Man hunted. But we must be equally prepared to accept the possibility that, to take the present case as an example, *Homo erectus* engaged in wholesale slaughter of *Gigantopithecus,* down to the last individual.

The distinction between scavenging and socialized hunting can become a bit blurry. Consider this scene: a young woolly mammoth has just been brought down by a carnivore, perhaps a big cat. A band of *Homo erectus* are out scavenging; hunting is the farthest thing from their minds. They come upon the dead mammoth—a scavenger's dream. The animal's huge carcass represents to them a month's supply of meat and fat, yards of fur for winter garments, large tusks and bones for toolmaking.

However, the cat is still there and is quite capable of ripping the whole band of human scavengers to shreds. The challenge to the human brain of how to get the mammoth for themselves constitutes a problem in many ways just as knotty as hunting itself. *Homo erectus* would have had no defense against the claws of a cat, so the strategy might well have been simply to wait. And yet—Occam's razor rules out such a safe hypothesis. The group of *Homo erectus* might just as easily have had a sophisticated scavenging strategy to wrest the kill from the original predator.

Yet for the sake of argument, let us take the dullest case, and say that our ancestors simply waited for several days, until the cat left the scene, and then moved in to appropriate its leavings. The human group would still have to contend with vultures and hyenas and other carrion feeders, and that would have required a strategy of some sort. Yet we may take it as a certainty that early man would have preferred freshly killed meat to rotting meat; our reaction of disgust to the smell of decaying flesh is an instinctive one, which is lacking in the animals that habitually feed on death. It is not romanticism to say that man is not an eater of carrion; it is a demonstrable truth.

Thus as experience provided our ancestors with the alternative between eating freshly killed prey, which might have been roasted to a juicy turn in a campfire, and the disgusting flesh of a scavenged corpse, it is reasonable to hypothesize that man developed hunting behavior in order to provide the more nutritious and healthful food supply—in a word, to adapt. For the one generalization most subscribed to by evolutionary scientists is that early man adapted by virtue of mental creativity. No one has yet invented a microscope that can reveal creativity in fossil hominids, but we know that it was there.

Another tack for validating the hypothesis of early human hunting is to seek, as we have done before, an analogy in the contemporary animal kingdom. Jane Goodall has demonstrated conclusively that chimpanzees in the wild hunt socially: a group of the animals surrounds the potential kill, and then the "hit men," in this case what truly are the killer apes, move in and bash out the brains of the prey. The fact that chimpanzees hunt certainly does not prove that *Homo erectus* hunted, a rigorous Occamist might say, and he would be right. Certainly it is a possibility, logically speaking, that human hunting behavior sprang full-blown from the brain of *Homo sapiens,* and was entirely lacking before that; yet it is reasonable to assert that such behavior evolved in pre-*sapiens* hominids, given the analogy with the behavior of modern monkeys and apes, and given the abundant (albeit inconclusive) juxtaposition of human tools and burned, butchered animal bones in the archaeological record.

"There Ain't No Moa"

That still leaves us with the question of whether *Homo erectus* in Pleistocene Southeast Asia turned his hypothetical hunting skills against *Gigantopithecus.* The associations between remains of the two species suffer from the same lack of sharp definition that prevails in most cases, and so at this point we can only speculate as to the human role in the extinction of Giganto. Nonetheless, the global record provides many instances where human hunting, whether for subsistence or other purposes, has been directly responsible for the extinction of vertebrate species in the preindustrial era.

For decades, the issue of the extinctions of megafauna at the end of the Ice Age has been hotly debated by paleoanthropologists, and we can look among these arguments for analogues to the possibility that an adversarial relationship between *Gigantopithecus* and *Homo erectus* might have contributed significantly to the extinction of the former. Species ranging from the woolly mammoth in North America and northern Eurasia to *Glyptodon,* the enormous armadillo of South America and the giant marsupials of Australia, all became extinct at roughly the same time, coincident with the expansion of human populations in these areas.

Each of these areas provides some support for the thesis that human predation contributed to the extinction of megafauna. In some cases, humanly caused extinctions of megafauna occurred in preindustrial contexts during the historical era, which makes it possible to achieve a high level of understanding of these events not possible for most of prehistory. One of the most fascinating cases along this line is that of the moa, a group of flightless birds in New Zealand. New Zealand was the last significant land mass to be inhabited by man, with the arrival of the Maori circa 1,000 years ago. Thus the island group makes an especially interesting and instructive laboratory for examining the impact of human occupation on a closed system.

And what a closed system it was! The fauna of New Zealand when the first Maori canoeists stepped on its shores was bizarre indeed, and among the zoological oddities there, none was odder than the moa. To Polynesians the word "moa" simply means "bird," but these birds were sufficiently unlike any other birds to be allocated their own order, Dinornithiformes. The moa ranged from the turkey-sized *Anomolopteryx parva* to the colossal *Dinornis robustus,* topping out at a height of twelve feet, which must have made an impressive and terrifying sight as it rumbled through the primeval forest. Within five hundred years of the Maori's arrival, the moa were all extinct; the kiwi is their closest relation among surviving avifauna in New Zealand.

The question of the human role in the extinction of the giant flightless birds has been a controversial subject, as you might expect, but the consensus now is that hunting was unquestionably a major factor, if not the overwhelming cause. For many years prehistorians resisted mightily the notion that the Maori had anything to do with these extinctions, but that has changed greatly in recent years. Two prehistorians in New Zealand named Michael Trotter and Beverley McCulloch published an entertaining study of the problem in 1984, called "Moas, Men, and Middens," which strongly supports human hunting as the principal cause of the extinction of the moa. According to Trotter and McCulloch, "Although the Noble Savage concept has taken a battering in recent decades, it lives on strongly enough to color our reasoning in such matters." They quote one heavily romanticizing source from 1949, which proclaims, "Essentially the Maori are believed to have lived in harmony with the region and to have altered its pristine character little if at all." As recently as 1976 another writer tells us that "the ancient Maori was a natural conservationist." Trotter

and McCulloch themselves have no illusions about the extinc-
tive capacities of primitive man. To support their thesis, they
quote, in addition to the usual battery of expert scholarly
sources, a popular New Zealand ditty that goes:

> No moa, no moa,
> In old Ao-tea-roa.
> Can't get 'em.
> They've et 'em;
> They've gone and there ain't no moa!

In the course of their article, Trotter and McCulloch examine
the various proposed nonhuman agencies for the extinction of
the moa, but ultimately they come down without equivocation
on the side of human causation: "We can find no evidence of
any convincing 'natural' causes for moa extinction, and more
importantly, we see no compelling need to continue to look for
them. Contemplating the monumental loss of native forms, not
only in New Zealand but elsewhere on oceanic islands, we are
inclined to agree with W. S. Gilbert, that 'man is Nature's sole
mistake.' "

One might object that an example from an island is an
inappropriate parallel for the issue of human responsibility in
the extinction of *Gigantopithecus* on mainland Southeast Asia,
since insular environments are obviously much more sensitive
to the destructive activities of man than are the open ecological
systems of Eurasia. Logically, this objection rests upon an unimpeachable premise, but the record indicates that human
agency in the extinction of species is not restricted to any
particular sort of environment. In fact, man has demonstrated
an eclectic and versatile talent for ecological pillage that knows
no parallel in the animal kingdom.

Indeed, habitat destruction by man almost qualifies as one
of those definitively human characteristics, associated most closely
in the archaeological record with agriculture. Everywhere that
the record permits us to document it, we have evidence indicating that massive land clearance, swamp drainage, overgrazing,
and other typically agricultural activities have had dire collat-
eral effects on the ecology. The scale of the extensive ecological impact wrought by agricultural man has tended to obscure

the fact that preagricultural hominids also had a negative effect on their natural environments, albeit in ways that are much more difficult to detect archaeologically.

Such difficulties are the result of the scale of the changes at issue: relatively small numbers of people can affect the environment in relatively specific ways that are sometimes indistinguishable from the effects of natural disasters. Yet we ought not to be lulled by this ambiguity of the record into thinking, especially after we have supposedly dispensed with the "killer ape" conjectures about human antiquity, that preagricultural *Homo* lived in some idyllic, Rousseauan harmony with nature.

Again, we must seek analogies with preindustrial societies in the historical epoch. For example, the aboriginal people of Australia's arid interior have been known since European contact to use fire as a tool in the capture of such game as the kangaroo, the emu, and the goana, a large monitor lizard. By setting fire to large tracts of grassland, aboriginal hunters are able to control the movement of game, and they rely on the fire itself to kill—and cook—slower-moving animals. Recently, it has become clear that the burning of open rangeland is also a sort of social activity for the aborigines. Since most native Australians travel in small bands, setting several thousand hectares of grass ablaze has the effect of letting everyone within a sixty-mile radius know of your whereabouts. If a few emus and goanas are roasted in the bargain, so much the better! The magic of the fire itself, and its awesome destructive power, is perhaps a part of the magic that gives the aborigines their justification to keep scorching great chunks of the outback, profoundly altering its ecology.

Perhaps a more pertinent and revelatory analogue, in terms of the possible adversary relationship between man and Giganto, is the great body of evidence proving how widespread, in all times and in all environments, has been the practice of human hunting of other primates. To begin with one of the most primitive groups of primates, the Malagasy lemurs, which are found on the island of Madagascar off the southeast coast of Africa, are threatened not only by the encroachment of agriculture and a burgeoning human population but also by persistent hunting with traditional weapons such as the blowgun and by trapping. In many tribes, lemur hunting is very much a part of traditional Malagasy culture; there is even one tribe which relentlessly hunts one particular species because it is considered a bad omen. Both native South American Indians and various West African tribes are regular consumers of monkeys. In some cases, this behavior has led primate species to the brink of extinction, even in areas that would, but for the presence of human hunters, be considered prime territory, capable of supporting a complex food chain, including a diverse primate fauna.

Yet by far the most powerful analogy we may adduce in support of the hunting hypothesis is the venerable and well-proved tradition of human hunting of the orangutan, after *Gigantopithecus* the greatest of the Asian great apes, and probably the most "human," at least in superficial terms, of the primates. The Pleistocene record is slim but positive: in 1957, Tom Harrisson, the curator of the Sarawak (Borneo) Museum discovered burned and broken fossilized orang remains in the Great Niah Cave, on the northwest coast of the island, very far from the current range of the ape. The rich cave deposits also contained the remains of a juvenile skull of *Homo sapiens,* quartzite flake tools, and a late Pleistocene fauna, all of which were carbon 14–dated to between 32,000 and 39,000 years B.P. Harrisson draws a number of interesting conclusions about his discoveries at Niah. He notes that the older the orangutan remains are, the larger the teeth are—and thus, presumably, the larger the animal.

The great majority of the specimens recovered are females and offspring, which would tend to indicate that the Ice Age Borneans either were incapable of hunting the larger, stronger adult males, or that they simply preferred the tenderer flesh of the female and her young. A devastating modern parallel exists: in the first part of this century, zoo collectors regularly went after mothers and their young, which probably contributed more than anything else to the orang's present precarious position. Harrisson also writes that there are "indications from the cave earth of Niah that far back in the Stone Age Orangs may have been kept as pets by cave-men." Unfortunately, he does not say what these indications are; if they are the presence of orangutan feces, the only explanation that springs to mind, then it is a highly suppositious notion. In any case, such a hypothesis ought to be taken with a healthy grain of Occamist salt.

Corroboration of Harrisson's find at Niah Cave comes, notably, from northern Vietnam, from a site in Bac Thai province called Nguom Rock Shelter, about 75 miles north of Hanoi. Here, too, hundreds of miles from the animal's current range, burned and butchered orangutan bones were found in the context of a human habitation by a major excavation undertaken by the Institute of Archaeology in 1982. The team found evidence of a long period of occupation at the rock shelter, spanning at least 10,000 years. At the top of the sequence they found a Hoabinhian occupation with hearths and faunal remains that can be radiocarbon-dated to 18,000 years B.P. Below this level is situated a Sonvian occupation, identified by its characteristic split-quartzite river cobbles. Here, at a level that has been radiocarbon-dated to 23,000 years B.P., the Vietnamese team found the burned and broken orangutan bones. Nguom Rock Shelter is the last dated occurrence of *Pongo* in peninsular Southeast Asia. It also provides near-certain evidence that the people who manufactured Sonvian tools hunted the orang for food.

Bones of orangutan and stone tools were also found associated in the two earlier levels, but by the time of the Hoabinhian occupation, about 18,000 B.P., no orang remains are present. This pattern is repeated at every cave site excavated in Vietnam. Either Hoabinhian people did not eat *Pongo*, or the orangutan had already become extinct in peninsular Southeast Asia by that time. If this evidence from Nguom Rock Shelter continues to hold up, it might one day be used as a benchmark to pinpoint the extirpation of the orangutan from Indochina at 23,000 to 18,000 years B.P.

Competitive Exclusion

It is almost a maxim in evolutionary biology that while nature's ability to speciate has, theoretically, no built-in limit, the resources required to support new species are limited. The result is competition, "the survival of the fittest"; and winning means access to those precious life-sustaining resources. Struggles between species are especially profound and clear-cut when the animals in question are higher vertebrates, and when the resources themselves undergo a reduction caused by some externally imposed condition, such as a sweeping climatic change. The result is the biological equivalent of "This town ain't big enough for the both of us." One species will control the food supply, the territory, the water—whatever it is that is in short supply—and the other species will be forced out. Ecologists call this "competitive exclusion."

If we apply the concept to the relationship between *Gigantopithecus* and our fossil ancestor *Homo erectus,* we may generate a testable hypothesis for the extinction of the former and the roaring success of the latter in Southeast Asia. When we examine the two of them side by side, we must avoid comparisons that make us think along the lines of one creature being "better adapted" or "more evolved" than the other. Such a perspective is irrelevant. *Gigantopithecus* was quite successful at being a large primate in a tropical environment. For all its great size and mass, *Gigantopithecus* had successfully adapted to the East Asian environment for several million years before the first members of our own evolutionary lineage, *Homo erectus,* appeared on the scene, and the two species enacted the scene of first encounter that has been driving our work in Vietnam. However, unfortunately for Giganto, an integral part of being successful meant becoming a specialized consumer of particular resources such as bamboo and various large fruits, which are sensitive to ecological changes.

As we have seen, the phytolith record and studies of the giant panda indicate that the vast majority of the diet of *Gigantopithecus* was the plentiful bamboo in the territory it inhabited during the Pleistocene. Yet bamboo's periodic fluctuations would have profoundly affected the populations of species heavily dependent upon it: the most recent bamboo die-off in China in the 1970's nearly wiped out the giant panda. It is estimated that fewer than one thousand pandas survived this disaster. While the natural pattern of ecological adaptation, forged over enormous spans of biological time, may have allowed Giganto to cope with episodes of bamboo failure at earlier phases of its history as a species, beginning in the middle Pleistocene, just under one million years ago, *Homo erectus* surely had a profound, debilitating effect, and may have in fact delivered the coup de grace to the great ape.

The "competitive" part of competitive exclusion does not function quite the way it might sound. There was probably never a time when *Gigantopithecus* and man came to blows over a particular bamboo stand, which resulted in the ape being driven away. Competition for similar territories and ecosystems, rather than specific resources, will do. For example, *Homo erectus,* the hunter-gatherer, might have brought about the extinction of Giganto by dominating scarce nonbamboo resources such as fruits. Thus, when one of the periodic dieoffs of bamboo occurred, the giant ape would have been deprived of its customary fall-back mechanism.

While human ancestors were consumers of bamboo, their modest need for the plant for toolmaking and other industrial uses would not have posed a serious challenge to *Gigantopithecus* for bamboo, even in times of the plant's decline. Yet if early Southeast Asians had a taste for bamboo shoots as marked as their contemporary counterparts, that might have been a more significant factor in the equation, for the large-scale consumption of the plant's first growth, obviously, would have constituted a more serious threat to its abundance. Moreover, another megaherbivore that relied almost exclusively on bamboo was also competing with Giganto for the grass: *Ailuropoda,* the giant panda. The bulk requirements of bamboo for the two animals would have been nearly matched, which would have constituted a more direct element of competition.

Yet even setting aside such a conflict between *Gigantopithecus* and *Ailuropoda,* it would not have been necessary in order to bring about the precipitous decline in populations of the great ape. Perhaps the simple fact of man's presence in the system was sufficient to throw out of kilter the delicate balance between Giganto and its resource base. A modern analogy that might be helpful is the precarious position of the mountain gorilla in present-day Rwanda. Despite laudable efforts on the part of local governments to reduce poaching on the ape, its numbers continue to dwindle. The reason is that people are steadily encroaching on the turf of the gorilla. As a technological creature, we humans have a tendency to consume all resources, not just food, at an awful pace. In the tropical highlands of central Africa, the gorilla's ultimate enemy is man, not because we hunt them for food or even because their hands, feet, and heads can be readily sold as grisly, tragic souvenirs on the tourist market. Rather, the gorilla's future is bleak simply because it has the misfortune to co-exist with *Homo*.

If we project just such a scenario back in time a few hundred thousand years, we may reconstruct a scenario for the extinction of *Gigantopithecus* that incorporates these elements: active human hunting, which can be shown to be the cause for other megafaunal extinctions; the concept of competitive exclusion, which posits populations of *Gigantopithecus* being forced into marginal, and perhaps much smaller, habitats because of their inability to compete with the more highly socialized, technologically adept hominid *Homo erectus*; and, finally, a possible simultaneous competition with the giant panda, on much the same terms as those stated for a possible rivalry with man.

The large territorial and resource requirements of a beast the size of *Gigantopithecus,* combined with an attitude of "I am monarch of all I survey" on the part of man—an attitude, we might add, as fundamentally a part of our definition of being human as the manufacture of tools or complex linguistic behavior—would have set the stage for Giganto's extinction. Schoolbook scenarios that suggest the only way in which prehistoric hunters could have affected the population of so large an animal was through direct intervention with trusty spear or club are just so much romantic twaddle. Take one large mammal, dependent for its livelihood on a specific, ecologically narrow resource for thousands of generations; add one highly successful, adaptive, and competitive newcomer, and the outcome for the former is, most likely, oblivion as a species.

CHAPTER 15

Myths of the Great Ape

First Glimpses

The allure of science—what makes us study the physical world, and what entices other people, nonscientists, to stay abreast of what we are doing—is the allure of the unknown. Just beyond the surface of the everyday world we inhabit lie its inherent causes, what we may call without exaggeration the secrets of the universe. To answer the basic questions that all people in all cultures have always asked about the world around them is the brief of the scientist. And among those questions none are more compelling than Who am I? and Where did I come from? These questions lie at the heart of our science, and their fundamental importance to us as a species explains why the study of human prehistory exerts such a strong fascination on the mind of man.

In the first chapter of this book, we examined the archaeological and ethnographical evidence that would tend to support the view that the collective memory of the human race extends back far enough to embrace the time when *Gigantopithecus* and man coexisted. We know that a confrontation between the two species occurred, and it could not have failed to stir our ancestors' imagination, just as recreating it stirs our imaginations today. Such a scenario strikes a deep and resonant chord in us, because in our collective unconscious we sense something familiar in the scene. It seems somehow *right*; in any case, that line of thinking is at least sustainable as a working hypothesis.

One of the reasons that Darwin's theory created such a furor in the intellectual community of his time was that it confirmed what perceptive people had long suspected. That the apes are indeed our "cousins," phylogenetically speaking, had always been apparent to anyone who had observed them carefully. The contemptuous jibes of pious Victorians, the cartoons caricaturing Darwin and Thomas Henry Huxley as apes, were nothing more than the hysterical reaction of a conventional society that saw its fallibilities being exposed. The great apes have always touched a deep, raw nerve.

The emotionally charged mythology of man's confrontations with the ape takes two divergent but parallel forms. The first is the deeply imaginative response of Western societies to the great apes, from the earliest reports of the hairy jungle men brought back to Europe by sailors and adventurers to modern treatments of the theme in popular culture. The second is the widespread complex of myths about the great ape among the traditional, prescientific cultures that coexist with primates in nature. In this case, the two parallel lines of myth and science ultimately meet—in the expeditions mounted by trained scientists who are still going to the ends of the world in search of the great ape-man.

Not until the latter part of the nineteenth century did Europeans and North Americans get their first real look at the great apes, but reports about them had been trickling back from the field since classical times. In the Western tradition, one of the difficult points in interpreting the literature about primates is that little distinction was made until quite recently between the apes and the native peoples who inhabited the apes' environment. For example, this quotation from the log of Hanno, a Carthaginian navigator, written in Punic in the fifth century B.C., survives in a Greek translation:

We came to an island full of hairy people, the greater part of whom were women, whose bodies were hairy and whom our interpreters called Gorillas. Though we pursued the men, we could not seize any of them; but all fled from us, escaping over the precipices, and defending themselves with stones. However, three women were taken; but they attacked their conductors with their teeth and hands, and could not be prevailed on to accompany us. Having killed them, we flayed them and brought their skins with us to Carthage.

Now, what was it that Hanno saw? The primatologist Vernon Reynolds, writing twenty-five years ago, conjectured that Hanno might have sailed as far south as the modern nation of Sierra Leone, well within the current range of the chimpanzee but hundreds of miles from that of the gorilla. Gorillas no doubt had a greater distribution 2,500 years ago, but it strains credulity to place them so far afield. The fact that Hanno calls them people might lead one to suppose that they were human natives, except for the fact that African people are not, of course, hairy.

Pomponius Mela, a Spanish writer of the first century B.C., included Hanno's report in his geography *De situ orbis,* in which he states that the "Gorillas" encountered by the Carthaginians were in fact Gorgons, the mythological monsters that were thought to dwell in the west. The creatures described by Hanno in no way resemble Gorgons, but no other explanation presented itself to Mela, who did not know of the chimpanzee or the gorilla. The elder Pliny, the greatest of the Roman naturalists, writing two hundred years later, declared that Hanno brought the skins of two Gorgons back to Carthage, where the Carthaginians hung them in the temple of Juno (what happened, one wonders, to the third Gorilla/Gorgon skin?).

In his *Natural History* Pliny also reported on two breeds of anthropoid beasts in India: "Among the western mountains of India dwell the Satyrs . . . the most swift in footmanship of all creatures; at times they run on all fours, and at other times they run on two feet like a man." The other ape-men were called *choromandae,* "a savage and wild people. Distinct voice and speech they have none, but rather they make a horrible gnashing and a hideous noise. They are rough and hairy all over their bodies, their eyes are red like an owl's, and they have teeth like a dog's." The satyrs and *choromandae* might have been langurs, or they could equally well have been pure fancy. In any case, at the time that Pliny was writing, even the most sophisticated intellectuals took it for granted that the earth was populated by wildmen and monsters.

In the Age of Discovery, beginning in the sixteenth century, sailors and adventurers brought back the first eyewitness reports of the great apes to Europe, and an accurate picture of the animals emerged—forming the basis of the first, tentative scientific studies. One of the most charming of these early traveler's tales, which were usually discounted by the leading intellectuals of the day as ridiculous fabrications, was the following description of the gorilla by an Englishman named Andrew Battell. Battell, who lived from 1589 to 1614, was an adventurer who was imprisoned by the Portuguese in South America and then transported to their African colony in Angola. He calls the gorilla by the name "pongo," a corruption of the African name "Mpongwe," and should in no way be confused with the scientific name of the orangutan, which is also *Pongo*. As an amateur naturalist, Battell acquits himself quite well:

> The Woods are so covered with Baboones, Monkies, Apes, and Parrots, that it will feare any man to travaile in them alone. Here are also two kinds of Monsters, which are common in these Woods, and very dangerous.
>
> The greatest of these two Monsters is called, *Pongo,* in their Language: and the lesser is called, *Engeco* [probably the chimpanzee]. This *Pongo* is in all proportion like a man, but that he is more like a Giant in stature, then a man: for he is very tall, and hath a mans face, holloweyed, with long haire upon his browe. His face and eares are without haire, and his hands also. His bodie is full of haire, but not very thicke, and it is of a dunnish colour. He differeth not from a man, but in his legs, for they have no calfe. He goeth alwaies upon his legs, and carrieth his hands clasped on the nape of his necke, when he goeth upon the ground. They sleepe in the trees, and build shelters from the raine. They feed upon Fruit that they find in the Woods, and upon Nuts, for they eate no kind of flesh. They cannot speake, and have no understanding more than a beast. The People of the Countrie, when they travaile in the Woods, make fires where they sleepe in the night; and in the morning, when they are gone, the *Pongoes* will come and sit about the fire, till it goeth out: for they have no understanding to lay the wood together. They goe many together, and kill many *Negroes* that travaile in the Woods. Many times

they fall upon the Elephants, which come to feed where they be, and so beate them with their clubbed fists, and pieces of wood, that they will runne roaring away from them. Those *Pongoes* are never taken alive, because they are so strong, that ten men cannot hold one of them: but yet they take many of their young ones with poisoned Arrowes. The young *Pongo* hangeth on his mothers bellie, with his hands fast clasped about her: so that, when the Countrie people kill any of the femals, they take the young one, which hangeth fast upon his mother. When they die among themselves, they cover the dead with great heapes of boughs and wood, which is commonly found in the Forrests.

What distinguishes Battell's description as a piece of natural history, as opposed to mythmaking, is that unlike his predecessors he has at least made the breakthrough distinction between man and animal (even if he does deem it necessary to point out that the *Pongoes* cannot speak). His usage of the word "monster" is in line with the accepted meaning of the word at that time, to signify a beast fearsome but real, not a figment of the imagination—although hominoid, clearly not human.

When the first reports of the orangutan came back to Europe, its uncanny resemblance to man prompted an even more explicit self-evaluation. As we shall see, man and orang have always lived in very close contact in Southeast Asia, and when European explorers first discovered the "man of the jungle," for that is how the Malaysian word *orang-utan* translates, nearly all of them expressed the notion that they felt as though they were seeing themselves. As the French naturalist the Comte Georges Buffon wrote in 1791, "This Orang-utang or pongo is only a brute, but a brute of a kind so singular, that man cannot behold it without contemplating himself. . . ." In his landmark *Natural History,* Buffon incorporated what appears to be the first eyewitness report of the orang by a Western observer, a Dutch doctor named Jacob Bontius. Bontius compounded the usual hodgepodge of reliable description and anthropomorphic nonsense, telling us, among other things, that female orangutans cover their sex in the presence of strange men, and that "the Javanese maintain that these animals can speak but refuse to do so for fear of being made to work."

The first eyewitness account of the orangutan in English comes from the captain of a merchant ship, Daniel Beeckman, who in 1714 published *A Voyage to and from the Island of Borneo.* Beeckman, in this charming description, does for the orang what Andrew Battell did for the gorilla:

> [They] grow up to be six Foot high; they walk upright, have longer Arms than Men, tolerable good Faces (handsomer I am sure than some *Hottentots* that I have seen), large Teeth, no Tails nor Hair, but on those Parts where it grows on humane Bodies; they are very nimble footed and mighty strong; they throw great Stones, Sticks, and Billets at those Persons that offend them. The Natives do really believe that these were formerly Men, but Metamorphosed into Beasts for their Blasphemy.

Linnaeus, Poe, and King Kong

Even so great a scientist as Carolus Linnaeus did not fare as well as Captain Beeckman in his treatment of the apes. The Swedish taxonomist composed a treatise called *On Creatures Resembling Man,* and in his system of zoological nomenclature he created the name *Homo nocturnus,* known alternatively as *Homo sylvestris orang-outang,* to describe a bizarre composite creature that lived in Ethiopia and the caves of Borneo. Linnaeus's description mixes science, pseudoscience, and metaphysical fancy: "Body white, walks erect, less than half our size. Hair white, frizzled. Eyes orbicular; iris and pupils golden. By day hides; by night it sees, goes out, forages. Speaks in a hiss. Thinks, believes that the earth was made for it, and that sometime it will be master again, if we may believe the travelers." Linnaeus also created the scientific name *Homo troglodytes* to accommodate the various semihuman bogeymen that have been reported with a frequency and regularity that seems not to have varied much from Hanno's time to our own. Not until 1847 was the lowland gorilla (subspecies *Gorilla gorilla gorilla*) first identified, by an American medical missionary named

Thomas Savage. Amazingly, the mountain gorilla (subspecies *Gorilla gorilla beringei*) was not known outside Africa until the twentieth century: in 1902 a Belgian soldier, the eponymous Captain Oscar von Beringe, shot one and sent it home.

If we may draw one generalization from the prescientific and pseudoscientific descriptions and fancies about the great apes over the course of Western civilization, it is that they do not differ significantly from the most fanciful tales of folklore of our own popular culture. For about the time that "real" science takes over, and the exotic tales of adventurers fade into obsolescence with the greater ease and availability of foreign travel, is just when the popular culture takes up the myth of the great ape.

In 1841, just three years before Darwin wrote his first essay outlining the theory of natural selection, Edgar Allan Poe published a short story called "The Murders in the Rue Morgue," usually described as the first detective story in the history of literature. In Poe's tale, the detective, Auguste Dupin, solves a double murder in which the mystery revolves around the fact that there appears to be no possible way for the murderer to have gotten away from the scene of the crime, a locked garret. Drawing upon the circumstantial evidence, Dupin concludes that the "murderer" was an orangutan. Dupin reads to the story's narrator a passage from Cuvier about the orangutan: "It was a minute anatomical and generally descriptive account of the large fulvous Ourang-Outang of the East Indian Islands. The gigantic stature, the prodigious strength and activity, the wild ferocity, and the imitative propensities of these mammalia are sufficiently well known to all. I understood the full horrors of the murder at once."

Poe's fiendish orangutan spawned a long line of ferocious killer apes that, as he says, are sufficiently well known to all—culminating in *King Kong*, the 1933 film classic by Merian C. Cooper and Ernest Schoedsack, in which "it was beauty killed the beast." (Before *Kong*, their first feature film, Cooper and Schoedsack had made a documentary called *Chang*, about life in a village in Laos, which included shots of tigers attacking men and an elephant stampede.)

The most recent myth of the great apes, if it is not stretch-

Even as great a naturalist as Alfred Russel Wallace contributed to the myth of the Killer Ape: an orangutan attacks a man in this engraving, the frontispiece to Wallace's classic *The Malay Archipelago* (1869). *(Collection of Russell Ciochon)*

ing the phrase too far, is the popular misconception that gorillas are completely harmless, lovable creatures who have an intelligence only slightly inferior to that of man—sensitive, poetic souls imprisoned in a fur suit. These exaggerated notions are the result of reports in the popular media about the work of Dian Fossey in Rwanda, the studies of primate intelligence at the Yerkes Primate Center at Emory University, in Atlanta, and the sign-language studies with Koko, by Penny Patterson at Stanford. It is true that gorillas are generally docile creatures, and not prone to go on murderous rampages. Nonetheless, in the wild they are ferocious if provoked, and quite capable of dismembering anyone who gets in their way.

Among the preliterate cultures of the world, myths about threatening, anthropomorphic beasts, typically very large and covered with dark hair, are not quite universal, but they are certainly cosmopolitan. In addition to the familiar Sasquatch of the North American Indians and the yeti of the Himalayas, there are remarkably similar legends around the world: the almas of Mongolia, the Chinese wildman, the *toonijuk* of the Eskimos, various hairy giants of Central America, the *didis* of Guiana, the *sedapas* of Sumatra, and many more, in all quarters of the globe, fit the same general description.

Interestingly, Southeast Asia seems to be particularly rich in ancient tales about the man-beast. In 1940, the American explorer Hassoldt Davis published this description of the *kung-lu,* whose existence is an article of faith among the Burmese people: ". . . a monster that resembled a gorilla, a miniature King Kong, about twenty feet tall. It lived on the highest mountains, where its trail of broken trees was often seen, and descended into the villages only when it wanted meat, human meat. We were told also that no one in Kensi [a village, now called Kawmyo, near the Thai border] had been eaten by the *kung-lu* for more years than the eldest could remember."

Cambodia, too, had such a beast during the Golden Age of Angkor. The Chinese diplomatist Chou Ta-kuan (in current orthography, Zhou Daguan), in his classic description of the Khmer empire, written after a year-long visit there at the end of the thirteenth century, states that "there are only a few lions, *sing-sing,* and camels." The *sing-sing,* according to Paul Pelliot, the French scholar who translated Chou Ta-kuan at the turn of the century, is "a kind of large monkey to which the Chinese attribute magical powers, and which devours humans. It is not known what animal gave rise to these legends." Incidentally, it seems quite unlikely that there were lions at Angkor at the time Chou was writing; the camel, it would appear, was never there. And recently, in Tucson of all places, John Olsen met a Laotian man who told him about the legend among the Lao people concerning a man-beast they call "Mr. Eight Cubits," yet another anthropomorphic bogeyman.

Of them all, the most famous and widely attested of the various manifestations of Bigfoot (as these creatures are sometimes termed collectively) are the Sasquatch of North America and the yeti, more colorfully known as the Abominable Snowman, of the Himalayas. The putative existence of these anthropomorphs is supported by a venerable tradition of folklore, a large body of eyewitness reports—and almost no physical evidence, though not for a want of looking.

Footprints in the Snow

From an objective point of view, the most persuasive Bigfoot casebook is the one made for the Himalayan monster, for the bulk of the testimony comes not from true believers, setting out with a firm idea of what they hope to find, but rather from pompous military men and brave mountaineers who spent their lives in the Himalayan highlands. While the indigenous legends of the "man of the snow" had existed since time out of mind, the creature was not well known to the outside world until 1920, when a mountain-climbing expedition was launched to explore the northern face of Mount Everest. At the height of 17,000 feet, the expedition leader, Lieutenant Colonel Sir C. K. Howard-Bury, saw a group of hulking, manlike forms ranging across one of the mountain's snowy, windswept passes. By the time the climbers arrived, they had fled, but Howard-Bury found their footprints, which he reported were three times the size of normal human footprints. All of the members of the party saw the "snowmen," known to their Sherpa guides as *Metoh-Kangmi*.

If the phrase "Abominable Snowman" seems to be just made for newspaper headlines, that is because it was. Actually, the phrase originated in a typo: when Howard-Bury's dispatch was wired to India, the transmitter accidentally typed *Metch-Kangmi*, and an English columnist in Calcutta translated it as "Abominable Snowman." The phrase, once it became known to editors, was never forgotten. Odette Tchernine, a longtime Bigfoot enthusiast, has compiled some twenty-two names by which the "snowman" is known to the peoples of the Himalayas, but among them only "yeti" has approached "Abominable Snowman" in currency.

Since Howard-Bury, the sightings of the creature have remained steady and more or less consistent, although they do not begin to approach the enormous quantity of Bigfoot sightings in North America. One of the most interesting pieces of evidence adduced in support of the Abominable Snowman is a famous photograph of a footprint in the snow, taken in 1951 by another English mountaineer, Eric Shipton, who subsequently climbed Everest with Sir Edmund Hillary. Shipton's photograph, unlike many others that are always being trotted out by Bigfoot boosters, cannot simply be dismissed as a hoax. It appears to be, simply, a well-exposed black-and-white photograph of an enormous anthropoid footprint; the presence in the frame of an ice axe, for scale, gives it a palpable aura of reality. Ivan Sanderson, one of the most knowledgeable and skeptical of Bigfoot scholars (if that is not a paradox), has declared the Shipton photograph to be the one piece of evidence that most stubbornly resists explanation (that is, any explanation other than the existence of the Snowman), primarily because of Shipton's unimpeachable integrity. Far from trying to capitalize on his brush with the Abominable Snowman, Shipton was always quite embarrassed about the incident, and refused comment on it ever after. All of which proves nothing, but if one does not believe that it is a picture of a yeti footprint (and we do not), it is nonetheless a good question what it is actually a picture *of*.

In large measure because of the Shipton party's report, a full-fledged Abominable Snowman Expedition was launched by the *Daily Mail*, a sensationalistic tabloid newspaper published in London. The expedition did not produce much: some photographs of footprints that look remarkably like windblown depressions, numerous conversations with local folk who knew someone who once saw a yeti, and a glimpse of a sacred yeti scalp that turned out not to be a scalp at all. Yet it was reported with breathless excitement in the press, and served to stimulate interest in the beast to an all-time high.

The evidence for the existence of Sasquatch, even more than for its Himalayan cousin, is entirely anecdotal. In the late 1950's and 1960's, Bigfoot sightings in northern California and the Pacific Northwest became so frequent, and the eyewitnesses so insistent, that some Bigfoot theorists have proposed that there might have been hoaxers—people in giant ape suits—marauding through the woods. Certainly, as Bigfoot proponents repeatedly point out, there must be some kind of explanation; and the most unsatisfactory of all is that hundreds of country people suddenly began telling lies, and remarkably similar lies at that, when the only apparent reward for doing so is to be treated like a liar.

There is a rational explanation for every phenomenon in the physical world, but it is a rather long leap from that

assertion to saying that the Himalayan glaciers and the woods
of America are populated by enormous anthropoid creatures,
of which we have no tangible evidence except for a few mysterious hairs and vaguely human-looking droppings. In 1967
there was a flurry of excitement over a bit of motion-picture
film shot by a man named Roger Patterson in the woods near
Bluff Creek, California. Twenty feet of 16mm film were exposed at fairly close range and in reasonably good focus. The
film shows a very large, hair-covered bipedal creature in a
clearing in the woods. It walks into the camera frame, turns to
look at the camera, and then strides into the woods.

The Patterson film was at first hailed as the concrete proof
of the existence of Bigfoot that skeptics had been demanding
for so long. Careful examination of the film, however, reveals
some queer details. To begin with, the physiognomy seems not
to resemble anything wrought by nature: the creature's pendu-
lous breasts, very like a woman's, are covered with hair, which
is quite unusual for a primate. A further objection is the
creature's gait, which is suspiciously human-looking. The film
has been analyzed extensively by all sorts of investigators, from
the most fervent Bigfoot believers, who naturally conclude that
it is genuine, to paid experts, presumably impartial, who arrive
at verdicts that vary in inconclusiveness. If the Patterson film is
a hoax, it is an extremely elaborate one; and what is most
surprising, given the immense amount of study devoted to it, is
that it has not been definitively exposed.

The Willing Suspension
of Disbelief

The myths of the great ape are irresistibly seductive for some
scientists. The most basic tenet of science is that one may give
credence only to what can be proved. Despite this, some fully
accredited and otherwise reputable scholars not only believe in
the existence of animals that have never been captured or
killed, they also think they know their taxonomic identity. Of
all the theories advanced to explain the zoological identity
of Bigfoot, perhaps the most popular is that the creature is

none other than *Gigantopithecus,* still alive in relict populations
and fist-walking among us. (Relict populations of Neanderthal
man run a close second.) For example, Geoffrey Bourne, the
former director of the Yerkes Primate Center and one of the
most respected primatologists in the world, wrote in *The Gentle
Giants,* his study of the gorilla published in 1975:

> We are suggesting that the Abominable Snowman of
> Tibet and the Susquatch [*sic*] of North America may be
> specimens of *Gigantopithecus* which may have survived to
> the present day. This does not appear to be out of the
> realm of possibility. An example of how evolutionary relics
> can remain in isolated areas for a long period of time is
> evidenced by the fossil man *Homo erectus.* . . . There is now
> evidence that some 1,000,000 years ago *H. erectus* probably
> got to Australia, where he found no other subhuman or
> other hominoid forms or even apelike forms to compete
> with because Australia had been cut off from the rest of the
> world for many millions of years. In this isolated situation
> *H. erectus* lived in modest numbers until some 50,000-odd
> years ago, when the predecessors of the Australian aborigi-
> nes came to the island on rafts or in dugout canoes. Appar-
> ently there was some racial mixing between the two, but
> there is now evidence that *H. erectus* lived in Australia until
> only a few thousand years ago. It does not seem impossible,
> therefore, that *Gigantopithecus* has survived in remote areas
> in Asia and North America and might be the animal that is
> responsible for the *Yeti* and Bigfoot sightings. It may in-
> deed have survived to the present day in very isolated areas.

Bourne goes on to state that Giganto might have come to
North America via the Bering land bridge and concludes,
"So perhaps *Gigantopithecus* is the Bigfoot of the American
continent and perhaps he is also the *Yeti* of the Himalayas.
Only the discovery of an actual animal and its thorough scientific examination can provide the answer." Only Bourne's last
sentence can be accepted as valid science. His analogy with
Australia is a faulty one, and it has no firm base in the fossil
record. The "evidence that *Homo erectus* lived in Australia" he
refers to is an isolated find of human fossils at an Australian
site called Kow Swamp. At the time they were found, certain
anatomical affinities with *Homo erectus* were perceived, but those

morphological similarities are now deemed superficial, and the specimens have since been determined to be much too young, perhaps as young as 12,000 B.P., to be *Homo erectus.* Paleoanthropologists do not currently accept the Kow Swamp hominids as *Homo erectus.* Even if it were in doubt, one would expect more evidence than one small group of *Homo erectus,* if the species had indeed existed in preaboriginal Australia for one million years.

In any case, Bourne's analogy is not apt, because there is no place in Asia or North America that is at all like Australia, in terms of remoteness. As a land mass, Australia was completely cut off, and developed its own unique and completely separate fauna; whereas even the most isolated glacier in Nepal is still connected with the rest of the terrestrial world. There exists a vast gulf of difference between infrequent contact and noncontact.

The case for relict populations of Giganto in North America is even more threadbare: in order to have a relict population of something, it has to have existed there before, and the incontrovertible fact of the matter is that the last North American primate species became extinct in the early Miocene, more than 25 million years ago. Moreover, this last surviving North American primate, called *Ekgmowechashala* (a Sioux word meaning "little cat man"), was a squirrel-sized prosimian, totally unrelated to the apes. Disregarding this overwhelming deterrent, a fervent Bigfoot believer named Grover Krantz, a professor of anthropology at Washington State University, has gone so far as to assign to Sasquatch the name *Gigantopithecus blacki.* By doing so, Krantz has stepped outside the bounds of science: zoological names are always assigned to type specimens, palpable and verifiable exemplars of an animal, something which is lacking in the case of Sasquatch.

Despite all the weight of scientific data and methodology that would tend to militate against them, well-established scientists around the world continue to join the ranks of those who subscribe to the existence of these anthropomorphic monsters.

ITEM: The Institute of Vertebrate Paleontology and Paleoanthropology (IVPP) in Beijing, probably the most important academic center of research in our field in Asia, and unquestionably a highly sober and conservative institution, sent a team of 110 people into central China in 1977 to search for the *almas*, a.k.a. the Chinese wildman. Huang Wanpo, a well-regarded paleoanthropologist on the staff of the IVPP who was on the expedition, has no doubts whatsoever as to the reality of the wildman. In 1988 Jamie James visited Huang in his office at the IVPP in Beijing; the anthropologist told him that the wildman expedition was quite extensive and lasted for a couple of years, yet they found nothing more than the stray hairs and droppings that Bigfoot parties always seem to turn up. Nevertheless, Huang remains convinced that *almas* do indeed inhabit the wild mountainous terrain of Central Asia. Huang is now excavating a *Gigantopithecus* site in Sichuan province, a cave called Wushan, where, as of 1988, he had recovered twelve Giganto teeth, as well as what he asserts are fossil remains of *Homo erectus*.

ITEM: In *Soul of the Tiger,* naturalist Jeffrey McNeely's account of his travels in Asia, he relates an interesting story about the noted biologist, the Earl of Cranbrook. According to McNeely, the earl "collected descriptions of a large unidentified primate called *beruang rambai"* in central Borneo. The Earl of Cranbrook says, "The people of the area are familiar with the orangutan," which would have been the most logical explanation, and describe it as a "hairy bear." The earl speculates that the *beruang rambai* is a relict population, but of what he does not venture to say.

ITEM: Vietnamese scientist Vo Quy is one of the most respected ornithologists in Asia, a staunch conservationist and the dean of the faculty of biology at the University of Hanoi. Quy has a collection of photographs and plaster casts of large (fifteen inches long) footprints that resemble those of man, which he has taken in the forests of northern Vietnam—not terribly far from Ba Thuoc. According to Quy, the local folks go out of their way to avoid the areas where the creators of these oversized spoor are said to live.

These are fascinating items, but that's all they are. The natural world is full of curious phenomena that have not yet been fully explained. Yet the essence of the scientific method—

what makes a scientist different from a politician or a novelist—is that our explanations must, by definition, arise from data, not from wishful thinking. What *might* be is often enough for other professionals, but it is never enough for a scientist.

The Ice Man

Our own closest brush with a myth of the great ape, and whether or not it has anything to do with science remains an open question, came on our first visit to Vietnam in 1987. After giving a very general, straightforward account of his paleoanthropological work at a lecture at the Institute of Archaeology, Ciochon was quite startled when, in the question-and-answer period that followed, one of the Vietnamese scientists asked him about the infamous Ice Man of Minnesota. We were astounded that news of the Ice Man, one of the more bizarre episodes of American pseudoscience, had reached Vietnam. Yet as we discussed it with our colleagues in Hanoi, and in our readings on the subject after our return, we learned that the affair has a direct link with Vietnam.

Our first awareness of the Ice Man came, it must be confessed, from an article in *Argosy,* the trashy men's adventure magazine, now defunct, and most of the rest of the literature on the subject comes from equally suspect sources. The gist of the story is as follows:

In December 1968, two zoologists named Ivan Sanderson and Bernard Heuvelmans received a mysterious invitation to the farm of a carnival huckster named Frank Hansen, near the town of Winona, Minnesota. Sanderson, an American, and Heuvelmans, who is Belgian, are well known as experts on the subject of cryptozoology, a word coined by Heuvelmans to embrace the whole study of "hidden" animals, species that are believed by some people to exist but are not known by a type specimen. Both men are trained scientists, known neither as overcredulous Bigfoot proponents nor as tough skeptics. They were summoned to the north woods to view the body of a hairy, hominoid creature frozen in a block of ice, which had been exhibited with some success on the carnival circuit by Hansen.

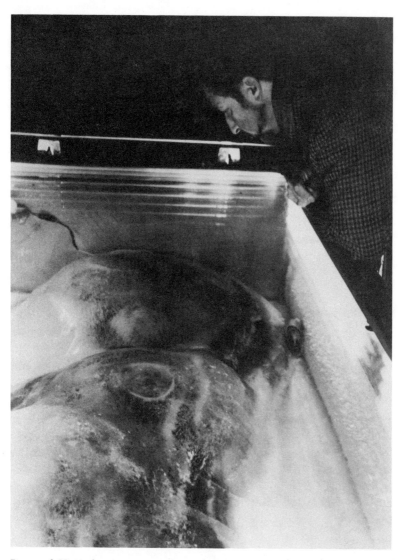

Bernard Heuvelmans contemplates the mysterious Ice Man of
Minnesota, in 1968. A trained zoologist, Heuvelmans was convinced that
it was real . . . but a real what?

The two men spent several days examining the thing, which was encased in a solid block of ice in a refrigerated, coffinlike case. They took photographs and made drawings, and at the end of their extensive observations, they both concluded without reservation that the specimen was genuine; of course, *what* it was, or purported to be, remains an unanswered question. Anatomically the creature was anomalous: its body was hairy and vaguely human, about six feet in height, with long limbs and very large extremities, and it had a simian face with a sloping forehead. Yet the important point is that both of these trained observers, after examining the thing at close range, were convinced that it had once been alive, and was no hoax.

Hansen told them that the creature belonged to "a well-known multimillionaire living on the West Coast," who had leased it to him. Hansen's story changed often, which cast a fishy pall over the affair from the beginning. First he said that the creature had been found floating in a block of natural ice in the Sea of Okhotsk by Russian sealers. Later the Ice Man's discoverers became Japanese whalers. The following year the carney artist "confessed" in an article in an *Argosy*-like magazine called *Saga* that the Ice Man was actually a native of the Minnesota woods, and that he, Hansen, had shot the creature himself and made up the story about the Sea of Okhotsk for his carnival spiel, in order to boost ticket sales.

Despite Hansen's shiftiness, Sanderson remained sufficiently convinced of the Ice Man's authenticity to involve the Smithsonian Institution. He called John Napier, the curator of the institution's primate collections who later published a book about Bigfoot, and the Smithsonian agreed to take a look at the specimen. At this point the story begins to unravel: when the Smithsonian got in on the act, Hansen suddenly announced that the anonymous millionaire owner of the thing had taken it back, and in its place Hansen planned to exhibit a latex model of the Ice Man he had made. It is clear from photographs of Hansen's new "Ice Man" that it was not the same thing Heuvelmans and Sanderson had seen in 1968.

Naturally, the Smithsonian withdrew its intention of having anything to do with so peculiar an enterprise. That gave rise to a number of conspiracy theories, including the persistent rumor that a real Bigfoot specimen had been found, but that the

Smithsonian had masterminded its disappearance and discredited Frank Hansen because, so goes the theory, the scientific establishment would be embarrassed if the existence of such a creature became known. It hardly needs to be stated how ridiculous such a notion is: real scientists would be the first ones to be fascinated by such a major find. The idea that scientists could ever collude in that sort of suppression of facts is more bizarre even than the tale of the Ice Man. The question remains, though: What did Ivan Sanderson and Bernard Heuvelmans see? Given the extremely shady circumstances, it is impossible to give the Ice Man any credence as a scientific find; yet it is nonetheless very hard to believe that two trained zoologists, whatever their expectations might have been, could be completely deceived by a fake.

Now, what does all this have to do with Vietnam? Our colleagues at the Institute of Archaeology knew all about the Ice Man, because the *Argosy* story detailing the whole adventure had been translated into Vietnamese and published in a popular science journal there, a circumstance which will seem almost inexpressibly strange to anyone who knows anything about Vietnamese publishing. Furthermore, yet another theory of the Ice Man's origin, one we were not aware of until our first visit to Hanoi, is that the creature was shot by an American soldier during the Vietnam War, and that its corpse was frozen and secretly shipped back to the States by U.S. military intelligence, which hid it in a coffin disguised as a war casualty. That particularly colorful version seems to be known to many American veterans of the war. Since the publicity about our research into *Gigantopithecus* in Vietnam, we have received several letters from veterans who say that they were face to face with huge, hairy apes in the Southeast Asian jungle when they were posted in Vietnam.

All of which goes to prove nothing, except that the myth of the great ape is firmly, deeply, and inextricably embedded in the human consciousness.

Epilogue

Scientific ventures only rarely reach a state of completion. Events such as the discovery of the moons of Jupiter or the development of the vaccine for polio are the exceptions, not the rule. Science is always arriving, becoming, particularly in the study of human prehistory. As we have emphasized throughout this book, science's ability to understand and recreate the world of early man is primarily restricted by the gaps in the archaeological and paleontological record, by the limitations on the data available to us, not by any failure of imagination. If anything, as we analyze what scraps of stone and bone do become available to us, we must learn to keep our imagination in bounds.

The temptation is always great to arrive at a grand synthesis, even where the data do not permit it, and it tugs at us now. Yet much work remains to be done in our field, and much more will remain long after our fieldwork days are over. So we cannot write THE END to this account of our search for the world of *Homo erectus* and *Gigantopithecus,* for through our further excavations, and through the efforts of other researchers, the fund of factual knowledge available to us will continue to grow and multiply, albeit unpredictably and at times very slowly.

Nonetheless, as we look over the goals we set forth in the joint agreement we drafted with our Vietnamese colleagues and signed in Hanoi on May 30, 1988 (published on the following pages as an appendix to this book), two things are most striking to us: first, how ambitious and even somewhat grandiloquent a statement it is; and second, how well we have succeeded at achieving those goals. We say this not to pat ourselves on the back, even if it may sound that way, but rather with a sense of amazement. As a rule, protocols such as these are drawn up more to express intent than to forecast reality. However confident the tone of such documents may sound, their real meaning is usually closer to "Wouldn't it be nice if we could ..." Yet as we write this epilogue, we can run down the list of promises made and note, with what we hope is a seemly sense of satisfaction, that they are promises kept.

In the most basic sense, we have accomplished, to a quite respectable degree, the scientific goals we set for ourselves. Through the fossil discoveries we made at Ba Thuoc, and through the extensive research we have done in the laboratory back home, the world of *Gigantopithecus* has, for us, taken on almost tangible life. The thousand-plus fossils we excavated at the Lang Trang cave system have provided a remarkably full portrait of life in mainland Southeast Asia during the Pleistocene. Through the use of the electron-spin resonance technique, we have been able to date firmly the fossils of *Homo erectus* we discovered, which have proved to be among the earliest yet found in mainland Southeast Asia. As Le Trung Kha phrased it, with his usual eloquence, the discovery makes the site important "not only for my country but for all the world." Through our application of phytolith analysis—original with us so far as we know—we have been able to pinpoint the diet of a fossil animal (in this case, of course, Giganto) with far greater accuracy than has ever been possible.

The other goals we set for ourselves, intended to establish a permanent scientific partnership with our Vietnamese colleagues, have all been realized: Le Trung Kha and Nguyen Van Hao made a very successful visit to the United States in the spring of 1990, which gave them the opportunity not only to continue the work we began in Ba Thuoc but also the chance to see first-hand the whole gamut of American life, from Tucson and Iowa City to New York City. The scholarly book we planned is close to fruition: to be entitled *The Prehistory of Vietnam,* it is scheduled for publication by the University of Arizona Press in 1991.

Yet most important of all, our fieldwork in Vietnam will continue. In March 1991, we shall return to Ba Thuoc with scientists from the Institute of Archaeology to renew our excavation. When we return to the beautiful uplands of Kha's country, we hope that we shall find the remains of *Gigantopithecus,* but whether we do or not, we know that we shall find something even more precious: friends.

Appendix 1

The Agreement

Research Agreement for the first
joint Vietnamese–American paleoanthropological excavation,
signed in Hanoi on May 30, 1988.

I. THE REPORT OF A VISIT BY
THREE AMERICAN ARCHAEOLOGISTS TO VIETNAM

As a part of the cooperation program between the U.S. Committee for Scientific Cooperation with Vietnam, RUSSELL CIOCHON, the University of Iowa, JOHN OLSEN, the University of Arizona, and JAMIE JAMES accepted the invitation of the Institute of Archaeology, under the administration of the Committee for Social Sciences of Vietnam. The American group worked in Vietnam from May 16 to May 30, 1988.

During their visit to Vietnam, the American archaeologists met and worked closely with Vietnamese archaeologists. They excavated and surveyed some archaeological and paleoanthropological sites in the western part of Thanh Hoa province and in Halong Bay. In Hanoi, at the Institute of Archaeology, they gave two lectures, on archaeology in western China and paleoanthropology in Southeast Asia.

The American group also visited and talked with the Institute of Geology, Hanoi University, and visited other cultural institutions in Hanoi. The group's working visit to Vietnam has been very successful, and in order to continue the cooperation, the Americans make the following proposal:

II. AN AGREEMENT

Between the Institute of Archaeology; the Committee for Social Sciences of Vietnam; the U.S. Committee for Scientific Cooperation with Vietnam; and Russell Ciochon, the University of Iowa, John Olsen, the University of Arizona, and Jamie James.

WHEREAS a spirit of scientific cooperation and warm personal regard exists among the above-named parties, and

IN ORDER to foster improved relations between the sovereign nations of the Socialist Republic of Vietnam and the United States of America, and

IN RECOGNITION of the significant accomplishments already attained by the above-named parties in advancing their mutual scientific work,

THEREFORE we agree in principle to the following terms for a scientific field research program:

1. The American and Vietnamese archaeologists will engage in a cooperative archaeological and paleoanthropological investigation in the western part of Thanh Hoa province, Vietnam. This research will entail surveying karst caves, those now known and others yet to be discovered, and excavating in these caves for fossils and archaeological artifacts.

2. This expedition will commence on January 2, 1989, and conclude no later than January 30, 1989. The American signatories wish to emphasize that this time frame is essential for their participation, as their professional teaching responsibilities preclude their participating at any other time in the near future.

3. The American signatories hereby guarantee that all expenses incurred by all members of the expedition for the time period described above will be borne by the American side, specifically by the National Geographic Society, the largest and most prestigious institution in the world devoted to geographical and anthropological research.

4. The American party will consist of: Russell L. Ciochon, John W. Olsen, Jamie James, Mary Kay Gilliland Olsen, wife of John Olsen and professor of women's studies, and geologist Katerina Semendeferi of the University of Iowa; and a team of still and motion picture photographers from the National Geographic Society. Under no circumstances will the National Geographic team exceed four persons. Thus there will be a total of nine Americans on the expedition. The American signatories wish to emphasize that since the National Geographic Society is underwriting the entire cost of the expedition, the participation of their four-member team is essential to the successful implementation of the project.

5. In order to facilitate our joint excavations, the American sig-
    natories agree to provide the following field equipment:
    a. one electrically driven rotary drill capable of cutting large
        blocks of breccia from the cave walls and ceilings,
    b. two portable petrol-powered electricity generators (1,500
        watts each) to drive the drill and a lighting system to be
        used in the caves,
    c. one small petrol-powered rock saw capable of removing
        small blocks of breccia from the caves,
    d. one optical light microscope for palynological and paleon-
        tological analysis of the breccia samples,
    e. one set of Rapidograph pens and a Dremel Moto-tool
        for grinding surfaces of bone and artifacts,
    f. other cave excavation equipment, such as safety helmets
        with lights, air-filter masks, eye shields, rock hammers,
        picks, etc., and
    g. special foodstuffs and beverages, sanitary equipment, and
        other items to improve the quality of life on the excava-
        tion, which will make the excavation team totally indepen-
        dent from the local economy of Ba Thuoc.

At the conclusion of the project, all of the above-named equipment will be left in the charge of the Institute of Archaeology for
future use. In addition to the above-mentioned field equipment,
the American signatories will also attempt to provide a video
cassette recorder and color television set, so the Institute of Archaeology staff can view the National Geographic television program that will result from this expedition, as well as other television
documentaries. The Vietnamese signatories agree to arrange ground
transportation, which will include two nine-passenger vans and
one multiton lorry, and accommodations at the District Headquarters in Ba Thuoc, the costs of which will be fully borne by the
American side.

6. After the successful completion of the excavations, the American signatories agree to sponsor two scientists from the Institute
of Archaeology as visitors to the Universities of Iowa and Arizona
for a period not to exceed two months each. The purpose of these
visits is to enhance the exchange of scientific information initiated
during the field expedition. It is further hoped that they will lead
to joint publications. It is proposed that these visits will take place
in either the Spring or Fall of 1989. The full costs of these visits to
the U.S.A. will be borne by the American side. The visas for the
Vietnamese scientists to enter the U.S.A. will be arranged by the
U.S. Committee for Scientific Cooperation with Vietnam.

7. The Vietnamese and American archaeologists also agree to begin planning a jointly edited book, tentatively entitled *The Prehistory of Vietnam,* which will be a cooperative project between the Institute of Archaeology and the American team. It is further agreed that this book will consist of approximately ten chapters on the archaeology of Vietnam written by Vietnamese scientists and translated into English, and at least one additional article by the American archaeologists. It is proposed that this book will be published in the U.S.A. by an American publisher.

8. The Committee for Social Sciences of Vietnam and the Institute of Archaeology welcome all of the above proposals and will present them to the offices of the appropriate jurisdictions to ask for their permission. When permission is received the Vietnam Committee for Social Sciences and the Institute of Archaeology will inform the American team, and together all parties will plan and discuss in detail how best to carry out this proposed research agreement.

9. This scientific project will be facilitated under the auspices of the U.S. Committee for Scientific Cooperation with Vietnam, based in Madison, Wisconsin, U.S.A.

Signed this 30th day of May, 1988, in Hanoi by:

Hoang Xuan Chinh
Vice-Director, Institute of Archaeology

Russell L. Ciochon
The University of Iowa

Nguyen Van Hao
Vice-Director, Institute of Archaeology

John W. Olsen
The University of Arizona

Nguyen Van Ku
Deputy-Director, Department of International Cooperation, Committee for Social Sciences of Vietnam

Jamie James
New York City

Fauna List of the Excavation

*Provisional list of the Pleistocene fauna
recovered from Lang Trang caves
during the January 1989 expedition*

PRIMATES

    Hominidae
      Homo cf. *erectus*
    Pongidae
      Pongo pygmaeus ssp. (orangutan)
    Cercopithecidae
      Macaca arctoides (stump-tailed macaque monkey)
      Macaca mulatta (rhesus macaque monkey)
      Macaca sp. (macaque monkey)
      Presbytis sp. (langur monkey)
    Hylobatidae
      Hylobates sp. (gibbon)

CARNIVORA

    Ursidae
      Ursus malayanus (Malayan sun bear)
      Ursus thibetanus (Asiatic black bear)
      Ailuropoda melanoleuca (giant panda)
    Mustelidae
      Arctonyx collaris (hog badger)
      cf. *Melogale moschata* (white-cheeked ferret badger)
    Viverridae
      cf. *Paguma larvata* (masked palm civet)

cf. *Paradoxurus hermaphroditus* (palm civet)
cf. *Viverra* sp. (oriental civet)
Canidae
  Cuon antiquus (Asiatic wild dog)
  cf. *Canis* sp. (wolf or jackel)
Felidae
  Panthera tigris (tiger)
  cf. *Panthera pardus* (leopard)
  Felis temmincki (Asian golden cat)

PROBOSCIDEA

Elephantidae
  Elephas cf. namadicus (elephant)
Stegodontidae
  Stegodon orientalis (stegodon)

ARTIODACTYLA

Suidae
  Sus scrofa (wild boar)
Cervidae
  Cervus (Rusa) unicolor (sambar)
  Cervus sp. (deer)
  Muntiacus muntiak (barking deer)
Tragulidae
  cf. *Tragulus javanicus* (Asiatic mouse deer)
Bovidae
  Bos (Bibos) gaurus (gaur)
  Bos sp. (ox)
  Capricornus sumatraensis (serow)

PERISSODACTYLA

Tapiridae
  Tapirus (Megatapirus) augustus (tapir)
Rhinocerotidae
  Rhinocerus sinensis (rhinoceros)

RODENTIA

>Hystricidae
>>*Hystrix subcristata* (porcupine)
>>*Atherurus macrourus* (brush-tailed porcupine)
>Rhizomyidae
>>*Rhizomys troglodytes* (bamboo rat)
>Muridae
>>*Rattus sabanus* (noisy rat)

CHIROPTERA

>Family Indet
>>Gen. et sp. indet. (bat)

GASTROPODA

>*Cyctophorus* (freshwater snail)

Bibliography

Andersson, J. Gunnar. "Topographical and archaeological studies in the Far East." *The Museum of Far East Asian Antiquities*, Stockholm (1939), 11:75–107.

———. "Researches into the prehistory of the Chinese." *The Museum of Far Eastern Asian Antiquities*, Stockholm (1943), 15:1–304.

Andrews, Roy Chapman. *On the Trail of Ancient Man*. New York: Putnam, 1926.

———. *This Business of Exploring*. New York: Putnam, 1935.

———. *Meet Your Ancestors*. London: John Long, 1949.

———, and Evette B. Andrews. *Camps and Trails in China*. New York: Appleton, 1918.

Austin, Robert, and Koichiro Ueda. *Bamboo*. Tokyo: Weatherhill, 1970.

Binford, Lewis R. *Debating Archaeology*. San Diego: Academic Press, 1989.

Black, Davidson. "Asia and the dispersal of primates." *Bulletin of the Geological Survey of China*, Peking (1925), 4(2):133–183.

———. "The lower molar hominid tooth from the Chou Kou Tien deposit." *Palaeontologia Sinica*, Peking (1927), series D, 7(1):1–28.

———, et al. "Fossil Man in China." *Memoirs of the Geological Survey of China*, Peiping (May 1933), series A, No. 11.

Boriskovskii, P.I. "Vietnam in Primeval Times." *Soviet Anthropology and Archaeology*. Part I (1968), 7(2):14–32; Part II (1968), 7(3):3–19; Part III (1969), 8(1):70–95; Part IV (1969), 8(3):214–257; Part V (1970), 8(4):355–367; Part VI (1970), 9(2):154–172; Part VII (1970), 9(3):226–264.

———. "The new problem of the Palaeolithic and Mesolithic of the Indochinese peninsula." *Archaeology and Physical Anthropology in Oceania* (July 1971), 6(2):103–106.

Bourne, Geoffrey H., and Maury Cohen. *The Gentle Giants*. New York: Putnam, 1975.

243

Bower, Bruce. "Asian human-origin theory gets new teeth." *Science News* (August 1989), 136(7):100.

Broom, Robert. *Finding the Missing Link.* London: Watts and Co., 1950.

Brown, Frank, et al. "Early *Homo erectus* skeleton from West Lake Turkana, Kenya." *Nature* (August 1985), 316:788–792.

Brown, Lillian. *I Married a Dinosaur.* New York: Dodd, Mead, 1950.

Cann, Rebecca L., Mark Stoneking, and Alan Wilson. "Mitochondrial DNA and human evolution." *Nature* (January 1987), 325:31–36.

Ciochon, Russell. "The Search for Fossil Man in Asia." *The Explorer* (Winter 1976), 18(4):26–36.

———. "Fossil ancestors of Burma." *Natural History* (October 1985), 95(10):26–36.

———. "*Gigantopithecus*: The King of All the Apes." *Animal Kingdom* (March/April 1988), 91(2):32–39.

———, and A. Brunetto Chiarelli, eds. *Evolutionary Biology of the New World Monkeys and Continental Drift.* New York: Plenum Press, 1980.

Ciochon, Russell, and Robert S. Corruccini, eds. *New Interpretations of Ape and Human Ancestry.* New York: Plenum Press, 1983.

Ciochon, Russell, and Dennis Etler. "The Asian Genesis of Primates." *American Anthropologist* (1990) submitted.

Ciochon, Russell, and John Fleagle. *Primate Evolution and Human Origins.* New York: Aldine de Gruyter, 1987.

———. *The Human Evolution Source Book.* Englewood Cliffs, NJ: Prentice-Hall, 1991.

Ciochon, Russell, and John Olsen. "Paleoanthropological and archaeological research in the Socialist Republic of Viet Nam." *Journal of Human Evolution* (November 1986), 15:623–631.

———. "Expedition to Vietnam." *Anthroquest* (Fall 1987), 38:1,12–18.

Ciochon, Russell, Dolores R. Piperno, and Robert G. Thompson. "Opal Phytoliths found on the teeth of extinct ape, *Gigantopithecus blacki*: Implications for paleodietary studies." *Proceedings of the National Academy of Sciences* (1990).

Ciochon, Russell, et al. "Anthropoid Origins in Asia? New Discovery of *Amphipithecus* from the Eocene of Burma." *Science* (August 1985), 229:756–759.

Coolidge, Harold J., and Theodore Roosevelt. *Three Kingdoms of Indo-China.* New York: Thomas Crowell, 1933.

Corruccini, Robert S. "Multivariate analysis of *Gigantopithecus* mandibles." *American Journal of Physical Anthropology* (January 1975), 42:167–170.

Davis, D. Dwight. "The Giant Panda: A Morphological Study of Evolutionary Mechanism." *Fieldiana: Zoological Memoirs* (December 1964), 3:1–338.

De Boer, Leobert E.M., ed. *The Orangutan: Its Biology and Conservation.* The Hague: W. Junk, 1982.

De Terra, Helmut. *Memories of Teilhard de Chardin.* New York: Harper & Row, 1964.

Dixson, Alan F. *The Natural History of the Gorilla.* New York: Columbia University Press, 1981.

Fleagle, John G. *Primate Evolution and Adaptation.* San Diego: Academic Press, 1988.

Fossy, Dian. *Gorillas in the Mist.* Boston: Houghton Mifflin, 1983.

Gilbert, Robert I., and James H. Mielke, eds. *The Analysis of Prehistoric Diets.* San Diego: Academic Press, 1985.

Goodall, Jane. *The Chimpanzees of Gombe Reserve.* Cambridge, MA: Harvard University Press, 1986.

Gould, Stephen J. *The Panda's Thumb.* New York: W.W. Norton, 1980.

Gowlett, John A.J. *Ascent to Civilization.* New York: Alfred A. Knopf, 1984.

Grün, Rainer. "Electron spin resonance (ESR) dating." *Quaternary International* (1989), 1:65–109.

Grün, Rainer, Henry P. Schwarcz, and Steve Zymela. "Electron spin resonance dating of tooth enamel." *Canadian Journal of Earth Sciences* (1987), 24:1022–1037.

Halpin, Marjorie, and Michael M. Ames, eds. *Manlike Monsters on Trial.* Vancouver: University of British Columbia Press, 1980.

Harkness, Ruth. *The Lady and the Panda.* New York: Carrick & Evans, 1938.

Harrisson, Barbara. *Orang-utan.* New York: Doubleday, 1963.

Harrisson, Tom. "The caves of Niah: A history of prehistory." *Sarawak Museum Journal* (1958), 8(12):549–595.

———. "Radio-Carbon—C14 datings from Niah: a note." *Sarawak Museum Journal* (1959), 9:136–138.

Herklots, G.A.C. *Vegetables in South-East Asia.* London: George Allen & Unwin, 1972.

Heuvelmans, Bernard. *On the Track of Unknown Animals.* New York: Hill & Wang, 1959.

Higham, Charles. *The Archaeology of Mainland Southeast Asia.* Cambridge: Cambridge University Press, 1989.

Hooijer, D.A. "The Orang-utan in Niah Cave Prehistory." *Sarawak Museum Journal* (July-December 1959), 9(15–16):408–421.

Jamieson, Niel. "A perspective on Vietnamese prehistory based upon the relationship between geological and archaeological data: Summary of an earlier article by Nguyen Duc Tam." *Asian Perspectives* (1984), 24:187–192.

Johanson, Donald C., and Maitland Edey. *Lucy: The Beginnings of Humankind.* New York, Simon & Schuster, 1981.

Kha, Le Trung. "First remarks on the Quaternary fossil fauna of northern Vietnam." *Vietnamese Studies* (1976), 46:107–126.

Kinh, Pham Van, and Luu Tran Tieu. "The Lower Palaeolithic site of Nui Do." *Vietnamese Studies* (1976), 46:50–106.

Leakey, Richard, and Roger Lewin. *Origins.* New York: Dutton, 1977.

——, and Alan Walker. "*Homo erectus* unearthed." *National Geographic* (November 1985), 168(5):624–629.

Lewin, Roger. *Human Evolution.* Oxford: Blackwell Scientific Publications, 1984.

——. "The Unmasking of Mitochondrial Eve." *Science* (October 1987), 238:24–6.

——. *In the Age of Mankind.* Washington: Smithsonian Institution, 1988.

——. *Bones of Contention.* New York: Simon & Schuster, 1989.

MacKinnon, John. *In Search of the Red Ape.* London: Collins, 1974.

——. *The Ape Within Us.* New York: Holt, Rinehart & Winston, 1978.

——, and Kathleen MacKinnon. *Animals of Asia: The Ecology of the Oriental Region.* New York: Holt, Rinehart & Winston, 1974.

Martin, Paul S., and H.E. Wright, eds. *Pleistocene Extinctions.* New Haven: Yale University Press, 1967.

Martin, Paul S., and Richard G. Klein, eds. *Quaternary Extinctions: A Prehistoric Revolution.* Tucson: University of Arizona Press, 1984.

Matthew, William Diller. *Climate and Evolution.* New York: Academy of Natural Sciences, 1939.

——, and Walter Granger. "New fossil mammals from the Pliocene of Sze-Chuan, China." *Bulletin of the American Museum of Natural History* (1923), 48:563–598.

McNeely, Jeffrey A., and Paul S. Wachtel. *Soul of the Tiger.* New York: Doubleday, 1988.

Mellars, Paul, and Chris Stringer, eds. *The Human Revolution: Behavioural and Biological Perspectives on the Origins of Modern Humans.* Edinburgh: Edinburgh University Press, 1989.

Morris, Ramona and Desmond. *The Giant Panda.* London: Macmillan, 1981.

Mortier, Jeanne, and Marie-Louis Auboux. *The Teilhard de Chardin Album*. New York: Harper & Row, 1966.

Movius, Hallam L. "Early man and Pleistocene stratigraphy in southern and eastern Asia." *Papers of the Peabody Museum of American Archaeology and Ethnology, Harvard University* (1944), 19(3).

———. "Lower Paleolithic archaeology in southern Asia and the Far East." *Studies in Physical Anthropology 1; Early Man in the Far East*. Philadelphia: Wistar Institute, 1949, pp. 17–82.

Napier, John. *Bigfoot: The Yeti and Sasquatch in Myth and Reality*. New York: Dutton, 1972.

Nitecki, Matthew H., ed. *Extinctions*. Chicago: University of Chicago Press, 1984.

———, and Doris V. Nitecki, eds. *The Evolution of Hunting*. New York: Plenum Press, 1987.

O'Brien, Stephen J., et al. "A molecular solution to the riddle of the giant panda's phylogeny." *Nature* (September 1985), 317:140–144.

Olsen, John W., and Russell L. Ciochon. "A Review of Evidence for Postulated Middle Pleistocene Occupations in Viet Nam." *Journal of Human Evolution* (November 1990).

———, Russell L. Ciochon and Ha Van Tan, eds. *The Prehistory of Viet Nam*. Tucson: University of Arizona Press, 1991.

Osborn, Henry Fairfield. "The geological and faunal relations of Europe and America during the Tertiary period and the theory of successive invasions of the African fauna." *Science* (April 1900), 11:560–574.

———. "Proving Asia the Mother of Continents." *Asia* (September 1922), 22(9):721–724.

Owen-Smith, R. Norman. *Megaherbivores*. Cambridge: Cambridge University Press, 1988.

Oxnard, Charles E. *Fossils, Teeth and Sex: New Perspectives on Human Evolution*. Seattle: University of Washington Press, 1987.

Pei Wenzhong. "Excavation of Liucheng cave and exploration of other caves in Kwangsi." *Memoirs of the Institute of Vertebrate Palaeontology and Paleoanthropology, Academia Sinica*, Peking (1965), series A, no. 7.

———. "Carnivora, Proboscidea and Rodentia from Liucheng *Gigantopithecus* Cave and other caves in Guangxi." *Memoirs of the Institute of Vertebrate Palaeontology and Paleoanthropology, Academia Sinica*, Beijing (1987), series A, no. 18.

Perry, Richard. *The World of the Giant Panda*. New York: Taplinger, 1969.

Pilbeam, David. "*Gigantopithecus* and the Origin of the Hominidae." *Nature* (February 1970), 225:516–519.

————. "Rethinking human origins." *Discovery* (1978), 13(1):2–9.

————. "New hominoid skull from the Miocene of Pakistan." *Nature* (January 1982), 295:232–234.

————. "The descent of hominoids and hominids." *Scientific American* (March 1984), 250(3):84–96.

Pilgrim, Guy E. "New Siwalik primates and their bearing on the question of the evolution of man and the Anthropoidea." *Records of the Geological Survey of India* (February 1915), 45(1):1–74.

Piperno, Dolores R. *Phytolith Analysis: An Archaeological and Geological Perspective.* San Diego: Academic Press, 1988.

Poirier, Frank, William Stini, and Kathy Wreden. *In Search of Ourselves.* Englewood Cliffs, NJ: Prentice-Hall, 1990.

Pope, Geoffrey G. "Current issues in Far Eastern palaeoanthropology." *The Palaeoenvironment of East Asia from the Mid-Tertiary,* Vol. II, eds. P. Whyte et al. Hong Kong: University of Hong Kong Centre of Asian Studies, 1988, pp. 1097–1123.

————. "Evidence on the age of the Asian Hominidae." *Proceedings of the National Academy of Sciences* (August 1983), 80:4988–4992.

————. "Bamboo and Human Evolution." *Natural History* (October 1989), pp. 49–57.

————, et al. "Earliest radiometrically dated artifacts from Southeast Asia," *Current Anthropology* (June 1986), 27:275–279.

Potts, Richard. *Early Hominid Activities at Olduvai.* New York: Aldine de Gruyter, 1988.

Qui Zhanxiang, and Qi Guoqin. "Ailuropod found from the Late Miocene deposits in Lufeng, Yunnan." *Vertebrata PalAsiatica* (July 1989), 27(3):153–169.

Reader, John. *Missing Links.* Boston: Little, Brown, 1981.

Reynolds, Vernon. *The Apes.* New York: E.P. Dutton, 1967.

Sanderson, Ivan T. *Abominable Snowmen.* New York: Pyramid Books, 1968.

Sarich, Vincent and Alan Wilson. "Immunological time scale for hominoid evolution." *Science* (December 1967), 158:1200–1203.

Sartono, S. "Observations on a new skull of *Pithecanthropus erectus* (*Pithecanthropus* VIII) from Sangiran, central Java." *Proceedings of the Academy of Sciences, Amsterdam* (1971), series B, 74(2):185–194.

Schaller, George B. *The Mountain Gorilla.* Chicago: University of Chicago Press, 1963.

————, et al. *The Giant Pandas of Wolong.* Chicago: University of Chicago Press, 1985.

Schwarcz, Henry, and Reiner Grün. "ESR dating of tooth enamel from prehistoric archaeological sites." *Applied Geochemistry* (1990), 4:329–330.

Schwartz, Jeffery H. *The Red Ape.* Boston: Houghton Mifflin, 1987.

Semendeferi, Ekaterini. *Upper Paleolithic Cultures in Late Pleistocene Cave Sites in Tower Karst Formations in Southeast Asia.* M.A. Thesis, University of Iowa, December 1989.

Shackley, Myra. *Still Living? Yeti, Sasquatch and the Neanderthal Enigma.* New York: Thames & Hudson, 1983.

Shapiro, Harry L. *Peking Man.* New York: Simon & Schuster, 1974.

Sheldon, William G. *The Wilderness Home of the Giant Panda.* Amherst: University of Massachusetts Press, 1975.

Sigmon, Becky A., and Jerome S. Cybulski, eds. *Homo erectus: Papers in Honor of Davidson Black.* Toronto: University of Toronto Press, 1981.

Simons, Elwyn L. "The phyletic position of *Ramapithecus.*" *Postilla*, Yale University, No. 57 (November 1961), pp. 1–9.

———. *Primate Evolution.* New York: Macmillan, 1972.

———. "Human Origins." *Science* (September 1989), 245:1343–1350.

———, and S.R.K. Chopra. "*Gigantopithecus* (Pongidae, Hominoidea); A new species from North India." *Postilla,* Yale University, No. 138 (October 1969), pp. 1–18.

———, and Peter C. Ettel. "*Gigantopithecus.*" *Scientific American* (January 1970), pp. 76–85.

Stoner, Charles. *The Sherpa and the Snowman.* London: Hollis & Carter, 1955.

Szalay, Frederick S., and Eric Delson. *Evolutionary History of the Primates.* New York: Academic Press, 1979.

Szalay, Frederick S., and Li Chuan-Kuei. "Middle Paleocene euprimate from southern China and the distribution of primates in the Paleogene." *Journal of Human Evolution* (July 1986), 15:387–397.

Tchernine, Odette. *In Pursuit of the Abominable Snowman.* New York: Taplinger, 1971.

Theunissen, Bert. *Eugene Dubois and the Ape-Man from Java.* Dordrecht, The Netherlands: Kluwer Academic Publishers, 1989.

Tobias, Phillip V. "The life and times of Ralph von Koenigswald: Palaeontologist Extraordinary." *Journal of Human Evolution* (September 1976), 5:403–412.

Trotter, Michael M., and Dwight D. McCulloch. "Moas, Men, and Middens in Quaternary Extinctions." *Quaternary Extinctions,* eds. Paul Martin and Richard Klein. Tucson: University of Arizona Press, 1984.

Turner, Christy G. "Teeth and prehistory in Asia." *Scientific American* (February 1989), pp. 88–96.

Tuttle, Russell H. *Apes of the World*. Park Ridge, NJ: Noyes, 1987.

Von Koenigswald, G.H.R. "*Gigantopithecus blacki* von Koenigswald, a giant fossil hominoid from the Pleistocene of southern China." *Anthropological Papers of the American Museum of Natural History* (1952), 43:291–326.

———. *Meeting Prehistoric Man*. New York: Harper & Brothers, 1956.

———. *The Evolution of Man*. Ann Arbor: University of Michigan Press, 1976.

Wallace, Alfred R. *The Malay Archipelago: The Land of the Orang-utan and the Bird of Paradise*. London: Macmillan, 1869.

Wang Danjun, and Shen Shao-Jin. *Bamboos of China*. Portland, OR: Timber Press, 1987.

Weidenreich, Franz. "Giant early man from Java and South China." *Science* (June 1944), 99:479–482.

———. *Apes, Giants, and Man*. Chicago: University of Chicago Press, 1946.

Weisburd, Stefi. "Creatures of the Dreamtime." *Science News* (April 1988), 133:248–250.

Wendt, Herbert. *In Search of Adam*. Boston: Houghton Mifflin, 1956.

White, Tim D. "Geomorphology to paleoecology: *Gigantopithecus* reappraised." *Journal of Human Evolution* (May 1975), 4:219–233.

Whitmore, T.C. *Tropical Rain Forests of the Far East*. Oxford: Clarendon Press, 1984.

Wolpoff, Milford H. "Multiregional evolution: The fossil alternative to Eden." *The Human Revolution: Behavioural and Biological Perspectives on the Origins of Modern Humans*, eds. Paul Mellars and Chris Stringer. Edinburgh: Edinburgh University Press, 1989.

Wu Rukang (J.K. Woo). "The mandibles and dentition of *Gigantopithecus*." *Palaeontologia Sinica*, Peking (1962), new series D, 11:1–94.

———, Lin Shenglong. "Peking Man." *Scientific American* (June 1983), 248(6):86–94.

Wu Rukang, and John W. Olsen, eds. *Palaeoanthropology and Palaeolithic Archaeology in the People's Republic of China*. Orlando: Academic Press, 1985.

Yuan Zhenxin and Huang Wanpo. " 'Wild Man'—Fact or Fiction?" *China Reconstructs* (July 1979), 28(7):56–59.

Zhang Yinyun. "Variability and evolutionary trends in tooth size of *Gigantopithecus blacki*." *American Journal of Physical Anthropology* (September 1982), 59:21–32.

———. "Enamel Hypoplasia of *Gigantopithecus blacki*." *Acta Anthropologica Sinica* (August 1987), 6(3):175–179.

Index